Also by Mikita Brottman

Guilty Creatures: Sex, God, and Murder in Tallahassee, Florida

Couple Found Slain: After a Family Murder

An Unexplained Death: The True Story of a Body at the Belvedere

The Maximum Security Book Club: Reading Literature in a Men's Prison

The Great Grisby: Two Thousand Years of Literary, Royal, Philosophical, and Artistic Dog Lovers and Their Exceptional Animals

Thirteen Girls

Hyena

Phantoms of the Clinic: From Thought-Transference to Projective Identification

The Solitary Vice: Against Reading

Offensive Films

High Theory / Low Culture

Funny Peculiar: Gershon Legman and the Psychopathology of Humor

Car Crash Culture

A DOUBLE LIFE

A DOUBLE LIFE

The Anatomy of a Premeditated Murder

Mikita Brottman

CITADEL PRESS
Kensington Publishing Corp.
kensingtonbooks.com

CITADEL PRESS BOOKS are published by

Kensington Publishing Corp.
900 Third Avenue
New York, NY 10022

All Kensington titles, imprints, and distributed lines are available at special quantity discounts for bulk purchases for sales promotions, premiums, fund-raising, educational, or institutional use. Special book excerpts or customized printings can also be created to fit specific needs. For details, write or phone the office of the Kensington sales manager: Kensington Publishing Corp., 900 Third Avenue, New York, NY 10022, attn Sales Department; phone 1-800-221-2647.

10 9 8 7 6 5 4 3 2 1

First Citadel hardcover printing: October 2026

Printed in the United States of America

ISBN: 978-0-8065-4556-1

ISBN: 978-0-8065-4558-5 (e-book)

Library of Congress Control Number: 2026938902

The authorized representative in the EU for product safety and compliance is eucomply OU, Parnu mnt 139b-14, Apt 123, Tallinn, Berlin 11317; hello@eucompliancepartner.com

CONTENTS

A DOUBLE LIFE

PROLOGUE

On the evening of Sunday, June 28, 2015, at 11:05 P.M., a video surveillance camera at Fort Myers airport catches the blurred image of a woman rolling a suitcase through the Arrivals terminal. She wears a sleeveless black dress and open-toed shoes. For a moment, she looks up. Then, like a ghost, she is gone.

The woman is Teresa Sievers, a forty-six-year-old physician returning home from a family trip to New York for her grandmother's birthday. Her husband, Mark, along with the couple's two young daughters, are staying on for another couple of days at his mother-in-law's house in Connecticut so the girls can spend more time with their cousins, but Teresa needs to get back to her office in Bonita Springs, Florida, to see patients the following morning.

On Monday, June 29, at 9:30 A.M., Mark gets a text from Teresa's office manager, Sandra Hoskins. "Mark," she writes, "I'm getting worried as Dr is not here we booked a sick patient at 9:30 and Dr is not answering her phone."

Mark is immediately concerned. His wife, an internist, is hardworking and reliable, never late. From New York, he checks the location of her phone: it's in their house in Bonita Springs, with a four percent charge. Alarmed, he calls his friend Mark

Petrites, a surgeon at nearby Naples Community Hospital. Could Petrites swing by and see if she's okay?

Of course, says the doctor. He happens to be at the post office anyway, just a couple of miles from the Sievers home. Five minutes later, he pulls up in the driveway and knocks on the door. Nothing seems amiss, but there's no reply. He knocks again. Nothing. He shouts Teresa's name. He tries the handle. Locked. He cranes his neck and peers into the living room window. What he sees worries him. The blinds are up, the lights are on, the dogs are running loose. Teresa's purse is on a stool by the kitchen countertop. But there's no sign of Teresa.

Mark has given him the garage code. As the door rises, one of the family's dogs runs out, giving Dr. Petrites a start. Inside the garage, he sees Teresa's white Mercedes station wagon on the left, next to Mark's blue minivan and Suzuki motorcycle. Oddly, her rolling travel suitcase is on the ground next to her car, its contents spilling out. Dr. Petrites steps into the small laundry room that leads into the kitchen.

He sees her at once, lying face down on the floor, her dress hitched up to her thighs. Has she fallen and knocked herself out? He reaches down to touch the middle of her back. She's stiff and cold. There's blood pooled under her head, some dry and coagulated, some still wet. He squats down to see more closely, then cries out in horror. The back of Teresa's head has been violently smashed in. Someone's beaten her brains out.

A few feet away, beside an elevated dog dish, lies a bloodstained claw hammer with hair wrapped around the handle.

• • •

Dr. Petrites calls 911. He's shaken, frantic.

"I'm at a friend's house," he tells the dispatcher. "He's out of town, and I came here to check on his wife. And she's dead on the floor . . . there's a hammer at the side, and she's been bashed in the back of the head."

"Are you with her now?"

"I'm outside the house. I don't know whether anybody's in the house."

"The deputies are en route and so is the ambulance," the dispatcher reassures him. "You're doing great. Okay?"

A paramedic crew enters the house—there's no one else on the premises. Teresa is lying face down in the kitchen, obviously the victim of blunt force trauma to the back of the head. Next to her body, on the kitchen floor, her wallet lies open with random items pulled out—an American Express card, a few receipts. Also on the floor are her phone, a bottle of water, an empty tumbler, her thong sandals, and a set of earphones. Blood splatter covers the bottom of the refrigerator. There's more blood on the floor, dried black and cracked into an unnerving mosaic.

Law enforcement officers immediately secure the premises, cordoning off the house with yellow crime scene tape. Paramedics take Teresa's body to the office of the Lee County Medical Examiner. The autopsy takes place the following morning, at 10:30 A.M. Teresa is described as "a middle-aged female approximately 46 years of age, 61 inches in height and 132lb, with hazel eyes and brunette highlighted hair." Her teeth are good. She's wearing black Maidenform underwear, size 6, a black-and-white Lola brand dress, size small, and black Okal high-heel thong sandals. Her hands show no cuts or bruising.

She's wearing a lot of jewelry, now stained with blood. Each item is removed from her body and catalogued. A pendant necklace. A pair of hoop earrings. A toe ring. From her right hand: a copper thumb ring. From her index finger: a large ring with a circular ethnic design. Two bangles and a bracelet, stained with blood. A watch from her left wrist, still ticking. Three rings from her left hand—a plain wedding band, a circle of five colored stones, and a diamond ring. Her stomach contains the residue of her last meal—something healthy, with spinach leaves.

The violence of the crime is indescribable. Teresa has been hit at least seventeen times with a hammer, leaving a circular crown of crescent-shaped lacerations on her crushed skull, causing parts of her brain to extrude. Her head, according to the report, is "pulverized."

Seventeen hammer blows to the head? Four or five would have killed her. After she was dead, whoever wielded the hammer went on. And on. And on.

PART ONE

Chapter 1

"Lord, It Is Night"

To describe Bonita Springs as a city would be both right and wrong. Officially, it's a city in its own right; geographically, it's one of a series of towns connected by suburbs to form a metropolitan sprawl: Naples, Bonita Springs, Fort Myers, Estero—it's hard to say where one ends and the next begins. To the west, a long barrier island connects Bonita Springs with the vibrant tourist haven of Bonita Beach, itself connected to a series of small islands crossing Estero Bay and reaching all the way up to Fort Myers.

Bonita Springs began as an encampment for the Army Corps of Engineers who, when mapping Southwest Florida in the 1870s, were posted here temporarily, and gave it the unimaginative name of "Survey." Early twentieth-century developers wisely resolved that the appellation lacked charm and came up with a more desirable name. "Bonita" means "pretty" in Spanish; "Springs" is after a local waterway, Indian Spring Branch, which later became Oak River.

A tony seaside town, Bonita Springs leans heavily toward the elderly, especially during the winter. If you see somebody pushing a baby carriage, it's more likely to contain a dog than a child. The population is almost entirely white and wealthy. Real estate is costly—the city is growing rapidly—and the highways are often clogged by commuter traffic. Estero Boulevard, bordering the beaches, is lined with condo construction projects. Out of season, there's not much going on. Summers are scorching. The area is prone to flooding and tropical cyclones—during Hurricane Ian in 2002, twelve-foot waves almost wiped out the city.

On the plus side, it's easy living. The shorefront condos, priced at a million dollars plus, are a haven for wealthy, white-collar retirees. The beaches are pristine, the winters mild, the skies clear, and the sunsets breathtaking. There's a little downtown area: faux-cobbled streets lined with ice-cream shops, beauty salons, souvenir stores, and dog-grooming parlors. You're close to rivers, lakes, campgrounds, and state parks. If you're into fishing, golf, or water sports, there's nowhere better.

27034 Jarvis Road, home of the Sievers family, was an impressive, modern, one-story house—the largest on the street, at almost 3,000 square feet (about the size of a doubles tennis court), with four bedrooms, three bathrooms, a lanai, and in-ground swimming pool. Jarvis Road is right next to East Terry Street, a busy four-lane freeway, so the neighborhood has some traffic noise, but otherwise it's a typical Southwest Florida suburb. Most of the homes are wide ranch houses, relatively new, many with in-ground pools and lanais out back. You might see boats in the driveways. On the lawns, sprinklers rotate all day.

On Friday, June 26, 2015, two days before the murder, the Sievers family—Mark, Teresa, and their daughters, Emma, eleven, and Olivia, eight—left home early in the morning and drove to the Southwest Florida International Airport in Fort Myers in Mark's car. To celebrate their mother's seventy-fifth birthday, Teresa and her siblings had split the cost and rented a large vacation house in New Windsor, New York, on the edge of Beaverdam Lake, halfway between New York City and where their mother lived in Connecticut.

The family took a Delta flight and arrived at LaGuardia between two and three P.M. on Friday afternoon. They rented a car for the drive to the vacation house—it should have taken an hour and a half, but rush-hour traffic slowed them down, and it was early evening by the time they arrived. When they were close to New Windsor, they stopped at an organic food store to stock up on healthy supplies. Teresa loved preparing gourmet vegan meals and never went anywhere without a bag of healthy snacks for the girls so they wouldn't end up eating junk—dried fruit, cashews, almonds, carrots, granola.

The vacation was boisterous and fun. Teresa's mother and grandmother were there, along with three of her siblings—Pat, Annie, and Frank—with their families. That Friday night, there was a big family dinner. Saturday was warm and sunny. The kids played in the pool; Teresa did some yoga, then, as usual, took control of the kitchen and bustled around cooking up healthy meals: guacamole with jalapeños and her famous vegan quesadillas. On Sunday morning, it rained; the family stayed indoors, catching up, playing Scrabble. There was a piano in the rental house. Both Annie and Teresa could play, although they hadn't done so for years. As Annie would later recall, it was a wonderful, busy, crowded reunion.

Teresa left on Sunday, June 28. That evening, Mark and the girls drove to LaGuardia to drop her off. The journey was stressful. Over the weekend, the Sievers daughters hadn't been on their best behavior, and during the drive, Teresa took the opportunity to give them a verbal dressing-down about respecting their parents. Then they got lost—Teresa had accidentally put her sister Annie's address into the GPS, and they ended up driving through downtown New York City. But they got to the airport in good time for Teresa to check in safely. Her flight, Delta 4319, left at 7:29 P.M.

After leaving the airport, Mark and the girls set off for Teresa's mother's house, in Connecticut. As they drove, while Teresa was still in the departure lounge, Mark put her on speakerphone and the family said their evening prayers, a ritual they'd followed since the girls were very young. They always said the same prayer, "Lord, it is night":

> *It is night after a long day.*
> *What has been done has been done;*
> *what has not been done has not been done;*
> *let it be.*

Teresa had overpacked, as usual: she had a large purple travel suitcase on wheels, a big carry-on bag, and a black faux-leather DKNY shoulder bag. She bought two bottles of water from an airport café, then checked in and went to the gate.

In a family photo taken earlier that day, everyone smiles for the camera. Teresa is wearing the clothes and jewelry that will be removed two days later, during her autopsy.

• • •

As soon as Dr. Petrites discovered Teresa's body, he called Mark Sievers in Connecticut and told him Teresa had been killed, and he needed to come home immediately. Soon afterward, Mark got a second call from a police officer who confirmed the terrible news: his wife was dead.

Disbelief, devastation, horror. Mark and his mother-in-law, Mary Ann, went into the front yard, where the children wouldn't hear them, and began sobbing and crying. They called to book the next flight from LaGuardia to Fort Myers, but neither of them was coherent. The gate agent at Delta noted, in a memo, that Teresa's tickets would have to be reissued or exchanged due to the passenger's death, adding, "Mother/Husband called too distraught to provide any details other than wife's name is Mrs. Sievers." The girls' tickets, too, had to be reissued. The agent also noted that the children hadn't been told of their mother's death, adding "do not mention to passengers."

For the whole three-hour flight, Mark and his mother-in-law, known to the family as Mimi, were praying desperately that the officer was wrong. Perhaps they'd mistaken Teresa's identity? On the outside, they kept calm for the sake of the girls and managed to pull it off. The children didn't realize anything was amiss.

After landing in Fort Myers, they drove to the home of Mark's mother, Bonnie, who lived just a few miles away from Jarvis Road. Shortly after they arrived, they were visited by Detective Jamie Nolen from the Lee County Sheriff's Office Homicide Unit. Now, there was no more doubt or denial. The family were formally notified of Teresa's death.

Nolen had been the on-call homicide investigator at the sheriff's office the morning Teresa's body was found. A middle-aged Brit who'd worked in law enforcement for eleven years, he became, for the first three months, the lead investigator on the case. Polite and soft-spoken, Detective Nolen knew how to break bad news gently. He didn't give away any details, just that Teresa had been killed some time the previous night during what appeared to be a home invasion. He took a brief sworn statement from Mark, then arranged for Mark, Bonnie, Mary Ann, and Teresa's sister Annie, who was flying in from New York, to come into the sheriff's office to be interviewed on Wednesday, July 1, two days later. He wanted to give the family time to grieve, and to start making funeral arrangements.

• • •

As soon as Teresa's body was discovered, crime scene technicians went to 27034 Jarvis Road to take photographs and retrieve possible evidence. The intruder, clearly, had pried open the side door to the garage, which was accessible only from the fenced-in yard. Mark told police that two or three weeks before the murder, he and his friend J. B. Tarrette had been trying to dog-proof the yard by adding concrete reinforcement to the privacy gate to be sure there were no gaps. The Sieverses' dogs, Nana and Lucy, were old, and never tried to get out, but sometimes the Sieverses would take care of the Tarrettes' dog, Murphy, who had a habit of slipping through the gap in the fence and turning up on the opposite neighbors' doorstep. The privacy gate was unbroken, so police assumed the intruder must have climbed over the fence. There were no security cameras.

Inside, the house signaled a family that was untidy, chaotic, a little spendthrift, and always on the go. Investigators started in the three-car garage, where, as well as two vehicles and a motorcycle, there were bicycles, mops and brooms, tennis rackets, a cooler, garden tools, an upright freezer, and a chest freezer, both full of organic dog food (the Sieverses were vegan and wouldn't have meat in the house). Teresa's large, wheeled suitcase was on the floor with some items pulled out. Her black travel bag had also been opened and rummaged through. On top lay the motivational book she'd been reading on the plane: *Letting Go: The Pathway of Surrender* by David R. Hawkins.

Officers entered a door in the garage that led to a small laundry area opening to the kitchen. Teresa had put down her purse on one of the counter stools, which suggested she'd been in the room for at least a few moments before she was attacked. The fridge on the left was covered in souvenirs of family life—baby pictures, party photos, prayer cards, children's drawings. The pantry was full of nutritional supplements, the freezer crammed with piles of organic, vegan food.

There were two sets of dog bowl stands, both elevated to assist the family's elderly dogs. One of the water dishes had been overturned. Opposite the fridge, on a countertop by the double sink, was a blender and basket full of more supplements, shakes, and powders. Mark's mother, Bonnie, who'd been taking care of the pets while the family was away, had left a bag of carrots and a note. "The carrots ran out for the dogs so here's some so you don't have to get. They were hungry and really liked the carrots."

The kitchen opened directly onto a bright, sunny, and modern living room, with tile floors and lots of windows. There were family photographs everywhere—hanging on the walls, standing in frames on shelves and dressers, made into playful collages. Children's toys, books, drawings, and colored pencils were scattered around the sectional sofa and coffee table. A set of sliding glass doors led to a large, lush, and shady lanai, lined with areca palms and clusters of the shrub known as Crown of Thorns. An oval-shaped swimming pool was surrounded by floats, sun loungers, picnic tables, a telescope, a hot tub, and a barbecue grill.

The office was cluttered, its L-shaped desk almost invisible, hidden under piles of documents, papers, magazines, DVDs, and computer equipment. One of the girls' bedrooms was painted lavender, with bells, butterflies, and dream catchers hanging above the bed. The other was messy—you could hardly open the door. Inside was a tent made from bedsheets, a play-kitchen, and a floor strewn with clothes and toys. On the vanity in the master bathroom, investigators found three plastic tubs full of pill bottles: eighteen contained prescription medications. The rest were vitamins, minerals, homeopathic remedies, and holistic supplements. A tub of makeup had been knocked over—by the cat, Zoey, it turned out.

In the corner of the master bedroom were a pile of free weights and an exercise ball. There was a book on the bedside table: *The Energy Healing Experiments: Science Reveals Our Natural Power to Heal* by Gary E. Schwartz, PhD, and William L. Simon. Teresa's side of the closet was full of brightly colored sleeveless dresses, some still in dry cleaning bags, purses, and high heels (at just over five feet, she was a big fan). Mark favored colorful Hawaiian shirts and leather jackets.

He also had an impressive gun collection. There was a rifle safe full of shotguns, fourteen or fifteen of them, some antiques. A smaller safe contained pistols and revolvers, many collectibles but still functional. In a nearby drawer were holsters, ammunition, a tray of rare and vintage coins (which Mark also collected), along with approximately 40,000 dollars in cash. Another small safe, accessed by a code, contained Teresa's more valuable jewelry and important documents such as the family passports and Teresa's medical license. There were also a couple of baggies of pot, and some rolling papers. Organic, of course.

Chapter 2

"A Modern-Day Mother Teresa"

In every homicide investigation, law enforcement officers begin by interviewing all those close to the victim, to understand who they were. The result can be like the parable of the blind men and the elephant—everybody knows a different side of them. Spouse, friends, family members, colleagues, neighbors, clients, ex-partners—each has a unique relationship. By putting these pieces together, investigators try to create a three-dimensional picture. But it doesn't always work. The process is complicated. In the days right after the crime, some people's memories are distorted by grief.

On television, the cops jump right in; in real life, they're trained to be sensitive about timing. True, they need to talk to family members as soon as possible, but in most cases, they hold off for a day or two so the shock can sink in. Even then, initial interviews are brief. The cops ask neutral, non-invasive questions to keep the lines of communication open. At this stage, they never accuse anybody of wrongdoing. They're trained to express sympathy but stay professional, to shape the path of the interview without pushing the subject in a particular direction.

They're also trained in body language (in police-speak,

"non-verbal communications" and "micro-gestures"). Some of this is obvious—if you fold your arms and look away, you clearly don't want to engage. Other signs are ambiguous. Your face is flushed. Are you lying, or just easily embarrassed? You're restless, shifting around and swinging your leg rhythmically. Are you anxious about being questioned, or do you have ADHD? Maybe you're just worried about getting a parking ticket. It's natural, whether you're guilty or innocent, to be nervous when being interviewed by the police, and while body language can be used to guide interrogations, it can't be used as evidence of guilt, even if apparently overwhelming. In one case, a suspect fainted when approached by the FBI, but when the state tried to use this fact against him, the judge concluded, "It is just as likely that he fainted from shock, surprise, or alarm at being accused of such a serious crime."

You didn't have to be an expert in body language to gauge the mood of Mark Sievers during his police interview—he was on the edge of a nervous breakdown. He'd already spoken to Detective Nolen when he was officially informed of Teresa's death at 7:12 P.M. on the evening of Monday, June 29, but he wasn't questioned at any length until Wednesday, July 1, two days after his wife's body was found. At 11:40 A.M., he arrived at the Lee County Sheriff's Office for a more formal interview.

Mark, forty-six, was a big guy, slightly overweight, with a fleshy face, shaved head, prominent ears, and closely clipped facial hair. His glasses, removed for the duration of the interview, lay on the table in front of him. He wore a gray T-shirt, black cargo shorts, and running shoes, and looked sweaty and disheveled, as if he'd been up all night (and maybe he had). Surveillance video from the interview room captured his behavior before Detective Nolen arrived. Frenzied and hysterical, he couldn't sit still. He sank his head into his hands, sobbed, then started to hyperventilate, performing breathing techniques to help him relax. He whispered to

Teresa. "I love you . . . give me strength . . . I keep hoping this is just a dream, so I can wake up with you in my arms. . . ."

Mark made odd movements, placing his arms in different positions, rapping and knocking on his head and his chest (a holistic "emotional freedom technique" known as "tapping" which is supposed to calm bodily stress). During the interview, he bit his nails, cracked his knuckles, wrung his hands, gesticulated wildly. When Nolen left the room for a few moments, Mark clasped his hands and prayed, shook, pounded his fists against the table and the wall. Later, he began gasping for air and could barely speak. When he did, he was distraught and often tangential, forgetting names and times, going off on unrelated sidetracks, becoming loud and overexcited. Detective Nolen encouraged him to breathe deeply and take his time.

The detective's immediate task was to find leads to follow—at this point, he was less interested in getting background information than in learning about the immediate circumstances surrounding the murder: the family's activities over the weekend, the layout of the house and garage, possible entryways for an intruder. Mark, too, seemed mostly fixated on what had happened during the attack—he kept saying he should have been there to protect his wife. But it was Mark's mother, Bonnie, who had the most useful information. She'd been in the house the day of the murder.

Bonnie Sievers, seventy-eight, had moved down to Bonita Springs from her home in Missouri to be close to Mark and Teresa, and to help babysit their girls. She lived with her partner, Melanie, just a few miles from the Sieverses' house on Jarvis Road. During her interview, Bonnie looked a little unkempt, in a green T-shirt, blue shorts, and sneakers. The room was cold, and she hugged her large black purse for warmth. She told Detective Nolen she hadn't been answering her phone because news stations had been calling nonstop.

Bonnie's style of grief wasn't dramatic, like Mark's. She'd

brought along a pad and pencil and made notes carefully. She was cautious, worried, and fretful, admonishing herself for not being more watchful.

Over the weekend of Teresa's death, she told Detective Nolen, she'd been visiting Jarvis Road twice a day to feed the family pets. She'd dropped by each morning, around nine A.M., then again in the afternoon, around four. She always entered the house through the garage, she explained. Mark had given her both the garage door code and the code to deactivate the house alarm system.

When she'd arrived at 27034 Jarvis Road on Friday, June 26, the morning the family left for New York, the security alarm hadn't been set. Bonnie didn't think too much of it—she assumed it was because they'd left early in a rush, and they knew she'd be coming by before long. She set the alarm on Friday after her second visit, and again on Saturday, but oddly, on Sunday, when she arrived at 7:45 A.M., the alarm appeared to have been deactivated.

Bonnie was confused. Had she forgotten to set it the night before? It was possible. When she'd left the previous afternoon, she'd had problems with the system and forgot what buttons to press. She'd called Mark in New York. "Don't worry about it," he'd told her. He didn't want her to set the motion sensor by mistake—the dogs would trigger it, and the cops would come out, which had happened before. Anyway, Teresa was getting back that night. Without setting the alarm, Bonnie left Jarvis Road between 4:25 and 4:30 P.M. on Sunday, June 28.

Now, afraid she'd unintentionally let the intruder into the house, Bonnie began blaming herself for Teresa's death. Nolen gently reminded her she wasn't responsible. "There's going to be a lot of things where you say, 'I should have done this, I should have done that,'" he reassured her. "You can't blame yourself."

Having established the immediate circumstances of the break-in, Nolen began collecting information about Teresa herself, starting with her family background. In this regard, the most useful informant was her older sister, Annie, who was interviewed by a detective named John Lathrop. Annie, on learning of her sister's death, had flown down to Bonita Springs from Connecticut the previous day. At fifty-two, she was a lively and attractive woman with long dark hair, dressed for the Florida heat in a black tank top, shorts, and thong sandals, with a pair of sunglasses pushed to the back of her head. She said she'd been crying the previous night, but her grief wasn't apparent on the surface—while waiting for Lathrop to enter the room, she sat examining her fingernails. During the interview, she was garrulous and talkative.

Annie explained the structure of her family, which was a little complicated. She, Teresa, and their younger brother, Patrick, were born and raised in Ansonia, Connecticut, a small town on the Housatonic River, eight miles northwest of New Haven. Their father, Jack Tottenham, was an auto mechanic.

After their parents divorced, their mother, Mary Ann, married a man named Frank, who suffered from bipolar disorder and took his own life at the age of thirty-nine. With Frank, she had another child, Frankie, who was raised with his three half-siblings as a younger brother. Their father, Jack, remarried too, and had a daughter named Nim, now a psychology professor at Columbia University. Also, a few years before Teresa's murder, the family learned that Jack had a daughter from an extramarital relationship, Dawn, who worked in emergency medicine. Since then, Mary Ann had married a third husband, Tom Groves.

Teresa's mother, seventy-five, was interviewed by Detective Nolen on July 2, at 12:48 P.M. She was a short, slight woman, neatly dressed in a white blouse and blue slacks, but her face was hollow, and her eyes circled with shadows. She wasn't frantic, worried, or desperate, just terribly sad. Like Mark, she was too distraught to remember dates, times, and names, but she had none of Mark's hysterical energy. She was tearful, sometimes breaking into sobs.

"We had a wonderful time," she said mournfully of the weekend in New York before Teresa's murder. "A wonderful time."

Mary Ann revealed to Detective Nolen that Teresa had been married before, "very briefly," but her daughters were both Mark's ("The children don't even know she was married before"). She explained that Teresa had gone to medical school at Ross University in Dominica, graduating in 1996. She completed a residency at the University of Florida Medical Center in Jacksonville, where she fell in love with the state, and eventually joined a medical practice in sunny St. Petersburg, two hours north of Bonita Springs.

Teresa met Mark through his sister Stacey, an acupuncturist. At that time, according to her sister, after the failure of her first marriage, Teresa was in a situation where she just wanted to be married with children, and Mark promised her "the whole package, including the white picket fence." But he wasn't all domesticity. Exciting, too. Mark told Detective Nolen their first date was at a gun range. He was a gun fanatic. He collected shotguns and rifles. Shooting was his favorite hobby. But Teresa didn't like guns. "I always told her, 'You're perfect for me, but there's one thing missing—you don't like shooting.'" But in the three months before the murder, she'd started to change her mind. They'd been going to the firing range together—Teresa enjoyed it. She'd already finished her safety training and received her concealed carry permit, but she didn't have a gun when she was attacked.

Mark was a licensed nurse, and after the couple married in 2003, he continued with his nursing career while Teresa worked as an internist. Eventually, the couple bought a home beside the ocean in Pinellas Park. "A lovely neighborhood. The Pink Streets," said Mary Ann, referring to an area where the roads were paved in concrete that had been dyed a pretty, soft reddish-pink. Both Annie and her mother said Teresa had preferred the family's previous home in Pinellas Park to their new house in Bonita Springs.

"She didn't want to leave beautiful St. Petersburg," recalled Mary Ann. "We all loved coming to visit her there."

The family—Teresa, Mark, and their infant daughter, Emma—moved from St. Petersburg to Bonita Springs when Teresa was offered the opportunity to invest in a new medical complex, where she could start a private practice as well as own real estate. The couple bought two lots on Jarvis Road and built what Annie described as "this big old stupid house," the biggest house on the street, completely out of place. Annie said the family "broke her bones" about it.

Mary Ann told Detective Nolen that right before she took her flight to Bonita Springs, Teresa had said evening prayers with her family via FaceTime.

"Was Teresa a religious lady?" asked the detective.

Her daughter had been raised Catholic, said Mary Ann, and although she didn't go to mass every week, she was deeply spiritual, in her own way. When the family did go to church, they usually went to Good Shepherd, an "inclusive Catholic community" ministered by Pastor Judy Lee, who later described Teresa as "an angel."

On other occasions, the couple went to Unity of Naples Church, where Bonnie and her partner, Melanie, volunteered as ushers. Sometimes they went to the synagogue, too—Mark's family was Jewish. But mostly, Teresa put her spiritual ideals into practice through her work. "She was on a mission to help people get well, stay well, take care of themselves," said her mother. I used to call her 'my modern-day Mother Teresa.'"

When the family moved to Bonita Springs, Mark stopped nursing and became Teresa's office manager—he kept the books and did the paperwork. He also did whatever needed to be done around the house. He wasn't exactly a handyman, but he could do more than the basics. He could install a fan or light fixture, fix the air-conditioning, mend the fence in the yard, even lay concrete.

But mostly, he was "Mr. Mom." He homeschooled Emma and Olivia, took them to their activities: swimming practice, theater, violin lessons, martial arts. As a father, he was very protective. He let the girls go on play dates, but they weren't allowed out in the neighborhood without supervision. He'd only leave them with people he trusted.

Over time, Mark and Teresa had become increasingly interested in holistic health, and in terms of their lifestyle, according to Mark, they were "as organic as you could be." They steered clear of canned and processed food. Teresa used organic makeup (expensive, noted Mark), organic perfume, organic shampoo and conditioner. Even the dogs ate an organic diet (they were allergic to beef). Teresa "investigated every product she used to be sure it wasn't tested on animals and was environmentally friendly and organic."

She was careful what she ate, took good care of herself, and exercised every day. She wasn't a big fan of prescription medication—although she wasn't against it—but she took a lot of vitamins, nutrients, and supplements. The children also took supplements. There were supplements all over the house. "We probably have more supplements in our pantry than we do food," said Mark.

Teresa would get up early to jog, meditate, and write in her journal. She was an expert multitasker; she and Annie often talked on the phone while they were putting on their makeup in the morning. And although she was something of a perfectionist, she wasn't over the top about it, according to Annie. Teresa's mother described her daughter as generous to a fault. She was on the board of a local charity. She'd lend money to friends and family members without expecting to get it back. She helped her sister, paid for her mother's iPhone plan. "She gave away probably more than anybody I've ever known," said Mary Ann.

Although Teresa ate healthily and exercised, the results were disappointing. As she entered her forties, her figure wasn't as trim as it used to be, and she had some self-esteem issues when it came to her body. When her dad, Jack, died in 2013, she used the money he left her to pay for a tummy tuck. Her dad was so vain, Teresa said, he'd surely have understood. And she was pleased with the result—she liked her improved figure. Finally, she had a waist. She was thinking about having a boob job, as well.

When Detective Nolen asked Mark if Teresa ever used drugs, he reluctantly admitted that she sometimes smoked marijuana. ("I don't want that out there in the press, because that's not who she was," he said. "Please don't let that out there. I don't want to see in the press tomorrow, 'Pot Smoking Doctor Died.'") She thought marijuana could help calm stress and saw it as a type of natural therapy, which she believed in.

Everyone said Mark and Teresa's marriage was strong. The only thing they argued about was Mark's forgetfulness. Annie described him as something of a scatterbrain who had to write everything down in his phone. His goofiness drove Teresa crazy. "He literally can't remember shit . . . it would make her insane. She'd say, 'I have to tell you everything fifty fucking times. You're exhausting me.'" Annie didn't beat around the bush: Teresa had a short fuse and a bad temper. She was loud. She yelled. She could be bossy, outspoken, demanding. Now and then, she rubbed people the wrong way.

Recently, the family had seen less of Teresa because she'd been trying to expand her practice, doing lectures, seminars, and media interviews, so she was very busy. "She had a very hectic schedule," said Mary Ann. "I can't keep track of where she went. She went everywhere. . . . She was being interviewed, talked about on TV. . . . She wanted to reach masses of people. And I always told her, 'I know you'll do it, Teresa, I just know you'll do it.' And she has." Mary Ann suddenly began to sob. "But not the way I thought."

• • •

On July 3, four days after Teresa's murder, the crime scene tape was removed from 27034 Jarvis Road, and Mark returned home with his daughters. The house held its breath. Six months later, the place was empty, the family gone.

Chapter 3

Targeted, Stalked, and Slain

Immediately after Teresa's death, the lurid story was picked up by the media, sending pundits and headline writers into overdrive. Always, she was described in ways that diminished her status as a hardworking, middle-aged MD. She became a "gorgeous young doctor," a "petite redhead," a "lady doctor," a "rising social media star," and a "doctor known for her holistic therapy and sexy high heels." Her murder was relayed in all its horror: the "beloved doctor" was "bludgeoned with a hammer," and "died on her kitchen floor, her skull shattered by seventeen blows."

Some media outlets were relentless. A producer for the *Nancy Grace* show kept calling and emailing the Lee County State's Attorney's office, requesting a copy of Teresa's autopsy report. A representative from Florida's WINK-TV sent an email, asking bluntly, "Good morning. Can you tell me if you have the body of Teresa Sievers?"

In media terms, the murder was compelling: a terrible, shocking act of violence against a beautiful, white female doctor committed, apparently, by a stranger. That same week, two Black men, Andrew Chisholm, thirty-nine, and Tarvese Johnson, seventeen, were killed in a double homicide in nearby Fort Myers, but few noticed or cared—it wasn't news. There were twelve other murders in Fort Myers that year, mostly of Black males—crimes that had no headline-grabbing glamour or public appeal. Teresa's murder was front page news for weeks.

The focus on her appearance and social status diminished her as a person. Yes, Dr. Sievers was popular, attractive, and charismatic. But she was also a well-regarded internist, a generous, compassionate healer. For a while, she chaired the board of a charity that helped homeless teenaged girls. She'd get up in the middle of the night to conduct emergency evaluations. To her patients, she was almost a saint.

Yet someone hated her enough to beat out her brains with a hammer.

• • •

Surprisingly, more people are killed annually in the US by hammers and other blunt objects than by shotguns or rifles (a statistic often trumpeted by NRA lobbyists). Of course, handguns (rather than shotguns) are by far the most common murder weapon—seventy percent of murders involve firearms of various kinds—but of the other thirty percent, blunt objects are high on the list. Most often, these are "weapons of opportunity" grabbed during a violent argument—bottles, dumbbells, vases, golf clubs.

The type of object used can provide clues to apparent motive, degree of intent, and relationship between victim and perpetrator. If you seize a baseball bat, you're probably thinking more murderously than if you pick up a flashlight or a paperweight. But this case was ambiguous. Wouldn't an intruder have carried a gun, or some other weapon more efficient than a hammer? Had the robber brought the hammer with him as one of his burglary tools, or did he grab the nearest thing to hand? Mark couldn't say whether the claw hammer found in the kitchen was his or not. He owned several hammers.

While Teresa's death was horrible, it came as a relief to her family when the medical examiner, Dr. Thomas Payne, testified that she was almost certainly killed by the third strike of the hammer, a "catastrophic blow to the occipital region" which would have sent her into what he referred to as "neuropathic shock." Everyone assumed the hammer found beside Teresa's body was the murder weapon, but this still needed to be officially verified. Dr. Payne confirmed that, although he couldn't say how many assailants were involved in the attack, the wounds on Teresa's head were exactly the kind found in forensic pathology manuals describing hammer injuries. "They're textbook wounds."

The number of violent crimes in Bonita Springs varied according to neighborhood and time of year—there were far more in tourist season, which meant the city's crime rate was slightly above the national average for a city of its size. Still, outside the tourist season and away from the beaches, most neighborhoods were quiet and safe, with fewer than two robberies per thousand inhabitants.

Jarvis Road was upscale: homeless people and shady break-and-enter types would stand out, and if there were suspicious lurkers, the cops rousted them quickly. Plus, unlike many of the other houses on the street, the Sieverses' home was surrounded by a high privacy fence. Sure, it was the largest house on the street, but wouldn't a potential robber have chosen a property that was more accessible?

And if it was a thief, why didn't they take anything from the house? Mark was concerned that the cops hadn't asked him to do an inventory to see if anything was missing, but there was no need: Teresa's wallet lay on the ground beside her body, open, cash and credit cards untouched. She'd been wearing expensive earrings and a diamond ring, but none of her jewelry had been taken. Nothing had been stolen—not the 40,000 dollars in cash in the safe upstairs; none of Mark's rare coins, foreign currency, guns, nor ammunition; not the ornamental samurai swords on the kitchen wall; none of the electronics, all easily accessible.

Teresa's safe, containing passports and more valuable jewelry, was also untouched. The only thing that had been disturbed was her suitcase, which she'd left by the door in the garage. Someone had rummaged through it—the zipper was open; clothes and a bag of makeup had been pulled out. A hairbrush, travel kit, and a tumbler had been placed on one of the storage freezers in the garage. All things considered, it looked as though someone had made a half-hearted attempt to give the impression of a robbery as they left the house in a rush.

No, this crime wasn't opportunistic: it was deliberately targeted. Someone had been lying in wait.

• • •

According to her sister, for the last couple of years, Teresa had been involved in a real estate deal that had started to get contentious. She'd been trying to get out of the contract for her medical office in Estero, where she and Mark owned five units. She was angry about the rent, which she thought was "astronomical," and she also felt the management company didn't understand the practicalities of running a medical center. They put competing doctors in the same building, including practitioners who offered the same kind of services as Teresa, but without the proper training.

Recently, a company had offered to buy the whole building, along with the doctors' practices. Teresa was relieved: this was the opportunity for her to free herself from a bad deal. She could get out of the rental contract, reduce her overhead, and find a better location. "We had a buyer and agreed to sell so we are getting out of this mess," she texted Mark in February 2014. But the deal had fallen through. "Teresa was devastated," said Annie.

Then, shortly before her death, a different management company had offered to buy the property. The building's board members wanted to the deal to close, but Teresa was against it. She didn't want to get involved with yet another real estate company, signing yet another ten-year lease. At the board meeting, she was vocal in her opposition. According to Annie, "she made people wake up and see what was going on." Annie wasn't sure whether Teresa was the only person who voted against the proposal, but she was surely the most outspoken. Some people had a lot invested in closing the deal. Did a stakeholder become irate and violent when financial promises weren't being fulfilled? "No one threatened her, but they didn't like it," Mark recalled.

• • •

Teresa's mother said of her daughter and Mark that "they lived a very simple life," but most people wouldn't think of it that way. Teresa didn't usually spend to excess, except when it came to food (on a single trip to the grocery store, she'd spend four or five hundred dollars), but the family had a huge house with a lanai and swimming pool. They took a lot of vacations. Teresa drove a Mercedes; Mark had a station wagon and a motorcycle. Investigators wondered whether there was anyone who might have been jealous or resentful of this happy, busy, wealthy family.

One avenue police explored was the couple's involvement with an organization called Our Mother's Home of Southwest Florida, a transitional housing program for teen mothers and their babies. These were girls who'd been left pregnant as the result of violence. Many had been homeless or were victims of human trafficking. It was Mark who first connected with the charity, donating food; Teresa came on board shortly afterward, getting increasingly involved. At one point, she even served as board president.

She taught a parenting class there on Tuesday evenings, showing the young mothers how to raise their children. She donated money (anonymously) if they wanted their babies circumcised. She organized birthday showers and hosted Christmas parties for the girls and staff. She and Mark had the teenagers over to their house for swimming parties and cookouts and took a group of girls to Disney World and Busch Gardens. The couple sometimes even let the girls and their babies stay at Jarvis Road while they were looking for somewhere to live.

For many of these girls, their future prognosis wasn't good. In the end, a lot of them returned to their abusers, or became addicted to drugs. Not long before her death, Teresa had vented her frustration to a friend—all she wanted, she said, was "to see one girl make it." In the previous year, she'd grown especially close to Nicole, a former drug user who was making amazing progress toward getting her life back on track. Teresa had enrolled her in a cake-decorating class and a fabric class. When she turned eighteen, Nicole had aged out of the foster system and had to leave Our Mother's Home. Mark and Teresa let Nicole and her son Anthony live at 27034 Jarvis Road until they could get settled.

But within two months of moving in, Nicole had gone back to live with her drug-addicted birth mother. Pretty soon, Nicole, too, was using drugs again. On January 5, 2015, she was arrested in Pompano Beach on charges of child neglect after Anthony, three, was found alone in a house with drugs and no food, no running water, no electricity. Child Protective Services proposed to remove him from Nicole's custody.

On May 18, just five weeks before her death, Teresa had advocated in court on Nicole's behalf, arguing for her parental rights. She said she'd worked with Nicole in the foster care system for over two years and she was "one of our stellar residents." The girl's problems, according to Dr. Sievers, were caused by her abusive upbringing, which had caused "long-term trauma to the brain." Did Teresa's strong-willed advocacy make someone angry? Detectives questioned whether Nicole might have associated with ex-convicts, pimps, and traffickers. Had she passed on information about the Sievers house to someone who wanted to commit a robbery? It was worth exploring.

• • •

Teresa's medical assistant, Sandra Hoskins, had worked at her practice for the last seven years (Sandra's husband, Frank, had also worked there until September 2014, when Teresa and Mark decided they no longer needed his services). Teresa and Sandra had been close friends in the past, but over the last couple of years, their relationship had gone sour. Teresa's sister Annie told police that Sandra had been "driving Teresa out of her mind." In February 2013, Teresa had complained to Mark about Sandra "badmouthing" her and "creating doubts in my patients about my capability." On February 25, 2014, Teresa texted Mark, letting him know "we need to talk . . . sandra has reportedly told other pts NOT to do what dr Sievers said about hormones . . ." Privately, to Mark, she called Sandra a "backstabber," a "pain in the ass," and a "vampire."

Mark and Teresa already knew Sandra had been looking for another job. At one point, according to Annie, Teresa had said to her, "Sandra, I'm sorry. I've tried so hard, but I just can't take your energy anymore. You're sucking me dry." Sandra knew Teresa was about to fire her. Could she have been disgruntled enough to want Teresa dead?

• • •

Investigators tracked down Kenny Cousins, Teresa's ex-husband. They'd met in 1999—their first date was on the beach in St. Pete's. Teresa had worn shorts and heels. Kenny couldn't believe she was a doctor. He was Teresa's type—a big, athletic man who lifted weights. They hit it off, married, and bought a home together in Pinellas County. But it wasn't a perfect match. Kenny, who was Black, was fourteen years older than Teresa, and although the marriage worked for a while, their differences came between them in the end. According to her sister, Teresa had been deeply in love with Kenny, and the ending of the marriage broke her heart.

Kenny and Teresa's divorce came through in February 2003, right before her marriage to Mark, but they kept in touch. "If there was a month that went by where we hadn't spoken, she would text me or she would call me," Kenny told NBC2 News, after Teresa's death. He learned about the tragedy through social media. "It was devastating," he recalled.

Investigators wondered: Had Kenny been harboring a long-held jealousy about Teresa's marriage to Mark? And if not Kenny, perhaps someone else was jealous, or simply obsessed with Teresa? She attracted a lot of male attention. Not only was she smart and outgoing, but she was also sexy. She loved to wear stylish clothes, jewelry, makeup, and four-inch heels. Her red hair earned her the predictable epithets: spitfire, bombshell, firecracker. According to Annie, "My sister loved to swear. I mean she *really* loved to swear." Everybody knew she could be loud, aggressive, and argumentative. Did she get into a confrontation with an obsessive stalker?

• • •

Teresa had a strong interest in transgender issues and had done endocrinology work for patients undergoing gender transition surgery. She'd recently appeared in the *Naples Daily News* discussing the use of hormone therapy in the case of a young girl who was transitioning from male to female. As late as May 6, less than two months before her death, she was talking to another young patient about transitioning. Could she have been murdered by an extremist who believed this type of surgery violated God's will? Or maybe a crazed parent blamed Teresa for changing the gender of their child? It seemed nuts—but again, anything was possible.

• • •

The strangest and most perplexing theory about Teresa's murder involved her disdain for mainstream medicine. Three weeks after her death, the Lee County Medical Examiner received a letter from John Hammell, an author researching an article for *Life Extension* magazine about "the deaths of several different alternative medical practitioners who have been murdered in different parts of the USA." He added, emphatically, that "the body count is now up to 10 by my count, although some are missing persons who have mysteriously disappeared. . . ."

Hammell was referring to a fringe conspiracy theory—it was far-fetched, although Mark didn't dismiss it out of hand—that holistic doctors like Teresa were being murdered because they'd discovered that certain vaccinations introduced cancer cells into the body. Those who believed this theory were convinced that Big Pharma, afraid of losing its huge profits from cancer treatment, was hiring assassins to silence naturopathic doctors. Each of the other practitioners who'd died or disappeared in apparently mysterious circumstances was described as a very healthy person with no major physical problems and no history of depression. All of them had harshly criticized the mainstream medical establishment and had had recent run-ins with the feds.

On June 19, 2015, Dr. Jeff Bradstreet, sixty, was found in a river in North Carolina with a gunshot wound to his chest. Bradstreet was a controversial naturopathic practitioner who believed vaccines caused autism. On June 21, outspoken holistic doctor Bruce Hedendal, sixty-seven, was found dead in his car in Boca Raton. No cause was given. And on July 21, Nicolas Gonzalez, also sixty-seven, collapsed suddenly from a suspected heart attack in New York. Gonzalez had been strongly criticized for his belief that cancer could be cured by dietary supplements and twice-daily coffee enemas.

While people have pointed out that these doctors were all in their sixties, had no connection with one another, and lived in completely different parts of the country, others were convinced something nefarious was going on. Could Teresa have been assassinated to cover up something she'd discovered?

Chapter 4

Bliss Oil

In 2006, Teresa opened her practice, Restorative Health and Healing, in the Estero Medical Center, a twenty-minute commute from her home on Jarvis Road, depending on traffic. Estero was an even more exclusive community than Bonita Springs—everything was large, bright, and modern. Mark ran the back end of the business, taking care of payroll, hiring and firing, HIPAA compliance, patient enquiries, and similar matters.

Estero, like many parts of Florida, has an elderly population; it's a good place for a doctor to set up shop. After tourism, medicine fuels the local economy. The Medical Center had enough doctors to fill a small hospital, but Teresa was unique. Like many physicians, she'd grown dissatisfied with western medicine's reliance on pharmaceutical cures and had begun practicing holistic techniques.

According to her assistant, Sandra Hoskins, Teresa's office wasn't a cold, clinical setting. "It wasn't a place where you sat in a traditional physician's office. . . . We served tea. . . . It was a living room. It wasn't a waiting room." Teresa's aim was to get patients to listen to their bodies and take responsibility for their own well-being. Her motto was, "Being healthy is your choice. Getting you there is my passion."

The premise behind naturopathic medicine is that the body has an inherent ability to heal itself. Natural cures have been around much longer than western medicine, and there's plenty of evidence to show that, for many patients, acupuncture, herbal remedies, ayurveda, and homeopathy are just as effective as modern pharmaceuticals, if not more so. Mistrust of the medical establishment, with its ties to insurance companies, is rapidly increasing; more people are finding relief in naturopathic practices and supplements.

None of the Sievers family ate dairy, gluten, or meat. Teresa didn't wear leather. She described herself as a "holistic healer," and her practices broadly concurred with the field's accepted traditions, combining the best of mainstream and alternative medicine. "I'm not against prescribing medicines at all," she explained in a 2010 interview in the *Florida Weekly*, "but I am against the wholesale and indiscriminate administration of medications. I don't want the side effects of a medication to be worse than the condition I am treating."

Cynics of traditional medicine come from both ends of the political spectrum, and sometimes espouse fringe beliefs in other areas, too. Left-leaning liberals like the Sieverses may turn to homeopathic cures because they mistrust chemical interventions, preferring the benefits of natural products. Right-wingers who avoid conventional doctors may do so because they're anti-vaccination, anti-government, or germ theory deniers.

Most naturopathic practitioners are well-trained and reputable, but some alternative healers make dangerous claims: that they can cure cancer, get rid of tumors, repair thyroid conditions, reverse Alzheimer's disease. Others promote methods of healing that have no verifiable effect except as placebo cures. They may also sell expensive supplements to those following their regimen.

Not to say all naturopathic healers push their products in bad faith—they may believe in the products and use them themselves—but in the world of alternative medicine, it's hard to tell the gurus from the shysters.

Additionally, some practitioners who disdain conventional methods have controversial relationships with medical authorities and licensing boards. After all, anybody can claim to be an "medical intuologist," or a "vibrational healer." While every field has its own training schools and colleges that give practitioners a lot of initials after their names, these are often self-governing, unaccredited bodies. Health benefits claims can be boosted by citing "peer-reviewed articles" in pay-to-publish journals with official-sounding names.

These kinds of scams may be why serious naturopathic practitioners are keen to assert their legitimate credentials, referring to themselves as "Dr. Bob," Dr. Mike," or "Dr. Nick" (even when their doctorate is a PhD). Defensively separating herself from any taint of hucksterism, Teresa garnered a long list of impressive qualifications beyond her MD. She had a Master of Science in Metabolic Medicine; she was certified by the American Board of Holistic and Integrative Medicine and certified in Functional and Anti-Aging Medicine and Energy Therapy. In May 2013, she earned a Master of Science degree in Medical Science, strutting across the platform in her gown and four-inch heels. Mark, overcome with pride, texted her picture to everyone he knew.

• • •

Anti-aging medicine is a huge industry, set to increase steeply as the world's elderly population grows. People have always sought out the fountain of youth, but today, many doctors see aging as a disease that can be cured—or at least temporarily reversed. This had become Teresa's main field. She described herself as an "anti-aging specialist," but again, there was a practical caveat.

"Anti-aging means many things to many people," she told the Naples *Florida Weekly*. "Too often, [anti-aging] is associated with the quest to look eternally youthful or to be slimmer—something that is mostly cosmetic. While that is fine, my practice involves finding imbalances in the body before they reach the disease state."

Teresa took anti-aging to another level. She'd come to believe the healing process wasn't just about repairing the body. It was also about the emotional blocks and stresses that people might not be consciously aware of. In the year before her death, according to Annie, Teresa had discovered the "missing piece of the puzzle," which was "understanding the energetic component" of her patients' lives. Teresa, said Annie, was "one of the first doctors in Southwest Florida to embrace energy medicine." These kinds of healing practices weren't covered by insurance, which Teresa had stopped accepting. Plus, the paperwork was getting in her way.

In 2014, Teresa met Lenka Spiska, a "quantum healer and intuologist" who could perform Reiki—the energetic laying-on of hands. Lenka specialized in techniques and practices that helped patients become conscious of their own intuition, their "deepest parts," their buried memories and emotions. She joined Restorative Health and Healing as a separate practitioner. If a patient had trouble getting better, Teresa would send them to see Lenka, who'd intuit how their emotional problems were manifesting in their bodies. Lenka might prescribe meditation, a Reiki session, or some other daily ritual for redirecting energy flow.

Before Teresa died, the two women had made plans to set up a new practice together: Sievers and Spiska: Where East Meets West. Together, they wanted to teach patients how to intuit when something was wrong with them, and why, and how to fix it. Another of Teresa's mottos: "I am passionate about empowering you to tap into the doctor within you."

The laying on of hands? Intuology? Quantum healing?

Energy flow? A lot of people saw it as, if not old-fashioned quackery, then New Age mumbo-jumbo. But Teresa didn't care. As far as she was concerned, it worked. Teresa's sister, Annie, admitted that the idea of "energy medicine" was "polarizing," but Teresa was convinced of its power. "Teresa didn't give a shit about what you thought about her," said Annie. "She didn't care if she lost every patient she had."

Energy is a slippery thing. It exists—it can be measured and harnessed—but it's difficult to grasp. The word is generally used to mean some kind of ethereal life-force. In some ways, "energy medicine" harks back to outdated theories of mesmerism, vitalism, or animal magnetism. Looked at more sympathetically, it's like sending prayers to someone—it operates outside the realm of scientific proof. "Healing energy" and "vibrations" can't be measured, and as with voodoo curses, success is largely a matter of whether you believe in them or not. And Teresa did. Perhaps to a fault. She talked about chi, tapping, frequencies, and contact healing. She was so attuned to "bad vibrations" that she wouldn't put certain objects on the floor and tried to steer clear of people (like her office manager Sandra Hoskins) with "negative energy" who "sucked her dry." Some said her zeal was more like superstition. Or, if not superstition, then obsession. She'd got Mark believing in it, too.

Could Teresa's obsession with "energy" have been symptomatic of a psychological problem? Lenka, who knew Teresa well, told investigators her friend "lived on the edge." What did she mean? Teresa, according to Lenka, was addicted to pot, to managing her self-image, controlling her food. She apparently took antidepressants, although the prescription was under Mark's name. She had "sexual orientation issues." She had an explosive temper.

Stress at home, stress at work, no escape. Teresa, said Lenka, had been "trying to shift the negativity." With this in mind, her interest in "frequencies" and "vibrations" made sense. If your life is spinning out of control, it's natural to find something to grab hold of. By tuning in to the energy around her, maybe Teresa felt she could keep everything on track.

But some felt she was going further astray, indulging in practices that were borderline unethical. Just as western medicine is entangled with Big Pharma, integrative healing has an unfortunate crossover with sales and branding: practitioners sometimes become associated with trademarked products like "electromagnetic cellular activation bracelets" and "biogenic lotions."

For a while, Teresa was listed by one of her mentors, Dr. Norman Shealy, as a Certified Bliss Oil Practitioner ("Bliss Oils" are a patented blend of essential oils "sacred to the Nemenhah Native American Church" that have been "developed specifically to stimulate the 13 points of The Ring of Crystal," and are "designed to enhance a sense of Bliss").

She'd also developed a profitable sideline in promoting Xymogen, a brand of "nutraceutical" supplements sold only by licensed health care practitioners. The American Medical Association doesn't approve of in-office sales by physicians of health products, but strictly speaking, it's not illegal. These are supplements, not prescription medications, but they're supplements that can only be obtained with a prescription. Some argue this is simply a marketing technique meant to make them seem more "medical."

Dr. Sievers had over a thousand patients, many wealthy, most of them elderly. Most of her clients paid between 150 and 250 dollars for an office visit, adding on another forty or fifty dollars for anti-aging supplements—RegeneMax, Ultra K2-D3 5000, OxyCleanse, ALAMax, VitalVasc, and ProbioMax—all Xymogen products. From 2012 until her death in 2015, Teresa got what her sister called "a nice big check" from Xymogen (which she believed in, and used herself); she also received yearly checks of up to 14,000 dollars from the supplement manufacturers MD Prescriptives, LLC, and around 400 dollars monthly from PureCapsPro.

• • •

By 2013, Dr. Sievers was getting to the stage where she wanted to start seeing fewer patients and, instead, to address the masses. She wanted to be a celebrity, speaking at large conferences, writing books, appearing on television. She had a website and was trying to spend more time on social media. She imagined restructuring her practice into "a twenty-first-century wellness center that included Reiki, transcutaneous acupuncture, and Emotional Freedom Techniques." She was planning to get a "crystal healing bed" for her patients.

She'd been practicing public speaking by giving talks to local audiences in Estero. She brainstormed her strategies with Mark, who did most of the promotional work, drafting his wife's talks and lectures. He started looking for someone to sponsor a TV show starring Teresa—perhaps a supplement company like Xymogen. His plans were ambitious. ("Get stars . . . to come on the show. . . . Have a website with links to Senators and other political contacts to make change to organic technologies.")

Intensive networking brought the couple into contact with Tamer Elsafy, an Egyptian entrepreneur who'd developed a joint supplement called Flexcin. Elsafy, himself a slick performer with mediagenic teeth, was looking for a charismatic MD to star with him in a series of infomercials endorsing the product. Teresa fit the bill. Eighteen months before her death, with great fanfare, she was appointed the new spokesperson for Flexcin International, Inc., "a joint nutritional product that helps to alleviate pain and stiffness associated with diseases."

According to the announcement, "Dr. Sievers will be introduced through a series of Flexcin informational videos on the internet and YouTube which will describe different types of arthritis. . . . National TV, Convention and Radio talk show appearances are in the planning stages." Mark, excited, began thinking of ideas, some a little shady ("get hormone expert and have it look like she uses flexcin").

At the time of her death, Teresa, dressed in a white coat, had already appeared in at least seven Flexcin "informational videos" (i.e., infomercials), one of them thirty minutes long, encouraging viewers to "call 1-800-End-Pain" and receive a tub of "awesome motion lotion" and a set of other Flexcin products discounted from 130 dollars to 49.95 (with free shipping and a lifetime guarantee).

While in Texas filming the infomercials, Teresa met a producer named Doug Kaufman, who was looking for a practitioner to host a show on the Doctor TV network. He thought Teresa was "a natural," and envisioned a series of short episodes in which she talked about her practice and interviewed other doctors and patients, with a focus on energy medicine. At the time of her death, the first season had already been completed. A second show, hosted with Lenka, would be called *Pathways 2 Healing*, and at the time of Teresa's death, they'd already filmed four short "taster" episodes, which are still available online. In the clips, as in her infomercials, Teresa looks fabulous—glossy, smart, sparkling, and full of life.

Once again, Mark jotted down some ideas they could use to market the show: "quotes from Einstein about intuition . . . something from John Lennon. . . . Pictures of people out in nature having a quiet moment . . . the importance of symbols. . . ." The more she strove for publicity, the more Teresa's focus veered toward the spiritual, and further away from science, even from integrative medicine. She began journaling about the "spiritual encounters" she'd had as a result of "sending out energy" into the world, such as seeing ladybirds and butterflies, and the recurrence of certain numbers.

In May, just a month before her death, Teresa appeared on the cover of *èBella*, a Southwest Florida magazine that publicized the accomplishments of local businesswomen. "She had a lot of contacts with a lot of different people," Teresa's mother told Detective Nolen. "She was involved with so many people who are famous."

But while Teresa may have networked with a few key players in the local wellness community, they were hardly "famous." They were people like Robert M. Korolevich, MD, founder of a healthy living protocol he called "the K process" and owner of a "concierge" medicine practice in Naples, Florida. Another was Mary Lynn Ziemer, a Bonita Springs-based "Master of Advanced Life Concepts" and "Master Life Coach" who had developed an educational course she called the "Joy Negotiator," which she described as "a new way of understanding and defining reality as you know it." Teresa, too, was hoping to set herself up similarly as a "health mentor" and "lifestyle specialist," ideally offering her followers programs of talks, meetings, online support, and a protocol of meals and supplements.

Nonetheless, although her star appeared to be on the rise, she was disappointed that things seemed to be going so slowly. Potential opportunities kept falling through. She often vented her frustration to Mark, her greatest supporter and biggest fan. "I am tired of hoping," she texted him wearily, in June 2013. He replied: "I'm here beside you for what it's worth."

• • •

When he was in his late twenties, Mark Sievers had a serious accident, hitting his head on the ground after slipping on ice. There was no brain damage, but afterward, he suffered from headaches and disturbing episodes of memory loss. Ever since Teresa had known him, he'd been absent-minded and disorganized, forgetting to do things, never putting things back where they belonged.

Teresa, who sometimes called him "a work in progress," had come to believe Mark's absent-mindedness was caused not by the head trauma but by an accumulation of heavy metals in his system. “My lead’s off the roof. My mercury’s off the charts,” Mark told detectives, during his police interview. Teresa had been administering “chelation therapy”—a series of intravenous infusions, usually given weekly, to remove heavy metals from the blood.

Chelation is a controversial process. Several medical practitioners, both traditional and integrative, believe it can help patients with autism and Alzheimer’s disease. Teresa offered chelation therapy to patients suffering from atherosclerosis, osteoarthritis, and other inflammation-related conditions, and believed it was a successful antioxidant. As she spent more time producing her television show and doing media appearances, she planned to reduce her office hours to three days a week, offering chelation on the other days, which could be administered by a nurse practitioner or physician’s assistant.

As of 2023, chelation is only FDA-approved to treat heavy metal poisoning. It hasn’t been endorsed for the treatment of heart disease, although champions of the process are convinced it works. It was endorsed by one of Teresa’s mentors, Norman Shealy, and his colleague, Dr. Roy Heilbron, author of *Healing Heart Disease with Chelation Therapy*. “Because of the toxicity of this world we live in today, it is important to be proactive in keeping your body as clean as possible,” advised Dr. Heilbron, a Boca Raton–based cardiologist, chelation specialist, and friend of the Sievers family. “As Norm and I try to live healthily to 120 years, we hope you’ll join us in cleaning your body. . . . Be elated, get chelated!!”

Roy Heilbron—who sometimes goes by Roy Jimenez, or Roy Heilbron-Jimenez—is an unnerving figure. In a series of 2010 lectures posted on YouTube, he appears as a youthful Hispanic doctor with hair slicked back into a thin ponytail, wearing a white coat even while speaking from the podium. He also appears as a talking head in *Unleaded*, a documentary alleging that "mainstream media actively covered up the National Institutes of Health's evidence that Chelation Therapy works."

In the *Unleaded* trailer, Dr. Heilbron appears twice. At first, he appears sitting at a desk wearing a white coat, with a turquoise pinky ring, and a stethoscope around his neck. There's a scientific-looking chart on the wall behind him. Identified as a "Board Certified Cardiologist and Co-Creator of the South Beach Diet," he has a full beard and no glasses. Oddly, the second time he appears, he seems to be in disguise. Without identification, he sits at a messy desk with a different backdrop—no stethoscope, no glasses, no pinky ring, no beard, and a constant, manic grin.

In another video uploaded to YouTube, Dr. Heilbron—white coat, stethoscope around the neck, never-ending smile—is interviewed by "Jim Healthy," a gentleman of indeterminate age with spiky white hair, an uncannily smooth, stretched face, and a pumped-up body. Mr. Healthy is the author, with Dr. Heilbron, of *The Thirty Day Diabetes Cure* and *The Thirty Day Diabetes Cure Special Reports* (both available from "Jim Healthy Publications").

In his 1857 book *The Confidence-Man,* Herman Melville describes the lineage of American charlatans: "Fellows who, whether in stocks, politics, breadstuffs, morals, metaphysics, religion—be it what it may—trump up their black panics . . . with a view to some sort of covert advantage." A time-honored fraudster Melville neglects to mention is the great American quack. From snake oil to superfoods, from e-meters to herbal fat burners, quack remedies have always had their pushers and promoters, who take advantage of people's trust, vulnerability, and ignorance of medical facts. Like most confidence men, quacks prey not on the rich but on people of ordinary means, especially the elderly and those whose health is failing. And there's always a market. If you've been sick for years and doctors haven't helped, it's natural to grow desperate and seek out alternatives.

Most people would agree that Roy Heilbron could legitimately be described as a confidence man. There are significant discrepancies in his own accounts of his educational background, qualifications, and work history. Many of the claims he makes are unsupported (nowhere, for example, is he accredited as the "founder of the South Beach Diet"). The Florida Division of Corporations includes various businesses registered under his name, including Caring Cardiology, Hart-Heilbron Realty LLC, Heilbron Baptist Church, Inc., A Well for Health Church (as Reverend Roy M. Heilbron), and Scrooge Collections.

In an event advertised on Facebook, his bio reads as follows: "Heilbron currently lives in Santa Fe, New Mexico where he is developing a cardiac rehab/retreat center, fully self-sustained with solar and wind power, water catchment system, and electric cars to teach lifestyle, exercise, jiu-jitsu, meditation and organic eating/farming. He has made 5 Himalayan Journeys where he studied under Babaji on how to combine Western and Eastern Medicine." (Perhaps these were spiritual journeys: Babaji died in 1895.)

The talented Mr. Heilbron: CEO, actor, author, cardiologist, chelation therapist, researcher, reverend, dietician, holistic doctor, public speaker, property manager, mystic, mountaineer, and collections agent.

And convicted felon. As with many confidence men, the law caught up with him in the end. In June 2014, Heilbron's license to practice medicine in New Mexico was suspended for three months when he was arrested for drunk driving. At the same time, Blue Cross Blue Shield terminated his provider agreement for "excessive, unjustified and fraudulent billing practices." Then on July 1, 2015, just two days after Teresa's body was found, he was indicted by a federal grand jury for a wide range of offenses related to health care fraud, including performing unnecessary tests, inserting bogus symptoms, observations, and ultrasound images into patients' medical charts, and submitting false claims to insurance companies. Apparently, he photocopied over one hundred patients' records and used them to fabricate identical records for others.

Heilbron appealed to the court to postpone his sentencing on compassionate grounds, submitting documents to show he had a rare form of prostate cancer and needed to be treated by a "holistic urologist" in Costa Rica. This added another charge to his indictment: obstruction of justice. The documents were shown to be faked. Dr. Heilbron did not have cancer, and, at the time he requested to postpone his sentencing, he was, in fact, happily vacationing in Europe.

Heilbron's indictment two days after the murder seemed frightening and suspicious. Investigators wondered: how and why was Teresa connected to this dodgy con man?

Chapter 5

"The Dictionary Definition of a Happy Marriage"

Although Teresa was pregnant when she and Mark married in 2003, the couple took their vows seriously. Before the wedding, they attended "Marriage Encounters," a "faith-based marriage enrichment program helping husbands & wives improve their communication." They believed in therapeutic exercises, journaling, couples' programs, workbooks, and "intimacy challenges" (such as having sex for several days consecutively). "Basically, the key to any successful marriage," noted Mark, "is Trust, Honesty, Open Communication, and commitment to each other and God."

Their dedication worked and saw them through the birth of their children—a difficult time for many couples. When selecting a romantic partner, we're unconsciously drawn to someone like our opposite-sex parent, even if we consciously think we're picking someone completely different. Because we choose partners from outside our immediate family, we're not hampered by the incest barrier. But once we become parents ourselves, everything changes. It's not unusual for new parents to go a year or more without being intimate.

It can be difficult, at first, to negotiate this new ambivalence, and sometimes couples never recapture their sexual love. Suddenly, breasts are for loving and nurturing, not arousal. Once a woman becomes a mother, she's no longer a sex object, but someone to be revered.

But for Mark and Teresa, the birth of their daughters sealed their bond even more tightly. In a healthy way, they brought an erotic element to their family roles. Mark's most common term of endearment for Teresa was *momma*, and she often called him *daddy*. The couple worked together to teach their children about sexuality in positive, unconventional ways. They encouraged Emma and Olivia to express their views freely and choose their own clothes. When their daughters were young, Mark and Teresa were happy with them going naked at home, and occasionally did so themselves.

By 2010, after seven years of marriage, the couple had settled into a stable routine. To friends, neighbors, and colleagues, the Sieverses were popular and outgoing, beloved in the community. They took the girls to recitals, violin lessons, and play dates, hung out at the dog park and the beach. They spent time with Teresa's friends and colleagues, as well as Mark's mom, Bonnie, and her partner, Melanie.

Often, Teresa's family visited from Connecticut, and the Sieverses regularly took trips to see them there. The couple were both involved in Our Mother's Home and other charities that fought human trafficking, such as Wings of Shelter and Safe House International. They shopped at Food and Thought, an organic store in Naples, ate at the café there, picked up drinks from the juice bar.

Teresa worked hard all day at the clinic. Mark helped with office management, took care of the finances, and did the grocery shopping, but most of his time was spent with Emma and Olivia, taking them to Seacrest, their pre-K day school (homeschooling came later), ferrying them back and forth from music lessons and dance classes. A popular, good-natured joker, he chaperoned groups of kids on field trips, holiday parties, and beach days. Emma and Olivia volunteered at PetSmart, were involved in a local community theater, and loved to swim; Mark bought them mermaid tails to wear in the pool and called them his "merms." He'd refer to babysitting as "mermaid watching." His motorcycle license plate read "MRMDS."

The couple were conscientious parents, but they had their outside interests, too. Mark would go on long motorbike rides. A firearms enthusiast, he'd inherited his father's impressive gun collection, and enjoyed taking Dr. Petrites's wife, Michele, to the shooting range. Teresa liked smoking pot (in April 2012, she texted Mark she was "ordering amazing grass"). She also enjoyed being pampered, going to the spa, getting her hair and nails done.

After the murder, Detective Nolen asked Bonnie about the couple's relationship. She described it as "the dictionary definition of a happy marriage." They were "wonderful, loving, caring . . . respectful," said Bonnie. "They were devoted to each other, devoted to the girls, and to having a happy, loving life. . . . Whenever you see them, they're always hugging and helping each other." Both Mark and Teresa, she said, were interested in "changing the world for a better place, teaching their girls how to love all people, and to be kind and considerate."

Like most couples, they weren't a perfect match. As Annie put it, "Teresa was more of a *Masterpiece Theatre* girl, a Scrabble girl. Whereas Mark was more of a World Wrestling and comic book guy." Naturally, they sometimes squabbled, but for the most part, they were too busy to fight. Teresa got annoyed with Mark's absent-mindedness, but in a playful, loving way: she called him a "dork," a "nut," and a "goose" ("i will never understand how u can make me so crazy but i can love u so much"). He called her a "goofy broad." She expressed gratitude for the way he took care of so many things ("I want to tx u again for being the kind of man that can deal with this"). Mark was a great booster, cheering his wife on in her career ambitions ("i told u that i envision u reaching people by the masses . . . this is just the beginning!").

During her police interview, Annie told investigators that Teresa was "kind of a drill sergeant" with Mark. "She would yell at him . . . but Mark worshipped the ground Teresa walked on. . . . Sometimes I'd ask him, 'how could you be so nice to her?'" It's true that Teresa could be demanding, especially when it came to food shopping. Every few days, she'd text Mark a grocery list, and in keeping with the couple's organic lifestyle, she was exacting about brands and ingredients ("box of regular [not GF] imported italian sm shells or elbows 2 bags of non organic tinkyada elbows or zitis if they have get 3 DeBoles gluten free multi grain rice [quinoa amaranth]").

Mark was a caring, devoted father deeply involved in looking after his daughters and managing his wife's career. But there was a quirky, needy side to his character, too. Women who knew him described him as a notorious flirt, but his text messages to female friends weren't flirtatious or playfully sexual—at least, not all the time—so much as unctuously overattentive. He gushed over Teresa, and other women, too. "When i said that u r Beautiful, i meant it, but not just ur physical beauty, more importantly, ur inner Beauty," he texted a female friend in April 2010. He'd often tell women how grateful he was to know them, to have them in his life, that they were "truly beautiful inside and out." He was always wishing somebody a happy birthday or anniversary, always "sending lots of light, love and happiness," prayers, sympathies, and healing energy, always texting people to remind them how grateful he was to know them. Even complete strangers got his blessing.

"They knew they were together for life," said Teresa's mother, Mary Ann Groves. When Detective Nolen asked if Teresa had ever been unfaithful, she said, "No. Not my Teresa. She did all that before she was married." The couple argued, she said, but that was natural. "Teresa had a temper . . . she was very animated. . . . It's just the way she was. We're a very vocal family."

Teresa's sister Annie also said things were good between the couple. According to Annie, "Teresa always said, 'I'll never leave Mark. I wouldn't do that to my girls.'" When investigators asked Annie whether she thought Mark might ever see other women behind her sister's back, she laughed. "There is no way on God's green earth," she said.

• • •

Sergeant David Lebid, a younger officer with a trendy fade haircut and laid-back demeanor, conducted Mark's second interrogation. After ten or fifteen minutes of small talk, Lebid homed in on the question of Mark and Teresa's marriage. Suspecting Mark wasn't coming clean, he pushed a little harder. As Nolen had done earlier, he asked: had there been any infidelity on either side?

"I've never cheated on her, and she's never cheated on me," said Mark.

To Lebid, this sounded cagey. "Do you guys swing with anyone?"

Mark hesitated. He lowered his voice. "I don't want this getting out, because it's so far out there," he said. "She liked to have another woman with us. She liked to watch me with another woman. She even liked to hear about me with another woman when she wasn't present. But it was very, very seldom."

Lebid wanted to know more. When did this start?

"We talked about it for two or three years before anything happened," explained Mark. "It was a fantasy. Strictly fantasy. Then one day she said, 'Let's do this.'"

The words *swinging*, *polyamory*, and *open relationships* are often used interchangeably, but they have distinctions. Normally, an open relationship is when a committed couple allow each other to have extra relationships on the side, sometimes on a "don't ask, don't tell" basis. Polyamory involves long-term commitments to more than one partner—sometimes, all partners share the same house. The primary difference between polyamory and swinging has nothing to do with sexual practices, but with the fact that swinging is a discrete sexual activity, whereas for polyamorists, their beliefs permeate every aspect of their lives. Swinging is generally considered "just sex," and usually refers to couples who experiment with many different partners, often at clubs or private parties.

People often think of swinging as something sleazy, practiced by men on the prowl and unwholesome couples with morbid tastes: orgies, cuckolding, voyeurism. In movies, swingers' clubs are found in dirty basements made to look like dungeons, or upstairs rooms with Gothic décor and velvet drapes. In fact, statistically, most swingers are educated, wealthy, and satisfied with their marriage and sex life. Most, like the Sieverses, are in their forties and fifties—when the children are grown, the relationship is solid, and there's more disposable income. Swingers' parties take place everywhere—in suburban homes, at fancy hotels, in the open air, at private resorts, and on cruises.

Mark told Detective Lebid that at first, he was very uncomfortable with the idea of swinging, because he loved Teresa so much and didn't feel the need for anyone else to join them in the bedroom. He didn't want to "go there," because his wife was the only woman he needed. She was amazing. Every time she walked into a room, all heads would turn. "Everybody's jaw would drop," he said. Still, even though Teresa was gorgeous, at first, Mark was concerned her desire for another woman was a "self-esteem" issue on her part—maybe she was trying to spice up their sex life just to please him? But eventually she persuaded him it was something she really wanted for herself.

Most couples begin swinging to act out sexual fantasies and reignite their relationship. To keep things on track, they often have rules—no kissing, for example, or no swinging without their partner present. Mark and Teresa's rule was that Mark could have sex with other women, but Teresa wasn't allowed to have intercourse with other men. While this seems hypocritical, Teresa didn't complain—outside of Mark, it was women that interested her.

In January 2011, the couple drove to nearby Naples to try out a swingers' club for the first time. Here they met John and Julie, a sympathetic couple, and the four got intimate. Mark and Teresa, in turn, had sex with Julie while John watched; then John made out with Julie and Teresa. Later, the two couples tried to hook up again. The party scene didn't interest Mark and Teresa—they wanted a more private situation that wasn't just about sex. Mark suggested getting together socially, going dancing at a club (Mark was into country; Teresa loved hip-hop). Texting back and forth, Teresa explained that she didn't want a "full swap." It wasn't because she didn't find John attractive, she reassured him, just that "I am looking first for the female connection." The feeling, apparently, was mutual, but a second get-together never happened.

The couple's next swinging adventure took place three months later, during a trip to Disney World in Orlando, when they got together with a woman named Marie. Originally, the Sieverses had been friends with both Marie and her husband Peter. Like the Sieverses, Peter and Marie had agreed to bring other women into their relationship, but Marie broke the rules by having sex with two men behind Peter's back. When he found out, the couple went through a "very nasty divorce." The Sieverses were no longer close to Peter, but they'd stayed friendly with Marie.

That weekend at Disney World, Mark hung out with the children at Splash Mountain while Teresa and Marie made love in the Sieverses' hotel room. Then they switched roles. Teresa watched the kids, while Mark had sex with Marie, filming the encounter on video. Later that year, with Teresa's permission, Mark hooked up with a woman named Sue; the idea of them together, Teresa told him, made her "hot and horny." (Later the same day, she was reminding him to pick up "salad ideally w romaine only and add avacado get 2 of their vinegratte dsg on side.")

In September 2011, again with Teresa's blessing, Mark got intimate with a local yoga teacher he knew named Brenda. This time, it wasn't just a one-off encounter. Mark and Brenda became close and stayed friendly for the next four years. Sometimes they hung out together, taking their children to the beach. They texted many times a day, sharing sexy pictures, reminiscing about the games they'd played in the Sieverses' hot tub. Despite her new lover's attention, Brenda was perennially miserable, always complaining about how lonely and unhappy she was. She couldn't find a boyfriend. She had no money. Her father was dead. Her friends hated her. Her new sandals got stolen at the beach. "You are a wonderful woman ☺" Mark reassured her in September 2011, promising she'd soon meet the man of her dreams.

As well as making notes in his phone calendar, Mark was a compulsive texter; he'd sometimes send forty to fifty texts a day, mostly loving and grateful messages to Teresa. He always appreciated their "adult time." He constantly praised her appearance ("You looked beautiful today!"; "u looked HOTTTT"). Teresa was often too busy to reply, but when she did, she was grateful, too. "i luv u baby thanks for being an amazing husband," she texted him in November 2011. "ur welcome, tx for tolerating me," Mark replied.

But Mark texted a lot of other women, too, and his muddle-headedness led to some embarrassing mistakes. He emailed Teresa's sister in Connecticut, telling her, "Hey mama, you look exceptionally beautiful today!" To Teresa's friend Daniele, he wrote "momma, i want to take you into my arms and devour your body inch by inch by inch until you scream . . ." Twice he texted Lenka calling her his "sexy mama." Both times she replied, tersely, "wrong mama."

Chapter 6

Profit Margins

"Did you guys ever talk about divorce?" Detective Lebid asked Mark, during his second police interview after Teresa's death.

Never in a serious way, said Mark. Teresa always described their marriage as a "sacred contract" she could never break, although he admitted she'd sometimes throw the word around. "She had a temper. She would get mad. 'Clear your office. This whole house is chaos. This kind of thing will lead to divorce.'" They told each other not to joke about "the *D* word," he said.

Passion was at the root of their relationship—"drill sergeant" Teresa yelling at a contrite and apologetic Mark. He was always letting her know how stunning she looked, how "damn sexy" she was, how much he adored her, how she was his "dream come true." Often, she would reply fondly, reminding Mark she loved him and cared for him, too. Sometimes, she'd spontaneously send him loving and erotic texts, but not as often as he wanted. Still, Mark had come to accept the situation. He knew Teresa loved him. "She has told me from day 1 that she doesn't love me the same way i love her," he reminded himself in the journal he kept on his phone. "Not mushy kind of sappy love. Writing notes holding hands. . . . It's not a bad thing, just reality."

Mark told Detective Lebid proudly that he and Teresa had a passionate marriage. “We enjoyed each other. . . . If we could, we'd do it four times a day.” It was true: the couple both had high libidos, and their sex life was dynamite. That year, in his phone, Mark started recording their encounters, noting how often they had sex, for how long, how many orgasms each of them had, and how. In 2013, they did it on the beach, on their hotel room balcony, in the car, in the pantry, in the (hopefully unisex) bathrooms at the pool, while upstairs fetching the girls' swimsuits. They did it stoned. They tied each other up. Teresa gave Mark a blow job while he was driving home. To ramp up the passion, while they were having sex, they shared fantasies about other people. As in the early days of their marriage, they tried “intimacy challenges,” doing it for a few days on the trot or seeing how long they could go without making love. “16 days in a row without sexual contact,” noted Mark in his calendar in April. “blue balls started.”

When it came to sex partners, Teresa was always Mark's first choice—he adored her more and more. Still, when she was too busy for sex, and when she wasn't available, he'd turn to other women to stroke his ego and reassure himself he was still virile. He still saw Brenda, although it was sometimes difficult for them to meet due to their busy schedules (in March, Mark texted her that he couldn't come inside for sex, as planned, because he didn't want to leave his kids in the car).

As usual, she was a drag, “sick of the drama” and “bored as hell.” She needed to borrow money. Her new boyfriend turned out to be a dud. Her neighbor cut down all her trees. “there is nobody under 70 interested in me,” she whined, complaining she'd “only had sex 15 times in 30 years.” Mark said he did it more times than that every month (“not trying to rub ur nose in it”).

When Mark got intimate with Kelly, another woman he'd been interested in, it didn't stop him from hooking up with Brenda. In fact, he'd send the same erotic pictures to both women one after another, sometimes sexting them the same messages. But, possibly at an unconscious level, the aim of his extramarital affairs was to bring him closer to Teresa—partly by reminding her what a stud he was, and also because he knew it turned her on.

When Teresa was at a conference out of town, Mark texted her that he was planning to hook up with Marie while Emma and Olivia had a play date with Marie's kids. "i'm so hot just thinking about you being with Marie," she replied. "even if nothing happens, I enjoy just thinking about it . . . wish I brought my vibrator." Mark told her he was planning to have intercourse with Marie. Teresa was fine with it (she reminded him to use condoms), but right on the verge of the act, Marie got anxious and texted Teresa to be sure she had her consent. Once they finally got going, Mark's mind seemed to be on Teresa, rather than Marie. He started giving her a play-by-play account of their lovemaking, with pictures, until Teresa got exasperated. "omg !!! stop texting me just enjoy it!"

• • •

At Restorative Health and Healing, without neglecting her regular patients, Teresa kept hoping to reach a "more affluent clientele." She started offering deep-tissue laser therapy, an FDA-approved treatment for musculoskeletal pain that uses light energy to reduce inflammation and promote healing. Laser therapy could be performed by anybody with the right training, so Lenka could do it, too. The women held several Open Houses (with vegan spreads) where they gave laser therapy demonstrations, offering treatment packages at discount rates. They bought mailing lists to send out ads, discussing the demographics of their ideal patients and potential "return on investments." (When Mark mentioned someone who worked at Our Mother's Home who was interested in laser treatments, Teresa responded, cynically, "unfortunately if they work at omh there're likely not going to be somebody we want here.")

More than ever, the couple hustled and pushed to promote Teresa's nascent media career. She spoke at meetings, conferences, and webinars. She set up a website, made an appointment with a publicist, enlisted a videographer to film her talks, planning to upload them to YouTube. In comparison to her high-flying ambitions, her workaday routine started to drag her down. She complained to Mark that she was getting tired of working with "a bunch of stupid and unmotivated patients." She told her sister, "I'm wasting my fucking time looking down people's throats and up their asses."

Building Teresa's media career came on top of the Sieverses' usual busy schedule. They were more occupied than ever, balancing work, play, childcare, and household duties. As always, there were trips to Connecticut to see Teresa's family. Annie and Mary Ann visited Florida; so did Teresa's brother Frank and his kids. Although preoccupied, Teresa and Mark continued, for the most part, to be loving and supportive. "Remember when you choose your husband someday," Teresa texted her daughters, "make sure he's a superman like ur daddy." Mark responded in kind. "i am proud of u! u continue to amaze me w what you accomplish & it is an awesome example (u r a great role model) for our daughters." As usual, Mark was the gushier one. His affectionate texts to his wife ("i love you momma ☺") were usually greeted by a brief "me 2." But then, she rarely had a free moment.

Mark told Detective Lebid that he and Teresa hadn't done any swinging in the last couple of years. "She didn't bring it up anymore, she didn't really need it." Mark had been relieved, he said. "It was done. Now, it's just us. It was so cool."

True, Teresa was no longer interested in swinging, mainly because she was so busy, and when she wasn't working, all she wanted to do was relax. It was Mark who needed it, although

Brenda, miserable and illness-prone, started to get on his nerves. In spring, she had a health crisis, telling Mark she had "deadly flukes or worms . . . possibly from snails" and didn't know what to do. A few days later, she called him in a panic on the way to hospital, rambling incoherently about "parasites" and "snail fever." Mark texted Teresa, asking for her advice, but she dismissed him. "I just saw all the nonsense and I have no time for it."

The busier his wife became, the more time Mark spent on his phone. He kept up a constant private dialogue, with "notes to self" following his daily encounters, however trivial—eating at a restaurant, sending in the dry cleaning, paying the girls' tutor, ordering from the juice bar. He reviewed meals he'd had at restaurants ("food not plated consistently, warm-cold & beans very dry, fish bland—no seasonings"). He jotted down the names of wait staff and delivery people, adding notes about their attitude and reviewing their performance in a way that seemed compulsive, even pathological, given the extraneous details. "His thinking is quite often from a different perspective than the accepted norm," admitted his stepmother, Jennie Weckelman.

After the snail fever episode, Mark lost interest in Brenda, though they kept in touch. As ever, the only woman who truly interested him was Teresa. They were still having sex at least once a week, and Mark continued to log their bedroom activities. In addition, as well as satisfying Teresa in the bedroom, Mark also helped with her speaking engagements. He kept track of what clothes and shoes she wore, and how she did her hair. When she went to conferences, he arranged her flights and rental cars. Teresa would give him long lists of items to pack, from underwear to sunglasses, toothbrush, and vibrator, and he took care to clean and fold everything neatly in her suitcase.

• • •

For sure, there were troubles in the Sieverses' marriage, but they were outside difficulties, not problems within their relationship. Finances, for example, were a major concern. Mark apparently had a head for money, but in time, his oversight began to slip, and the couple became surprisingly laissez-faire. Neither of them paid much attention to their personal day-to-day bank balance. Why would they? Teresa had a full load of patients, and her rates were high. There was also income from the laser clients, and significant payments from Xymogen, as well as other supplement companies. In addition to their home, the couple owned five units in Teresa's office building. There was Mark's rare coin collection, and the 40,000 dollars he kept in his upstairs safe.

In the past, though, the Sieverses had been through some financial tension. In 2009, their house was placed temporarily into foreclosure. Since then, things had improved, but the situation was complicated. Both Mark and Teresa had separate bank accounts in their own names. There was also a joint account and an account for Sievers and Co. PLLC, a company registered in 2005, two years after the couple married, as well as a business registered in 2009 called Your New Beginning, LLC. Teresa had a separate account for her business, Restorative Health and Healing.

They had another account for a company called Universal Communications Unlimited, a data and information processing company set up in Mark's name and registered in Florida in 2003 (this was also the account used for Teresa's supplement sales). Another complication: Mark had helped the Sieverses' two daughters set up a company for their own charity venture—selling bracelets on behalf of Our Mother's Home—called U2 Can Make a Difference LLC.

After Teresa's death, the media reported that Mark and Teresa were down to their last thirteen dollars. This was a huge exaggeration. Admittedly, at one point there was only thirteen dollars in Teresa's bank account, but this wasn't their only account. Still, often, they didn't have enough liquid cash to cover their daily expenses. Mark could be careless, neglecting to juggle money between different accounts and writing Sandra's paycheck late. Sometimes, she had to remind Mark to deposit it at all (and occasionally, it didn't clear).

In 2011, the couple started getting anxious about "back taxes." In August of that year, the landlord of Teresa's office complex complained about their "outstanding bill"—apparently, they hadn't paid rent since April. Her Bank of America card was cut off temporarily. The couple were 130 dollars away from their credit limit with American Express. The IRS filed a federal tax lien against them for $32,833.24. Mark was ashamed ("i am sorry i am not the manager both of us wanted me to be").

Teresa, normally on top of things, was at sea when it came to money. She'd text Mark asking him what account she should use. During a trip to the museum with the girls, she texted him to ask whether she could buy them a telescope ("most expensive is 90 bucks"). At other times, she'd call and ask him to put money on her credit card. Nonetheless, she kept up her 500-dollar trips to Whole Foods ("Please bring home five vanilla shakes and a large container of amazing meal the red one the pomegranate Mango and bring a vanilla up to cleanse plus also if there is L glutamine I can use that").

To put it simply, in the two years before Teresa's death, the couple had started to live beyond their means. The office units they owned at Restorative Health and Healing were worth less than 20,000 dollars, and the couple tried to offload them because they needed ready cash. On top of the usual mortgage payments, taxes, and insurance bills, there were classes, camps, and private tutors for the girls; vacations; Teresa's continuing education; lawn care; cleaning; dog grooming; spa dates; club memberships. When the couple started to launch Teresa's media career, expenses skyrocketed: airfares, limousines, hotel bills, publicity advisors, videographers, software, a makeup artist and hair stylist (at the Ritz-Carlton spa). To save time in the kitchen, they hired a private chef, who'd bring meals to their house every week.

To some degree, the couple recognized the extent of their difficulties. Teresa would tell her sister, "I can't believe I'm a doctor and I've got no fucking money." When Mark's brother-in-law texted him to help with his sister's 1,080-dollar car repair bill, Mark said he couldn't do it. "We are hemorrhaging money," he wrote. At the same time, the couple were convinced their investments in Teresa's career would pay off. When she went to take yet another training course, Mark noted it would be "an additional 10,000$ loss of revenue." Nonetheless, he was convinced things would come around. "it will b fine financially ☺"

The couple were also dancing around the issue of Medicare, and after Teresa's murder, the media brought up rumors of possible fraud. It was true that the couple's texts suggested things at Restorative Health and Healing may not have been completely aboveboard. They both seemed confused about the process of insurance reimbursements. In May 2012, Teresa, reading up on the rules, texted Mark in a panic: "omg there is no gray area w medicare, We cannot bill medicare then charge cash . . . only way to avoid is not seeing any medicare pt . . . omg we r fucked. . . . I'm scared."

The couple were worried about having to pay "big bucks," debating about whether to hire an attorney to help them resolve the issue. This was another reason Teresa wanted to "go concierge." Mark made notes in his phone. Could the same doctor have more than one tax ID? How about the same doctor with more than one business name? Does nutritional testing and counseling imply a doctor-patient relationship? Could they charge for advice given online or by email, and what disclaimer should they use to waive liability?

Patients had complained about billing practices at Restorative Health and Healing. The clinic was cash only; at least one patient complained that Mark told her the practice took Medicare, but after her visit, he sent her a bill. Sometimes Mark asked Teresa to sign prescriptions for people she hadn't seen. Mark Petrites recalled Mark Sievers saying to him, "I got this figured out. I'm not taking Medicare anymore; I'm going to take cash for patients coming in, and I'm going to still bill Medicare." Dr. Petrites said it came up in various conversations—that Mark had told him "he'd figured out a way to get around the system."

Despite the couple's financial concerns, Teresa was still fantasizing about her future media career. She imagined big-scale conferences at upmarket hotels—the Shangri-La in Bonita Springs, the Naples Beach Hotel, and the Universal Hotel in Orlando—where people could attend talks by all the "anti-aging bigwigs." She envisaged hosting conferences and health expos "mixing nutrition advice with energy healing." While she was giving the lectures, Lenka, like a psychic, could walk around the room and "call things out that she's picking up in the audience." People "need to see something to believe," she reminded herself. "Lenka will show how she sees beyond her eyes."

Another possibility was to offer conference attendees—"special guests only"—the opportunity to have an "intimate cocktail with Dr. Sievers," where she'd tell them she had a "special announcement" that would cause "a big hubbub, a big secret about what's going on." Then her PR advisor could spin it out into a great story: "what is Dr Sievers secret event?" There might be musicians or bands playing, too. "The possibilities are limitless."

But for all her plans to bring energy healing "to the masses," Teresa was also thinking clearly about the bottom line. "Sales should be a big part of things," she noted. Too, these large-scale events would put her name up there, helping her attract the "affluent clientele" she was hoping for. Then "when we go to sell our other conferences . . . we can charge more."

Mark was equally excited. "i love u baby!" he texted her. "You are taking off NOW!! I could not be any prouder of you ☺" But for all her YouTube videos, infomercials, plans, fantasies, and hobnobbing with "big cheeses," Teresa's media career never seemed to launch. In her mind, she was walking on a stage addressing huge crowds ("keep eye contact," she reminded herself. "Stay away from the cutsie as most women walk the line between bitch and femininity"), but in real life, she was still stuck in her office with the day-to-day grind. It wasn't because she didn't try hard enough—Teresa had poise, style, presence, and charisma. But to many potential patients, her message was off-key. Holistic treatment, hormones, and supplements were one thing, but intuition, spirits, and "crystal healing beds" quite another.

When Tamer Elsafy finished post-production on the Flexcin infomercial, he sent it to a few advertising agencies to get their opinion on it; "all thought it was exceptional and has the potential to be a runaway hit," he said. And: "one of the guys at the agencies said and I quote (no joke) 'where did you find her?' Meaning she's awesome!" They were "chopping at the bit," he said.

Ultimately, he hoped to place the ad on various TV channels in Southwest Florida after first "testing it out" elsewhere, and "tweaking as we test." But by mid-April, the infomercial still hadn't been aired, and Teresa hadn't received any money. She and Mark were both getting pissed off with Tamer. "We are trying to get that financing I told you about lined up," he explained. "They want to see our profit margins, accounting etc so they are comfortable with spending the money."

In the absence of any progress toward her imagined stardom, Teresa felt increasingly unhappy with her current life. "I want to work on educating public on how to stay healthy and make lots of money," she wrote. "I want to be on TV. I want . . . to see patients 1 day per week and make 1 million dollars take home every week." But in real life, she was exhausted and broke. "11:30 A.M. at work . . . currently I just feel sad. I'm tired I would rather lay down and sleep."

Chapter 7

Wayne

Mark Sievers was born in 1968 in Columbia, Missouri, and grew up in Manchester, a small town twenty miles west of St. Louis, right on old Route 66. As with the outskirts of most big cities, the St. Louis suburbs blend into one another; to an outsider, they seem indistinguishable. For the most part, these are insular, formerly blue-collar communities, but by no means backward. Most of the neighborhoods are safe, with decent restaurants and easy access to highways. In other words, ordinary subdivision living—cookie-cutter housing and big box stores. The only real danger is the possibility of flash flooding.

When he was nine, his parents divorced. Mark and his three siblings shuttled between mom and dad. His mother, Bonnie, moved in with a same-sex partner. His father, Michael, after marrying Mark's stepmother, Jennie Weckelman, died of pancreatic cancer in his fifties, when Mark was twenty-four. His two sisters had health problems. Stacey, the sister who'd introduced him to Teresa, died at forty-six, from Graves' disease. He rarely saw Jaemea, his second sister. His brother, Scott, an accountant in St. Louis, lived a stable family life, although he and Mark were so busy, they rarely had the chance to connect.

But none of that mattered. Mark had a friend in Missouri who was even closer than family. His name was Curtis Wayne Wright, Jr.

Wayne was born in 1968 in Kirkwood, Missouri, five miles from Mark's home in Manchester, but he grew up forty miles south in Hillsboro, a small, rural town in Jefferson County, right off Route 21. The area is sparsely populated—derided by some as the home of hillbillies, bumpkins, rebels, and isolationists.

Wayne and Mark met in grade school and soon became tight. But Mark had moved on: his wife was a doctor, he lived by the beach in Florida, ate an organic diet, practiced yoga, and believed in energy medicine. Nonetheless, his friendship with Wayne didn't diminish over time; it grew stronger. They'd moved in such different directions, people found it strange they stayed so close. But there was something even stranger.

Wayne looked exactly like Mark.

• • •

The resemblance was uncanny. They could have been twins, or doppelgängers, especially after they both shaved their heads. Wayne was the first to pick up the razor, around 2000, when he started to go bald. Mark followed suit four years later. They were both big guys—not in terms of height, but stocky (Mark was a wrestler in high school). A school friend of both men said they didn't look alike when they were younger. "They morphed into each other over the years. If it was by chance or by their plan, I don't know."

Of course, the similarity waxed and waned over time—one of them might gain or lose weight, wear different glasses, go clean shaven, or wear a beard. And up close, there were obvious differences: Mark was a little taller, his face fuller and fleshier, his ears more prominent. But at a glance, to someone who didn't know them, the two men were startlingly alike. When they knew they were going to be photographed, at parties and weddings, they deliberately hammed it up, wearing the same facial hair, the same clothes, the same kind of glasses. At Mark and Teresa's wedding, even Teresa's mother admitted there were times when she couldn't tell them apart.

Most people didn't see anything sinister about the resemblance. "I just think it was a joke to them," said Mark's stepmother. "They got a kick out of it, like twins would get a kick out of fooling people." But identical twins, or siblings who look alike, are usually irritated to be mistaken for each other—it disregards their individuality and uniqueness. There was something strange about the way Mark and Wayne tried to confuse others, to appear interchangeable. In a way, they were inverse versions of each other, just as M is the upside-down version of W.

Mark had moved to Florida with his smart, talented wife, and his standard of living had improved enormously. He moved from the post-industrial, down-at-heel Midwest to breezy, beachside Southwest Florida. To his friends in the St. Louis suburbs, Mark had "made it." And he had. But not without ambivalence. Perhaps working as Teresa's office manager and homeschooling his daughters had made Mark feel, to some extent, robbed of his identity. Wayne, to the contrary, owned nothing more than a trailer, but he worked for himself, when he wanted to work, and was—at least, compared to Mark—his own man. Their ongoing connection, despite their differences, suggests that maybe for each of them, the other's life represented the "road not taken," and by merging with each other, they could escape the limits of the self. Or perhaps their deliberate resemblance was simply a kind of narcissistic enjoyment, with each functioning as an empathic mirror for the other?

At school, Wayne was known as a likable guy, smart, charming, a smooth talker, fun to be with. Friends recall riding around town with him looking for women—Wayne was a pro at scheming to get girls. He was tough, too. He was trained in boxing, karate, judo, and mixed martial arts. But he wasn't a rebel: he was dubbed "most dependable" at school and voted senior class president.

The one thing everybody remembered about Wayne is that he was a wizard with computers. From an early age, he could program, work on complicated databases, and build seamless websites. He kept up with all the changes and developments. He loved learning new technical languages, getting familiar with the latest systems. State-of-the-art technology fascinated him. When it came to software and programming, he was always trying to do things nobody had done before.

Mark and Wayne met in ninth grade, when Wayne's girl, Carrie, introduced Mark to her best friend, Gloria, who became his first great love. The two men stayed close, getting to know each other's families. After graduating in 1986, they went in different directions but stayed close. Mark majored in psychology at the University of Missouri, living on campus, but dropped out after his freshman year, when his father was diagnosed with cancer. He worked a few jobs full-time before finishing his degree at a smaller local campus, working on and off between classes and semesters. Eventually, he also got a nursing qualification from a private college. Wayne studied electrical engineering and computer science at the Missouri University of Science and Technology in Rolla, although he dropped out before graduation.

After college, both lived locally. Their lives stayed intertwined. Wayne worked as a software programmer at a home security company. Mark found work as a card flipper at Harrah's Casino in St. Louis. Here, he was in his element. Although he was never a gambler, he loved playing cards and meeting people. He stayed on at Harrah's after graduating, making his way up to supervisor. Eager and talkative, he engaged strangers wherever he went. For his upbeat disposition and friendly nature, he earned the nickname "Smiley."

When looking to invest his savings, Mark decided on real estate. He put down a deposit on a condo in Fenton, Missouri, which he and Wayne shared for a while. He bought a house there, too, which he mortgaged to Wayne. Always an entrepreneur, he set up a company that mounted satellite dishes; Wayne did the installation work. When Mark's sister, Stacey, moved to St. Petersburg, Mark bought a house there, too, which he intended to fix up and rent out. When Wayne set up his own IT consulting company and ran into financial difficulties, Mark gave him money. He didn't expect to Wayne to refund the investment. "Just pay it forward," was Mark's credo.

• • •

Oddly enough, Wayne, like Mark, also had an accident that left him with episodes of forgetfulness. Wayne's accident was more serious—he'd been in a car crash in 2005 that caused a traumatic brain injury so incapacitating, he had to go on disability. Like Mark, he experienced short-term memory loss. Too, he lost the capacity and stamina for the long, demanding hours he used to spend programming computers. He had bouts of dizziness and seizures, suffered from insomnia and sleep apnea, and needed to use a breathing machine at night. The accident also led to symptoms of fibromyalgia—burning sensations in his arms and legs caused by damage to the nerves. He took anti-inflammatories, and whenever he went to Florida, Teresa treated him for pain. While driving, he had trouble keeping his hands on the wheel. The seven-hour trip to visit his dad in Alabama became a two-day drive. He'd always suffered from depression, anxiety, and mood swings, but after the accident, they got worse—he experienced fits of aggression and was diagnosed with bipolar disorder.

Although he was no longer able to work full-time, Wayne picked up small jobs here and there, helping people fix viruses and update software. He also built, installed, and maintained video cameras and alarm systems. Generally taciturn and distant, he could be engaging, with a nervous, gentle smile. He liked going to estate sales and dabbled in antiques, especially vintage coins, like Mark. He went to church regularly—he was a Baptist—and at one point was a deacon and youth pastor, although he lost that position for unknown reasons. People murmured that he was getting too close to the kids. According to another rumor, he was fired because he and a second pastor had taken the children to a homeless shelter so they could see how poor people lived. Apparently, the church disapproved.

For the most part, people enjoyed Wayne's company. Neighbors said he was reserved and respectful. One of his trailer park neighbors said he always waved when he saw her, asked after her husband, and helped unload groceries from her car. Others called him polite and helpful, if quiet. Everybody said he was a very loyal, moral person who lived by his own personal code of ethics. If he thought something wasn't being handled properly, he dealt with it himself. In other words, his inner code of right and wrong trumped society's moral protocol.

But Wayne was a complicated character. Some called him a career criminal, although if this were true, he didn't have much of a career. His court record went back to his early twenties, but it mostly consisted of minor infractions: driving offenses, failure to pay bills, tax liens, trespassing, property damage, custody disputes. Fines. Eight days in jail here, ten days there. There were only two serious criminal cases, both involving meth.

The first occurred in May 1996, when he was twenty-eight. The cops in St. Louis pulled over his red Chevy Camaro. In the back, they found a .22 caliber revolver, a black plastic scale, and three glass vials of a white, powdery substance. For possession with intent to deal, he got two felony convictions and five years' probation. He stayed clean for the next fourteen years, until 2010, when was he was arrested for manufacturing methamphetamine, resulting in three more felony convictions and an eleven-month prison stint.

Wayne had been renting out his house to a female roommate for three months, he told the police, while he was in Texas taking care of his brother, who'd been in a motorcycle accident. When the house was raided and the woman found herself facing jail time, she told the cops the meth lab belonged to Wayne, causing him to be sent to prison instead. According to Wayne, investigators framed him for the meth charges because they didn't have enough evidence to arrest him for a far more serious charge: the unsolved murder of a local preacher.

• • •

On July 10, 1996, a homeless man spending the night inside the Zakar Car Wash on Florissant Avenue in North St. Louis, a derelict area known for drug dealers, was woken in the early hours of the morning by a loud argument. Preferring to keep a low profile, he didn't bother looking out to see what was going on. When the altercation was over, he went back to sleep. The next morning, in front of the car wash, employees found a white Subaru with the front driver's door hanging open and the keys in the ignition. They tried to start the car, but the engine was dead, so they pushed it into the parking lot. That afternoon, when nobody turned up to claim it, the car wash owner called the police.

The Subaru, it turned out, belonged to thirty-three-year-old Ronnie Bolin, an ordained minister in the Church of God who'd been reported missing the previous day. When he wasn't preaching, he worked as a temporary clerical and computer processor.

Ronnie had been on a downward spiral. He was broke and owed a lot of back rent. According to his brother Greg, Ronnie's future had seemed bright until, a year before he went missing, his wife of ten years filed for divorce because she'd discovered he was bisexual. Her suspicions were fortified when, while searching through his property, the cops found risqué photographs of a young man posing suggestively at the Hosanna Christian Center, the church Ronnie founded three years earlier that had recently been dissolved for failure to file annual nonprofit reports. When the youth was tracked down, he told police he'd always wanted to be a model, and Ronnie had offered to help him out by taking photographs, but apparently the preacher had become "obsessed" with him, and the young man, feeling uncomfortable, broke off the relationship.

After his divorce, as well as indulging in unchristian sex, Ronnie also started drinking heavily and got addicted to meth. The last person to see him before he disappeared was Wayne Wright, Jr., who told the cops that he'd lent Ronnie 900 dollars, allegedly to buy crack, and never saw him again. Others said it was the other way around—Ronnie had lent money to Wayne and was having trouble getting it back. Regardless, after Ronnie went missing, Wayne left Missouri for a Florida vacation.

A compelling break in the case came in April 2001, five years after the preacher disappeared, when Missouri police got a letter from Corey Fox, an Illinois prison inmate awaiting trial for murder. In the letter, Fox wrote that he had information about "the man of the altar" who'd been missing since 1996 (according to the police report, Fox would only give "bits and pieces of information at a time," and "liked to talk in riddles"). Investigators took his claims seriously, because he seemed to have inside information about the crime. His description of Ronnie was accurate—"a white male who was kind of round, balding in the front, and was a preacher at one time." He also added, "Let's just say that Ronnie was a weak person. . . . Let's just say that his sexual preference may not be the same as most people's." But Fox, who had mental problems, was playing games. He led police on a wild-goose chase, and soon they were back at square one. Still, they had no shortage of leads. Dozens of people came forward with stories about what might have happened to the missing preacher, some plausible, some off the wall. None of them led to Ronnie, but a lot of them led to Wayne.

On August 21, 1996, one of his ex-girlfriends told the cops that Wayne liked to brag about beating people up and "running them off the road." She said he'd complained about Ronnie "whining all the time" and said he'd like to "punch him in the face." Her parents lived directly across the road from Wayne in Hillsboro, she said, and for the last three weeks, they'd "smelled something like a dead animal or body in the woods behind their house." She added, "I don't know if Wayne killed Ronnie, but I would not put it past him, then burying him in the woods. . . . Wayne knows the woods very well." Cops took the tip seriously, searching the area with cadaver dogs, but nothing suspicious was found.

On Valentine's Day in 1998, two years after Ronnie disappeared, a second woman decided to allay her guilt by going to the police. She said that right before Ronnie vanished, a man named Rusty Meddows turned up at a friend's trailer and asked to borrow a shovel. When asked why he needed it, Rusty apparently replied that he, his brother, and Wayne Wright "had killed a preacher and needed to bury his body." He said they'd murdered Ronnie because he'd threatened to tell the police about a bunch of computer equipment the men had stolen; the body was buried on a thirty-acre lot in the Lynnview Acres subdivision, where Wayne lived. Police were dubious—wouldn't somebody planning to bury a dead body bring their own shovel?—but they checked out the tip anyway. Rusty Meddows and his brother, who were both in prison, had nothing to say. The thirty-acre lot was searched, but to no avail.

Finally, in 2014, eight years after Bolin's disappearance, detectives at the Jefferson County Sheriff's Department got a call from a man named Kevin who said he had information about the case. He knew Ronnie and Wayne did some work together involving computers, and he'd heard they got into an argument when Bolin discovered money had gone missing. Kevin said Wayne and another man had killed Ronnie Bolin, dissolved his body in a cast-iron tub, used a woodchipper to crush his bones, and scattered them around Wayne's property. They couldn't get his skull through the woodchipper, said Kevin, so they crushed it with a hammer and threw the pieces all along the highway "from Missouri to Kentucky."

Ronnie Bolin was never found; due to the suspicious circumstances surrounding his disappearance, his case is no longer classed as that of a missing person, but of a suspected homicide. The investigation is still open. "I have no doubt," said Greg Bolin. "Wayne Wright killed my brother."

• • •

Those who knew about his connection with Ronnie's disappearance were understandably wary of Wayne. He wasn't the kind of person to run his mouth, but sometimes he said things that made people think twice. They might have been lies, maybe not. He said he had a goat farm in Potosi. He said he was a licensed electrician. He said he was a "ninja" and knew how to "disappear." He told people he'd been paid 150,000 dollars to design software for Build-A-Bear toys in St. Louis. One person who knew Wayne wondered: "Why do you live in a trailer park in Hillsboro if you're some bigwig software engineer programmer guy?"

He also said he'd murdered someone. When he talked about it, he made choking motions with his hands and described watching the life leaving their eyes.

• • •

Mark was the kind of man who kept in touch. From Florida, by text and phone, he loved to catch up with his old buddies in Missouri, including a few he'd known since kindergarten, as well as four or five ex-girlfriends. "He was constantly on the phone, sometimes two phones," said his stepmother, adding that a lot of people found his energy "tiring." In Bonita Springs, he was overshadowed by Teresa, but in the outskirts of St. Louis, Mark was a big fish in small pond. He went back whenever he got the chance, and if he didn't have time for a trip up north, he'd invite Wayne to Florida.

In May 2014, the patient management system at Restorative Health and Healing needed upgrading. Their go-to tech support guy was costly and inefficient. Although Mark was handy with computers, he couldn't manage more complicated tasks, and the billing codes were changing constantly. When he had trouble, he'd call Wayne to walk him through it. Eventually, he suggested to Teresa: Why not put Wayne on the books? "It would probably get our issues resolved quicker," he suggested.

Wayne could do most of the work remotely, from Missouri—he'd gotten things set up where he could access the office servers via his phone. If he needed to come down in person, all the better—they'd have time to catch up and hang out. And it wasn't just the computers—Wayne could troubleshoot anything: the servers and modem, the printers and fax machine, Windows, QuickBooks, all kinds of software, audio, voicemail, even the EKG machine. At first, he insisted he didn't want to be paid, but Mark knew he was barely getting by and persuaded him to accept a small salary of one hundred dollars a month (which, to Wayne, was a lot of cash). There was no written contract, just a spoken agreement.

• • •

On the surface, Mark and Wayne were separate men with different lives. Their personalities were different; sometimes they seemed like opposites, or alternatives—Alpha and Beta males. Mark was loud, outgoing, and demonstrative. He could be cocky, effusive, and brash. He loved a crowd. When he'd been drinking, he could have people doubled over with laughter. Wayne was more reserved and softer spoken, preferring to stay in the background—although, like Mark, he liked to drink, and if somebody pissed him off, he could be threatening and aggressive.

A person who has a doppelgänger, writes Freud, "may identify himself with another and so become unsure of his true self." A look-alike is a counter-self, an uninvited reflection, both familiar and strange, recognizable but also peculiar. In art, literature, and myth, a person with a doppelgänger often becomes unmoored and destabilized, swaying back and forth between different possibilities.

People said that when Mark was around Wayne, his personality began to shift and merge. Florida Mark was tied to the social demands of homeschooling, play dates, and charity work; Missouri Mark enjoyed heavy drinking, partying, and dirty jokes. Too, Florida Mark—"Mr. Mom"—had a distinctly feminine personality, while Missouri Mark was more hardline and macho. On one level, taking pleasure in your double could be seen as simple ego-inflation. It could also imply estrangement from the self—a single personality split in two halves. But most psychologists would agree that, unconsciously, cultivating a double suggests a homosexual identification, however repressed.

Of course, things were more nuanced than this. Mark's shadow-self didn't come to life only when he was around Wayne, for example. In Florida, too, he had a secret life—swinging, sexual experiments, multiple partners. For that matter, so did his wife. Still, the relationship between Mark and Wayne was something different; it was secretive and intense. On his Facebook page, Mark called Wayne his "brother," but it might have been better to call him Mark's shadow. Or was it the other way around? With doppelgängers, you can never be sure.

• • •

After Wayne came on board as Mark's tech guy in 2014, the two men were in touch weekly, sometimes more often. Most of their communications concerned problems with the faxes and computers in Teresa's medical office, which seemed to consistently malfunction, but the tech advice was interspersed with daily updates, giving side-by-side snapshots of the two men's parallel lives.

Wayne's daughter passes her driving test. Mark cuts ten pounds of frozen dog food into individual servings. Wayne's delinquent stepson is arrested by juvenile officers. Snowstorms in Missouri. Wayne, at an estate sale, contemplates buying a menorah. He takes his daughter to a volleyball game. The shifter bearings on Teresa's Mercedes are worn down; Mark wants Wayne's guidance (his advice: it's not a big deal). Wayne, worried about his growing potbelly, experiments with weight-loss drinks. The two men can't talk because Wayne's babysitting his grandbabies. "25 years ago . . . who would have thought that those words would have been uttered?" marvels Mark. "I hear that!" Wayne concurs.

In April 2014, Mark bought Wayne a plane ticket to come and stay with him in Bonita Springs. Teresa, as always, was thoughtful and considerate. She worried about his flight status ("there were a lot of tornadoes last night"). She made sure they had half-and-half for Wayne's coffee (rather than their usual organic coconut creamer) and wondered whether they should buy any meat for him, since theirs was a meatless household ("Wayne will eat some kind of chicken baby," texted Mark. "He likes chicken fingers & tenders, he's not big on coleslaw"). Teresa gave Wayne advice about his aches and pains. Later, when listing her daily blessings, she mentioned "having wayne come down to work on the computers."

Teresa was generous and appreciative: Mark and Wayne's texts were less open-hearted. Their exchanges were regularly interspersed with private comments and personal jokes, often sexually explicit. Mark, inordinately proud of Teresa, boasted about their sex life. He sent Wayne erotic photographs of his wife with other women. In January 2015, he sent Wayne a close-up of a woman's genitals. "That was my breakfast and lunch today !!!" quipped Wayne. ("Mine too," Mark replied.)

Sometimes, the men's communications seemed tender, even romantic. They seemed hyper-aware of each other's moods and concerns. "R u ok?" Mark asked Wayne, in January. "noticed something when we were talking this morning, but I was in a crowded environment and could not say anything." In April, Wayne mentions a certain country song is playing on the radio that reminds him of Mark. Mark often calls Wayne "baby" or "sunshine." Sometimes they text each other just to say good morning (Mark asks: "is it up?").

Their relationship was secretive and intense. They knew each other's proclivities, inside jokes, quirks, secrets, and sexual fantasies. The two men had been close for almost thirty years, and while it may not be unusual for longtime buddies to share explicit pictures and sexual boasts, Mark and Wayne's relationship went beyond locker-room braggadocio and sniggering *double entendres*. There were playful references to shared girlfriends, group sex, cross-dressing. Their unusual intimacy led people to wonder: Was their brotherhood sexual in nature? To some, there was no doubt. Others weren't so sure. But one thing was undeniable—even if the men weren't lovers, they were happy with a threesome if there was a woman in the mix.

Was the woman ever Teresa? Mark and Wayne shared everything—why not their women? There's no doubt that Mark and his wife indulged in light sex play in Wayne's presence. In one journal entry, Mark mentions putting his hands up Teresa's skirt in the kitchen while Wayne was standing nearby, happy to watch, although he didn't join in. On another occasion, Mark noted, of Teresa, that he "played w her . . . w Wayne there talking." Also: "played w Teresa on couch. movie w Wayne." Teresa, according to Mark, had told him she fantasized about "Wayne I & her being blind-folded & having to tell us apart." One night, after smoking pot and drinking wine, Mark noted, of Teresa, "she mentioned wayne, said she really enjoyed having door open when he was in town . . . she said it would b cool to give us both simultaneous head side by side." And then there was the time when Wayne was in Bonita Springs to work on the office software. While Mark wasn't around, he'd whispered something exciting in Teresa's ear:

"Maybe next time."

Chapter 8

The Delgado Protocol

The Sievers marriage was surely unconventional, but it worked. Anger plus adoration plus lust made for sizzling alchemy. But everything changed when, at a conference in Orlando, Teresa met one of her mentors, Dr. Nick Delgado, whom Mark later described as "a very big name in the anti-aging field" and was the author of *Mastering the Powers of Your Inner Health* (1992) and *Grow Young and Slim* (2000).

A short, muscular man in his early sixties with thick hair and a permanent tan, Delgado described himself as a "Diplomat of the American Academy of Anti-Aging Medicine, Leader in Health Nutrition, Speaker, and World Record Holder" (for lifting 50,640 pounds in one hour). He was also the originator of the "Delgado Protocol," which involved a patented brand of "regenerative biomedical technologies" called "DocNutrients." On top of that, he promoted himself as a sex guru with "the stamina of a young stallion." He believed in the "full building of passion and release weekly," and promoted his own guides to sex and intimacy, endorsing, as a supplement, his "special testosterone booster."

Until then, apart from her teasing fantasies about Wayne, Teresa had only shown interest in other women, but when she met Delgado, the spark was instant. "T met nick. (major attraction-flirting)," Mark noted in his phone. Apparently, they'd dined together in an intimate setting. Nick had touched her leg, caressed her cheek, rubbed her shoulders, and put his arm around her. Teresa characterized it as "flirting and foreplay," nothing more. After dinner, they went back to their separate rooms. Still, Mark was jealous and upset. "I guess I'm just dealing with my own double standards," he told Teresa by text. ". . . its just a new scenario for me to digest (u texting/talking very sexually with a man)."

If his orgasm stats are reliable, Mark, too, had the "stamina of a young stallion," but in other respects, compared to Mark, Delgado was a magnificent Achilles. Just as Wayne was Mark's double, Nick was his opposite. Nick was a doctor: Mark was a nurse. Nick was forthright and dominant: Mark was submissive. Nick had thick black hair: Mark was bald. Nick had hundreds of contacts in the anti-aging field; Mark knew no one. Nick was toned, tanned, and muscular; Mark was pale and flabby.

It was true that, for a sex guru, Nick's own track record wasn't great. He'd just divorced his fourth wife, and perhaps for this reason, he'd grown cynical about marriage, believing it could often hurt a relationship, and "it's more of a tax write-off." Still, some of his ideas about pair-bonding may have struck a chord with Teresa. Nick believed "the best correlation to longevity is not cholesterol, blood pressure, diabetes, it's the quality of your relationships." Teresa was profoundly impressed.

• • •

When the couple had first started swinging, Mark had assumed they'd be doing it together. If Teresa wasn't there in person, he'd share his sexual adventures through texts, pictures, and videos. But Teresa and Nick's relationship excluded Mark, who'd never even met his rival. Sex apart, Teresa was thrilled to be in personal contact with a major figure in the world of anti-aging. She and Nick kept in touch after the conference, by phone and text. Mark could hardly prevent her from some important networking, but he was dismayed to realize Teresa's encounter with Nick wasn't just a one-off. There'd be more conventions, more dinners, more chances to pet and flirt.

Time and time again, Teresa reassured Mark that she loved him and wasn't planning to have sex with Nick (who was also in a relationship), but just as she'd given Mark free rein to act out his fantasies with other girls, she felt she had a right to daydream about Nick. "It's no different than if I'd had a crush on another woman," she assured Mark. He "kept trying to rationalize it and accept it," but he couldn't let it go. Still, there was an upside to the situation: "since all this happened, Teresa has been far more receptive to sex." The couple started sexting and sending each other erotic photos during the day. Teresa never mentioned Nick, but if he was in her head, Mark didn't want to know—as long as he was the one getting her off.

In the past, the couple had shared their problems openly, but after Nick came into their life, Mark started hoarding his anxiety, keeping it to himself. On May 22, he saw a text on his wife's phone from Delgado saying, "can u talk." Mark said nothing but wondered whether she would delete it ("she didn't!"). The next night he dreamed that Teresa had "cheated on our marriage" and woke up in a "foul mood." To make matters worse, he didn't feel as though he could tell his wife because "i feel like a baby, being this affected by a nightmare." But he couldn't help wondering: what if the dream was an omen?

"And so, we have spikes and adrenaline and so anger and hurt and jealousy—all these negative emotions. People need to learn how to let that stuff go," writes Delgado in his Protocol. But Mark couldn't do it. Obsessively, he kept going over the idea of Teresa flirting with Nick. He dictated his feelings into his digital calendar via voice-to-text recognition. "i am frequently wondering if they r privately talking, texting or emailing. she says they r not but it is hard for me."

To make matters worse, Teresa was openly recommending the Delgado Protocol to her friends, pushing Nick's remedies and supplements. One afternoon, she accidentally sent Mark a text intended for her friend Karen, with a link to the Delgado Protocol. Mark was shaken. He thought she'd done it on purpose, and texted her back saying she was "mean," then backtracked. "I wasn't insulted by ur prior text I was just playing with you baby," he wrote. Teresa ignored him; she was more concerned about getting her office toilet fixed. But Mark couldn't get over it. He felt upset whenever he heard Delgado's name. "It is hard for me to think about much less type," he admitted.

• • •

Everyone who knew Teresa came to learn she had a short fuse, and by 2014, she'd stopped finding Mark's muddle-headedness endearing. After a hard day at work, it was difficult to deal with his absent-mindedness. He never did the simple things she asked of him, even though he was home all day. His office was a disaster, full of trash and empty boxes. He forgot to do the laundry, and when he did, he mixed up the whites with the colors, then left everything in the dryer. He lost the TV remote. He couldn't fix Teresa's computer. The toilet in her office was still broken three weeks after she'd asked him to deal with it; then the plumber turned up during work hours while she was seeing patients.

"It just seems like everything you do frustrates me," she texted him, enraged by his incompetence at office management. "You do not understand how frustrating it is to work with you. . . . I don't have time for that shit Mark . . . your failure to accept responsibility makes me absolutely crazy." Despite grocery shopping, ferrying the children around, and keeping them busy, her husband, it seemed, could do no right. In October, to cheer her up at work, he sent her a cute picture of himself. Her response was dispiriting. "Looks great now take that light green blanket and cover up the cushion I don't want the dogs on that without the blanket." Mark was downcast. "T seems to have little respect for me," he noted, glumly.

Sound carried on Jarvis Road, and the neighbors had overheard loud arguments. Salomon Bernal, directly across the street, said he'd heard the couple fighting on several occasions. Pamela Metz, two doors down on the opposite side of the street, had also heard the couple arguing. Rick Mosher, opposite, said he heard a loud argument about a year before Teresa's death, with Teresa clearly the aggressor. Donetta Contreras, who lived behind the Sieverses, said she heard constant arguments from their house.

The neighbor on the right, Kimberly Torres, mentioned a loud fight she'd overheard between Mark and Teresa just a month before the murder. Teresa's sister, Annie, during her police interview, was asked about these reports, but she waved them away. "My sister was extremely loud. She would yell. She was a screamer. . . . We enjoyed watching her get fired up, because you never knew what would come out of her mouth."

In the past, Teresa had been happy that Mark spent all day homeschooling and caring for Emma and Olivia, but by 2014, she'd started to want more from him. She complained about how he dressed, his appearance, the fact that he wasn't going to the gym, hadn't cleaned the house, hadn't filled her car with gas. She got easily annoyed with the girls ("tell Olivia to shut up"). Her texts grew increasingly demanding and aggressive ("cut the shit"; "are you fucking crazy?"; "what the fuck"; "are you fucking kidding me"; "Wtf is taking so long?"; "what's so fucking hard").

Her perennial complaints didn't stop: his office was full of empty boxes ("I cannot take the constant clutter . . . I don't think you realize how absolutely insane it makes me"). He still left the laundry in the washing machine or the dryer. Her office toilet was still on the fritz ("get a new plumber or tell them to get out here and fix it"). He said he'd mended the computer, but it was always balky ("I am ready to jump off a fucking cliff"). And then there were the groceries. Water had to be Voss. Dental floss had to be Glide. Honey had to be raw and local. "Please go to the freezer section and get the lands bakery special or Millet regular but remember do not get the gluten-free one. . . . Good marinara sauce or spaghetti sauce you check by making sure the ingredients of olive oil there's a couple from Italy in Tuscany . . ." She simply didn't trust him to buy the right products, demanding he text her a photograph of the list of ingredients, or get a store clerk to help him.

Most upsetting to Mark was her anger with him for texting her at work, when she was busy (even though, hypocritically, she'd sometimes get irritated with him for failing to pick up the phone when she called). "What the fuck do you want," she'd ask him. "Do not text me again." "you're sending me these bullshit texts." "you think you're being so fucking cute." "you are so fucking annoying." More and more, she accused him of "smothering her," demeaning him when he reached out to her ("please stop your passionate talking so I can relax"). Mark never responded with anger, although he was sometimes passive-aggressive, referring to himself as "ur concierge," and to Teresa as "boss." But for the most part, in response to his wife's belligerence, he was sheepish, even craven. To reassure himself and counter the blow to his ego, whenever Teresa was rude to him, he'd immediately text another female friend, often an ex, "just to see how you're doing."

Mark remained anxious about his wife's continuing relationship with Nick, whom she still spoke to, as she explained, either as a friend or in a professional capacity. Mark didn't believe her. He couldn't stop thinking about the two of them, wondering what they talked about, analyzing his feelings. He still couldn't deal with the fact of his wife being sexually attracted to another man. He felt "betrayed," in thoughts if not in deeds, but possibly in deeds, too. Was Teresa telling the truth that she hadn't had sex with Nick? "she gets high, horney w a hot guy . . . and NOTHING happens?" He thought about checking her deleted text messages but withstood the temptation.

On April 17, 2014, he acknowledged that he'd had sex with plenty of women outside the marriage, and it was hypocritical of him to envy Nick. And after all, "it is great for her to hang with the big boys of anti-aging!" In the past, he'd never felt jealous, because he was so good in bed. If she wanted a sex with a woman to spice things up, that wasn't a problem. "i have something that no woman has." But he was worried. Nick, if his hype was anything to go by, was also a red-hot lover. "if she fell in love with a man who can do to her and for her in bed what I can do, there goes my advantage."

The following night, Mark had put Emma and Olivia to bed, and he and his wife got cozy, smoking pot and listening to music. At 10:30 P.M., Teresa's phone pinged. It was Nick. "she wants to interrupt 'us' to call him. she lit up at the prospect." Mark was hurt. "it was devastating!" After that, he started checking her texts and emails. He was unhappy to learn that Teresa had told her friends and family about Nick—their sexy dinner together, and Mark's jealousy. Everyone agreed that it wasn't a big deal, because nothing had happened between them. They all confirmed Teresa's point of view—that Mark should "get over it and move on."

When it came to sex, Mark was at war with himself. Teresa's fantasies about Nick made her hot and eager, and this was something Mark couldn't resist. They were having more—and better—sex than ever before. In the heat of the moment, Mark could relax and forget or deny the fact that Teresa's mind was elsewhere, but as soon as the passion was over, he felt repelled. And she didn't necessarily want to keep it to fantasy. She'd suggested that perhaps one day, in the future, she and Mark could have a foursome with Nick and his girl. This he found abhorrent. "She wants to include him in our fantasy and maybe in real-life sex life," wrote Mark, and "I can't go there." He told Teresa he wanted their sex to be private, without the lurking specter of Dr. Delgado, even just in Teresa's head. The situation was making him crazy. "i want our sex back. No nick needed."

On May 14, he got a new idea. "Wow okay, something I haven't tried yet is I'm going to ask God for strength to help me through this." The strength he got from God lasted until Nick sent Teresa a LinkedIn request, when, once again, Mark started writhing in jealous agony. "Every time I think of his name I think of her cheating, think of them holding hands and its driving me crazy. I can be doing fine and then I think about his name . . . and here goes that fucking emotional floodgate and I don't know how to control it!"

With Teresa's encouragement, he talked things over with his friend J. B. Tarrette's wife, Nancy, who was a therapist. She didn't think couples' therapy would be much help, but recommended that Mark start seeing a different therapist alone, for his "trust issues." He followed her advice, but it didn't seem to assuage his mounting jealousy and insecurity. He may have gotten more benefit from the long, rambling monologues he made on his phone recording his feelings, anxieties, hopes, and grievances, and "speaking what's on my mind."

What was on his mind was Teresa, sex, and the lack of it. On Father's Day of 2014, he'd wanted to have sex with Teresa while he was blindfolded, but she wasn't into it. Although their sex was still great, she was too tired to get intimate more than once a week (not enough for Mark—"quality is exceptional, quantity sucks ass"). When his wife came home after work, all she wanted to do was lie down, read, and relax. For this reason, she didn't mind Mark meeting his needs outside the marriage. She sympathized with his "blue balls," encouraging him to find "another hot mama."

But Mark didn't want another woman: he wanted more of Teresa. At one stage in their swinging, according to the notes on his phone, Teresa had "fallen in love" with a woman—possibly Marie—and "got her heart broken." To Mark, although he sympathized, he could accept Teresa's feelings. It was no big deal. But when it came to Nick, everything was different. "I don't know how I could deal with my wife falling in love with another man." He found it hard even to contemplate. Teresa, as always, encouraged him to "move on." She said her texts with Nick were "just an energy exchange, like a higher connection on a more intimate level," and he should be okay with that (although Mark found it suspicious that she couldn't give him any other example of a "intimate higher-level energy connection").

His anguish kept flaring up. On December 19, he sent Teresa a long, passive-aggressive text insisting he was working to get over his jealousy but was finding it difficult. He even brought up the specter of divorce, though denied he was interested in it ("I do NOT want a divorce!"). He was "in it for the long haul," he told her. But he was struggling. "I am just working hard to get that TRUST back . . . I have never experienced such core betrayal & it is not as easy to just simply 'move-on.'" He added, "I would be foolish to think that it MAY not go deeper." Her feelings for Nick had shattered his confidence, he told Teresa. "This is by far the most difficult thing I have ever had to deal with."

• • •

In the past, Mark and Teresa had often been at odds and had always managed to reconnect. Their marriage was passionate, tempestuous, fiery. Sometimes Teresa's fury seemed unsustainable, but she'd always been quick to anger, and often recognized that she was being unfair, explaining how tired she was and apologizing for being "bitchy." Plus, rage doesn't always have to be negative and destructive. Sometimes it can be a vital force powering intimate relationships, bringing couples closer together. Violent arguments may have been a way for Mark and Teresa to reignite their passion. The problem was the aggression was all on Teresa's side. Mark sulked and fumed.

The busier his wife got, the more frustrated Mark became. He'd spend all day with the girls, waiting excitedly for her to come home; then when she did, she didn't want to deal with him. All he wanted was some "adult conversation every evening before she does her own thing." Reduced to the role of "a glorified baby sitter," he wasn't even getting "the basics"—"just simple things" like "holding and kissing each other, expressing affection."

Still, when he expressed his complaints, Teresa was usually receptive and understanding. She didn't take him for granted, she said. She loved him as much as she could, and "that's something she's always felt guilty about." Teresa, Mark reminded himself, was "not the kind of person to show affection or need displays of it." She also reminded him, patiently, that she'd borne the family's financial burdens for the last eleven years, and after work each day, needed time to relax and recharge. She was happy to spend time as a family, but Mark groused about that—he'd been with the family all day. He wanted "some time with my wife so we can be growing together, not just . . . with the girls."

In early September, trying to be positive, Mark agreed that he was too focused on Teresa. "I am missing something in my life, friendships and other adult outlets," he concluded, resolving to spend time every Friday getting into shape and working out at the gym. But then, on September 22, something unfortunate happened. In the middle of intimacy, Mark, fumbling for the lube, accidentally grabbed Dr. Delgado's "Grow Young" spray, which was on Teresa's bedside table. Mark was indignant. "She took it from me and used it!" It didn't stop him from having sex, but once they'd finished, he lost his temper and threw the "Grow Young" spray across the room. After that, Teresa was careful never to use Delgado's products when Mark was around.

Teresa and Nick were still seeing each other—they were still collaborating on their anti-aging outreach—but Teresa reassured Mark the relationship was friendly and professional. He kept trying to deal with it. He didn't complain when she went to Texas and, with Nick's help, filmed a new video for her website. He was begrudgingly grateful when Nick sent Teresa a text "stating that her video was the best one next to his."

• • •

Mark and Teresa's open marriage began as a success; "when we started all this a few years ago with another woman, we actually talked a lot of this stuff out before we ever invited somebody to join us," Mark mused. They'd even discussed moving from swinging into an open relationship—"we've talked about adding a third person, a woman into our bedroom on a more permanent basis." But when Nick came along, things changed. Despite having lovers all over town, Mark started to think of Teresa's fantasies about Nick as a form of infidelity ("cheating starts in the heart and mind and then actions"). And even if it wasn't Nick, might a similar situation come up again in the future?

By 2015, Mark was feeling torn between making sure Teresa was happy and keeping their marriage stable (in the past, these hadn't been mutually exclusive outcomes). He now regretted opening their marriage to other people. "We allowed this intrusion into our union our marriage our lives so I guess it would be our fault. . . ." He realized that they'd never stopped and thought: "Do we really know what we're getting into with all this?"

By 2015, the couple's relationship was seriously damaged. As Annie put it, "the higher Teresa soared professionally and spiritually, the more Mark tripped her mid-stride." The furious texts got more frequent, but now they had a new theme. Instead of seeing Mark as a useful but infuriating helpmate, Teresa started to regard him as a "leech," living through her and off her. After Mark texted her at work to remind her where she'd parked, she grew livid. "This kind of helicoptering is driving me crazy and it shows me you are more focused on me than you. Get off the fucking couch and fucking do something with yourself. Get off my ass and stop living vicariously through me for fuck's sake."

Mark was hurt. He'd never thought of himself this way. "She feels stressed overwhelmed trapped in our lives," he realized. "I'm not bringing in an income . . . I had not really thought of myself as leeching off Teresa until tonight . . . she wants a man who can multitask and has it going on." For a while, he thought about going to law school, but nothing came of it.

Even when there was no contact with Nick, his ghost still hovered. Teresa, following the Delgado Protocol, didn't believe in compromises, because "by compromising u are giving up power." In her eyes, Mark realized, he was weak, both mentally and physically. "I know I'm overweight and I'm trying to work on that." Teresa told him it wasn't the weight, it was just that he wasn't motivated to take care of himself. But later, she admitted: he was losing his sex appeal.

Mostly, Mark kept his resentment to himself, but it continued to fester. He was upset that Teresa hadn't worn her hair the way he liked it for almost a year (although she did it "sort of" for the Our Mother's Home gala). He wanted sex daily, and she wanted it weekly or less (recently it had been "a little bitty peck and then she's out"). Mark needed a real kiss now and then, genuine hugs, intimacy. "I cannot keep settling with the lack of these basic things in my life." Often, he sensed Teresa wanted to avoid being around him. He felt he was always frustrating her, crowding her. "she thinks i only think about sex." She had a point.

One night, the couple went for a long walk on the beach and

had a soul-searching conversation. Teresa admitted that they might have married too hastily, because she'd been pregnant. If they met each other today for the first time, she suggested, they might not even want to date. Mark understood that his wife had launched on a new journey in life, with new horizons and new prospects. Was she leaving him behind?

The couple went back and forth: their marriage was broken, they were both unhappy, and their future looked bleak. Neither could see a way out. At the same time, neither was willing to take the first step toward separation. "We do not want to make any decisions about giving up," Mark resolved. They staggered on, struggling and fighting. Mark admitted: "I do feel myself becoming a little numb ☹"

But during the weeks leading up to the murder, things began to turn around. The couple started working on their relationship, planning for their future together. "T lay in my arms in bed," Mark noted happily, on April 18. In May, he thanked Michele Petrites for lending him a book about couples' healing. "I think things may be getting slightly better," he wrote. He began suggesting family trips. On June 9, he sent Teresa a link to Discovery Cove, a theme park in Orlando. "I think we should go there during our vacation," he wrote. "The scenery is worth the price of admission (starts at $190 depending on time of year)." On June 24, a week before the murder, he noted, "T & i are in a good place, she has been kissing me unsolicited . . ." They even had sex on June 26, the first morning they spent in New York.

Three days later, Mark was planning her funeral.

Chapter 9

Best Man

In the summer of 2002, a series of high-profile kidnappings shook the country, causing a national frenzy. Relentless news coverage made the missing girls—Elizabeth Smart, Samantha Runnion, Michelle Knight—into household names, and the media began referring to "the summer of child abductions." So when six-year-old Casey Williamson disappeared on Friday, July 25, police immediately took it seriously.

Casey lived on Benton Street in Valley Park, a small, blue-collar town twenty miles west of St. Louis. The residential areas, cut through by railroad tracks, were surrounded by factories, many abandoned. Casey's mom and dad, Angie and Ernie, were separated, but still close, and purportedly trying to "work things out." The night of Thursday July 24, 2002, Angie and her three kids stayed over at Ernie's house, right across the street. Also at Ernie's house that night, sleeping on the couch, was a twenty-four-year-old family friend named Johnny Johnson, whom the couple had known since he was a kid. When Johnny told them he had nowhere to stay, Ernie invited him to sleep over.

The next morning, Ernie got up early for his seven A.M. shift—he was a union carpenter at a nearby cement factory. Casey got up, too, and turned on the television while her dad got ready for work. Ernie, about to pour Casey a bowl of cereal, went to the bathroom for five minutes. When he emerged, the television was still playing, but Casey was gone. And so was Johnny Johnson.

Within half an hour, St. Louis County deputy sheriffs and FBI agents were searching the nearby factories, woods, and parks. Local volunteers knocked on their neighbors' doors. Police helicopters surveyed the town. Boats explored the Meramec River; bloodhounds sniffed through the undergrowth. The case made national news, and the local media ran a constant feed. Angie was beside herself. She stood outside her house, wailing. Neighbors held her, reciting the Lord's Prayer. Against the side of the clapboard home, Casey's little pink bicycle leaned forlornly.

In the early afternoon, police discovered the child's nightgown—white with red flowers—in an abandoned glass factory less than a mile from her home. Then Johnny Johnson turned up, walking down Benton Street. Dirty, covered with mud, and soaking wet, he said he'd been for a swim in the nearby Meramec River. No one believed him, and when pressed by the cops, he quickly confessed.

When he woke up on the couch, Johnny told police, he saw Casey standing beside him, and decided he wanted to have sex with her. He gave the barefoot girl a piggyback ride, taking her to the most fitting spot that could be chosen for the perpetration of such an appalling crime. The abandoned glass factory was a place of deep solitude, full of overgrown tunnels and muddy silos. Johnny took the child to a dark pit, molested her, crushed her skull with a rock, then concealed her body under leaves and pieces of concrete.

Johnny Johnson had a long history of mental illness. Six months before Casey's murder, he'd been hospitalized after hearing the voices of dead friends and seeing "cracks everywhere, shadow people, and hands coming out of the walls." He believed he was being "eaten alive," that bugs were crawling into his brain, that he had "the power of making tornadoes." Unbeknownst to Casey's family, he'd been diagnosed with paranoid schizophrenia, and was addicted to meth, alcohol, and cocaine. He also had a learning disorder, a history of suicide attempts, and had spent time in prison. After his arrest, he was convicted of first-degree murder, kidnapping, and attempted rape, and held without bond in the county jail. After a trial, despite his mental illness, he was sentenced to death.

In memory of her daughter, Angie got a huge tattoo at the top of her back: Casey's name above a picture of her face with a halo and angel's wings. On the wall of the family room, she installed a photograph of Casey superimposed on a picture of Jesus. The child's death had a terrible impact on the family—Angie and Ernie divorced. Angie's brother had a complete mental breakdown, and her father drank himself to death. Then, thirteen years after losing Casey, on March 12, 2015, Angie lost her oldest daughter, Chelsea, twenty-four. Heavy drug use caused an infection in her lungs that spread into her bloodstream, and her organs failed. Chelsea left behind a son, Jackson, and a daughter, Ava, who was confined to a wheelchair and needed constant care.

Chelsea's death was particularly tragic because Angie was about to get married. At first, she thought about calling the wedding off, but decided there was no point prolonging the grief—life must go on. Her fiancé was a man she'd dated many years ago, but things hadn't worked out. His name was Curtis Wayne Wright, Jr.

• • •

It was Mark Sievers who'd introduced them: the bonds between the three were almost incestuous. Back in high school, Mark had dated Angie's Aunt Shelley, whom Wayne also dated briefly. At the time he'd introduced Wayne to Angie, to complicate matters further, Mark was involved with Angie's glamorous mom, Kathy, seventeen years his senior. Their relationship was short-lived but passionate. Many years later, Wayne told Mark that Kathy often reminisced about how great the sex was. "She said that in bed you are the best she has ever been with . . . and she thinks of you a lot," Wayne texted Mark. "She said she would love to have you around for an anytime booty call." ("Where does she live again? just kiddin," Mark replied.)

With Angie, too, Mark was more than just a friend. Wayne enjoyed showing her off, sending Mark sexy pictures of his bride-to-be. On April 2, 2014, he sent Mark a risqué photo. "beautiful!!!" Mark responded. "Want to see more . . . up close and Very personal." Wayne told him: "I will see what I can do." He added, later, "she said maybe in person."

When the couple announced their engagement, in 2014, Wayne, forty-six, was a burly guy, with a small potbelly, a shaved head, metal-framed glasses, and a reddish goatee. Angie, forty-one, was a stout, strong-featured woman with short black hair and blue eyes. After reconnecting after twenty years, they'd been living together in Wayne's trailer for about fourteen months. The manufactured home was crowded—it was shared, at various times, with the couple's children (Wayne's two daughters and Angie's fifteen-year-old delinquent son), as well as Angie's grandchildren, Jackson and Ava.

The couple planned a spring wedding—the date they chose was Saturday, May 2, 2015. They decided to hold the ceremony in De Soto, a quiet little town whose main street faced the freight tracks of the Pacific Union Railroad. Although Teresa and the girls couldn't make it, Mark—the best man—was so psyched about the wedding that he started calling up his Missouri buddies and old flames, letting them know he'd be back in town, counting down the days. As May approached, the risqué texts between Mark and Wayne ramped up. "What should I wear to your wedding" asked Mark on April 13. "(no, not Angie's panties again.)" "she said you have to!" joked Wayne. "ok, but on the outside?" wondered Mark. Later that day, he texts: "You know we sleep *au natural*." Wayne responds, "I don't care how you sleep, you are not sleeping with us!" (Later, he revised his message: "I meant to say you are not *sleeping* with us.")

But one text was not so playful. "hopefully we can talk privately tomorrow," wrote Mark. "nothing about u or angie, but its personal."

• • •

Mark arrived in Missouri on Thursday, April 30, two days before the wedding. Back on his home turf, he was determined to squeeze in visits to all the friends he could manage. His plane landed at 8:50 P.M. Right away, he dropped in on a buddy who lived close to the airport, then drove to see his brother in nearby St. Charles. In the early hours of the morning, he visited another friend in Des Peres, fifteen miles south, then drove ten miles south to his condo in Fenton, where he spent the night. The next morning, he got a text. "Good morning honey ☺" wrote Wayne. "hello sugar . . . what u wearing?" Mark replied. He tried to get Wayne to send him a sexy picture of Angie, because ". . . I just woke up & you know what that means ☺" Wayne asked his bride-to-be, but she wasn't in the mood. "she won't let me send one," he wrote. Mark was disappointed. "☹ I guess I will have to use my imagination."

Located on S. Old Highway 141, Mark's condo was a small, plain, two-bedroom unit in an ordinary suburban complex. In the past, he'd rented it out, but in the last few years, he'd been using it as a place to stay when he visited Wayne, and it was full of clutter and junk—piles of clothes, computers, printers, and exercise equipment. He spent the morning of Friday, May 1 cleaning out the condo, garage, and storage unit, dumping boxes of paperwork from his old satellite business. By lunchtime, things were in better shape, but not much. Mark was a lifelong hoarder.

He finished cleaning around noon, locked up his condo, and drove over to Wayne and Angie's place. The couple lived in an aluminum-sided single-wide manufactured home in Chapel Hill Court, about twenty minutes from Mark's condo in Fenton. The small, shabby trailer park was built on a slope overlooking a drainage ditch; Wayne and Angie's trailer, indistinguishable from the others, was at the bottom of the slope. It was an unsavory spot, but since she'd moved in, Angie had made some attempts to cheer things up. She'd put some plants on the stoop outside the kitchen door, and hung a butterfly windchime above the steps. Angie had a thing about butterflies. She always wore butterfly jewelry, and had butterflies tattooed on her right breast and her right wrist.

That afternoon, the couple hosted a cookout outside the trailer for their closest friends—just nine or ten people. The kids ran around by the ditch while Wayne fired up the grill. The adults were all old buddies, many of whom hadn't seen one another for years; inevitably, there was a lot of drinking, and things got rowdy. As usual, Mark was the center of attention, doing impressions, recounting anecdotes, telling jokes. Still, he found time to check in with his daughters in Florida—so often, in fact, that Teresa got annoyed. She, too, was attending a wedding that weekend, and didn't want Emma and Olivia on the phone all the time. "I can't believe how much your texting the girls," she wrote. "just do your thing."

After partying in the trailer park, the happy couple and their guests went to a karaoke bar in Bonne Terre, about half an hour away. Those who were still there when they got back—five or six people—wanted to keep drinking, so they joined Wayne and Angie inside the trailer for what Wayne euphemistically described as "a combined bachelor/bachelorette party." More carousing ensued. Things got wild. So wild that when Angie was later asked if she'd ever had sex with Mark, she replied, "Not that I know of." What did she mean? "I was pretty drunk the night before my wedding, and I don't remember bits and pieces of it," she admitted. "But Mark and my husband look an awful lot alike . . ." An exchange between Mark and Wayne two days after the wedding suggests Angie's inkling was right. "How is 'our' Angie?" asked Mark. "She is great!" Wayne replied. "Should have offered her a blindfold the other night ☺," texted Mark. "Why would she need a blindfold?" wondered Wayne. "Nobody can tell the difference between us in the pictures from the wedding."

On Saturday morning, hungover or not, people had to start setting things up. There was no more drinking—it was a liquor-free ceremony, partly because the wedding was sanctioned by the church, but mostly because they couldn't afford it. The service would be taking place outdoors, at Walther Park, a long strip of recreation ground between the highway and a creek, containing a soccer field, walking path, and children's playground. When they first arrived, Wayne recalled, there was "a big dramafest" when the pavilion they'd reserved for the wedding was "overrun by soccer moms," but the confusion was swiftly resolved, and the preparations began. There were decorations to hang, chairs to bring over from the church, folding tables to set up, meat to grill.

The couple couldn't afford a fancy wedding; it was basically do-it-yourself, with no caterers or photographers. Everything was cheap and cheerful. Nobody cared that it was all was plastic: the flowers, the plates, the utensils. There were plastic champagne flutes for the fake champagne. Angie wore a filmy white dress with a butterfly print, a butterfly necklace, shiny blue nail polish, and a white hairclip festooned with a silk rose. Decorative butterflies adorned the wedding cake.

It was hot, but not too hot—the thermometer barely grazed eighty. Wayne and Mark, as they liked to do on such occasions, deliberately played up their resemblance. Both wore goatees, glasses, short-sleeved gray shirts, and black pants—the only difference was that Wayne wore a striped tie. They changed in the public restroom at Walther Park. In a photograph of Wayne taken right before the wedding, it's not clear whether he's facing Mark, or looking into a mirror.

PART TWO

Chapter 10

"Something's Not Right"

On Saturday, June 27, 2015, the day before Teresa's murder, Rose Grunert, a registered nurse from Mount Vernon, Illinois, was spending the day in Ballwin, Missouri, with her close friend, Kathy Moran (Angie's mom). Rose and Kathy had grown up together and still talked almost every day. They visited whenever they got the chance, even though they now lived two hours apart.

That day, Rose and Kathy had been shopping at a tag sale, then spent the afternoon making wedding bouquets. In the evening, Angie came by for her mom to color her hair—Kathy, fashionable and stylish into her seventies, was a hairdresser by trade. When the bouquets were finished, the three women went into the kitchen, where Kathy wrapped a towel around her daughter's shoulders and pulled on a pair of disposable gloves.

Angie was antsy and distracted. Kathy asked her what was going on.

"It's Wayne," she told her mom. "There's no way I can get hold of him. He's down in Florida. He left his phone at home."

Kathy was surprised. Wayne was on his phone all the time, calling and texting.

Angie agreed: while Wayne often forgot things, he never

forgot his phone. Plus, he'd told her he'd be staying in a hotel, so she didn't see why he couldn't call her on a landline.

Rose wondered what Wayne was doing in Florida. Angie explained that he was visiting his best friend, Mark Sievers, to work on his computers. He was Mark's tech guy, said Angie.

Rose was confused. "Wait. He drives all the way to Florida to work on Mark's computers? Can't Mark get somebody local to do it?"

"Wayne's a genius with computers," Angie boasted. "And he doesn't charge a whole lot. He told me I had to stay home and work. He said we needed the money."

"Didn't you say his car was in the shop?" asked Kathy, as she was mixing the color.

"He got a rental," said Angie.

Rose slept over at Kathy's house that night and returned to Mount Vernon on Sunday. The following evening, after dinner, she was watching the HLN channel and, as often happened, she fell asleep on the couch. In the early hours, she woke up suddenly—the clock said 1:37 A.M.—and they were re-airing the *Nancy Grace* show. Rose didn't care for the program and normally she'd turn it off, but something seized her attention. On the screen was a picture of a pretty woman with red hair—a doctor, said Nancy, who'd been brutally murdered in Florida. When Rose heard the name "Sievers," her heart missed a beat. She grabbed her phone and called Kathy.

It was the middle of the night, but her friend was awake. Yes, Kathy told Rose. The doctor was Mark's wife, and she'd been bludgeoned to death. Nobody could believe it. Apparently, Wayne had gotten home from Florida about six o'clock on Sunday evening. The next day, he got a text from Mark's brother telling him Teresa was dead.

Rose had only met Wayne once, and she hadn't been impressed. She thought he was kind of rough. He didn't say much. A little intimidating. She knew he'd been in prison before. Kathy told her he was a champion kickboxer and cage fighter and was supposed to have a metal plate in his head. According to Angie, his hands were registered as lethal weapons, although Kathy didn't believe that was a real thing. She found it weird that he'd been at Mark's house in Florida the same day Teresa was killed. Rose agreed. Very creepy.

"I've got a gut feeling something's not right," said Kathy.

"Listen, Kathy. You should talk to the police."

Her friend was reluctant. Wayne was her son-in-law, after all. Angie would go nuts. "Let's wait and see," Kathy decided. "It might just add up to a whole lot of coincidences."

While Angie and Wayne were in Florida for Teresa's funeral, Rose and Kathy talked every day. "We've all got a feeling that something's not right," Kathy told her friend. "My sister, my husband . . ." She described an alarming conversation she'd had with Angie right before she and Wayne left for the funeral. Kathy had said something about how spooky it was that Wayne had been at Teresa's house just a few hours before she was murdered.

Angie corrected her. "No, Mom, I didn't say he was going to Mark's *house*, I said he was going to work on the computers at Teresa's *office*."

"You told me the house," said Kathy.

"I did not tell you that," said Angie.

Conversation closed.

"Kathy, you've got to call the police," said Rose.

"I can't," said Kathy. "We're all scared to say anything. Wayne's not the nicest person in the world. If I went to the police, my daughter would never speak to me again. And if he was involved, Angie is so hung up on him, she'd probably commit suicide."

Rose could understand her friend's reluctance. Angie's life had been one tragedy after another. If it turned out her new husband was a murderer, best let the cops figure it out. "The police are smart people," was Kathy's opinion.

The next day, Rose got a call from Kathy's husband, Ed Moran, a retired contractor for Anheuser-Busch. Ed didn't like Wayne. Never had. In his mind, there was no doubt—Wayne had murdered Dr. Sievers. But he couldn't talk to the cops, because Kathy wouldn't let him. "If there was an anonymous number I could call, I'd do it," he said.

Rose thought of herself as a Christian. It was her personal belief that, in situations like these, you should follow your best instincts. After all, it might be God telling you what to do. A friend of hers knew a police officer, Jeff Hamilton, who worked at the airport. Maybe she should talk to Jeff.

• • •

It's July 9, eleven days after Teresa's murder. Detective Jamie Nolen is working late in the Lee County Sheriff's Office, going over the Sievers homicide file. At the desk next to him, also working late, sits Michael Downs, an ambitious young detective with receding hair. Downs, who's been at the Lee County Sheriff's Office for around ten years, accompanied Nolen to the murder scene at Jarvis Road and has an active interest in the Sievers case.

Around six P.M., the phone rings. The caller identifies himself as Chief Jeff Hamilton of the Southern Illinois Airport Authority; he wants to speak to Detective Nolen. A friend of his has just provided him with a tip about the Sievers case, says Hamilton—it's credible and consistent, and if it proves accurate, could be vital. He offers to put the tipster on the line.

Detective Nolen thanks him, and puts the call on speakerphone, so Mike Downs can join them, along with Lieutenant Jim Amrich, another investigator who happens to be in the office.

Rose is nervous. She won't give her name. "I don't know anything for sure," she says. "I was wanting to hopefully point you in the direction that you could check it out. I don't know that he did this."

Nolen assures her that everything she's telling them is completely anonymous and confidential. Nothing will ever be repeated back to anybody. She'll never be implicated. They'd certainly never put her in any kind of danger.

Tentatively, Rose tells the detectives what Angie Wright had said while Kathy was doing her hair, about Wayne being in Florida at the same time Mark's wife was murdered. "He's the best friend of the husband," she explains. "They've been friends for several years." She tells them about Wayne's criminal history and Angie's tragic past. She describes how she woke in the night and saw Teresa's picture on the *Nancy Grace* show. She recounts what Kathy told her, about Angie changing her story. She mentions that Kathy's husband, Ed, had always mistrusted Wayne. When she tells them what Ed said about wanting to call in an anonymous tip, Nolen asks Rose for his number.

"That's not something I'm comfortable with right now," says Rose. "He's scared to say anything. They're all scared."

Mike Downs tries to put her at ease. "You're doing a very noble thing," he tells her. "There's two little girls without a mother. . . . You're going to keep this from happening again. But we'll cross that bridge when we come to it. Right now, you're just pointing us in a direction. That's all." He asks her to gather more information, including dates, times, and details.

"I'll do what I can," she promises. "My heart goes out to this doctor and her family. And this has bothered me ever since I found out about it. So, I'll do what I can."

Immediately after their conversation with Rose Grunert, the homicide team checked out Mark Sievers's phone records for any communications with Wayne Wright in Missouri. Shockingly, they learned the two men had been in contact almost daily for the last few months. This, along with Rose's testimony, gave the investigators more than enough reason to take the next flight to St. Louis.

• • •

The Sievers homicide investigation was a huge case for the Lee County Sheriff's Office, involving a large team of law enforcement personnel whose roles, for various bureaucratic reasons, changed over time. It was Detective Mike Downs and his partner David Lebid, rather than Jamie Nolen, who flew to St. Louis on July 11 to meet with officers from the Jefferson County Sheriff's Office in Hillsboro and fill them in about their suspicions. Between Rose Grunert's statement and Wayne and Mark's phone contacts, the investigators decided they had enough evidence to search Wayne's trailer and Mark's condo, and to take DNA samples from Wayne. The warrant was signed by a Jefferson County judge that same afternoon.

Brutal early-morning raids are a common police tactic used to surprise someone who might otherwise try to flee or to hide evidence. Whether intentionally or not, they also intrude and humiliate. The suspect is usually in a vulnerable state, generally undressed in bed, which was the case on July 12, at 5:45 A.M., when a SWAT team from the Jefferson County Sheriff's Office donned their protective gear, drew their guns, and swept down on Wayne and Angie's trailer at 8894 Chapel Hill Court.

They hammered violently on the door. When no one responded, the cops let off a "noise flash diversion device" at the back of the house—a machine that makes a huge bang and shines a blinding light "intended to cause confusion and distraction to provide a tactical team with a few seconds of advantage." Still no response. A last resort: the police broke down the door with a battering ram. Neighbors, jolted awake, emerged from their trailers rubbing their eyes, dazed by the sudden violence.

Wayne and Angie were sitting up in bed, half-naked and

petrified. With them was Angie's terrified grandson, Jackson, six. The child was taken into another room while the newlyweds, after grabbing some clothes, were handcuffed and taken to police headquarters in separate squad cars. Here, they were photographed. Wayne, bare-chested, looked stoic. Angie, braless in tank top and purple pajama shorts, glowered defiantly. Police obtained buccal swabs from the pair and took their fingerprints. Jackson, too, was photographed—a wary kid in a dirty blue T-shirt with drool on his face. He was held at the station until Kathy, his great-grandmother, could come and pick him up.

While Wayne and Angie were being interviewed, law enforcement officers searched and photographed their residence, described by Angie's mother as "an old, dirty, beat-up trailer." The sordid hovel made a tawdry contrast to the Sievers home in Bonita Springs. The newlyweds' family room contained a few feeble attempts at bourgeois life—a framed picture of Jesus, porcelain figurines, family photographs, a couple of dying plants—but the other rooms were, as the police report curtly put it, "excessively cluttered," the floors and beds covered with computer equipment, children's toys, tool chests, and piles of dirty laundry. In the bathroom, someone had installed an elephantine Jacuzzi. Hanging over the shower curtain: a towel memorializing Wayne and Angie's marriage, clearly a wedding gift. In the closet hung Angie's filmy, butterfly-themed wedding dress, a weak stab at happiness.

The couple were interviewed separately. The cops were convinced Wayne was involved in the murder. Surely Angie had to know? After all, they were, as everyone said, "inseparable." David Lebid, who had a reputation for relentless questioning, worked on Angie's conscience, giving her the opportunity to rat Wayne out without feeling bad about it.

"You're a victim, in my opinion, because you're put in this situation you didn't fully appreciate," he told her. Then he offered her an out. Maybe Wayne was a decent guy who simply "made a bad choice?" If not, then he was "a calculated predator" who was trying to manipulate her. "They find people like you and me, and they'll use us to their benefit," he said. Then he went even further. He asked her, "Did you know you married a murderer?"

Angie wasn't biting. "My husband's an awesome man," she said. Later, she complained to Wayne about the way the detective tried to insinuate that he cared about her. "'How're you doing, Angie? How are the kids? How's your mom?' He was asking me all these questions. . . . He was pissing me off . . . I'm like, 'take your fake ass somewhere else.'" Wayne agreed. "They say they want your help, then everything you say to try to help, they turn around and try to twist into something."

Wayne's interview began at 8:49 A.M. He insisted to Sergeant Lebid that, during the weekend of Teresa's death, he'd been working on a car belonging to Christian Taylor, the landlord of Chapel Hill Court—he often repaired Chris's cars, said Wayne, in lieu of rent. While working, he'd started to feel weak and dizzy, so he took a break and went to bed, resting alone until Monday evening. When Detective Lebid told him Angie said he'd been in Florida that weekend, Wayne apparently "got nervous" and said he didn't want to talk anymore. This was his prerogative, and at this point, the police weren't especially concerned. The raid wasn't an attempt to get information but a sudden shock wave, meant to frighten Wayne, show him what they knew, and send ripples through the community.

At 9:40 A.M., Angie's mom and stepdad, Ed and Kathy Moran, came down to the sheriff's office to pick up their daughter. Before being allowed to see her, they, too, were interviewed by Detective Downs. The couple admitted that, after learning about Teresa's murder, they'd turned to each other in fear. Wasn't that the weekend Wayne went to Florida without his phone?

"Do you think Wayne is capable of killing Teresa?" Downs asked.

Kathy was circumspect. "I know he's a martial arts expert," she said. "I also know that he was in prison for three years. I'm sure that if you're in prison for that long, you have to know what to do to survive."

When Downs asked for her husband's opinion, Ed didn't beat around the bush. "I don't trust that son of a bitch," he said, "and I never have."

The cops had no arrest warrant, so after interviewing Wayne and Angie and searching the trailer, they had to let them go. They also had a search warrant for Wayne's storage unit, at 11349 Pounds Road, but they found nothing of evidentiary value, only plastic tubs full of children's toys and clothes, and a pile of newspaper cuttings about the murder of Angie's daughter in 2002.

• • •

Over the following days, investigators approached Wayne's friends and relatives, hoping to get further tips. But his family were wary of the cops. On Saturday, July 18, law enforcement officers contacted Wayne's father, Curtis Sr.; his mother, Jane; and his brother, Jerry, but none of them would talk. Neighbors in the trailer park shut doors in their faces. The only person who agreed to be interviewed was Wayne's friend Jerry Lubinski, a pleasant guy in his seventies, slightly heavyset, with slicked-back gray hair.

On July 13, at eleven A.M., Detectives Lebid and Downs interviewed Jerry at his home, where he lived with his girlfriend, Sundaye Harrison. Jerry explained he'd been a bricklayer for thirty-two years. After his retirement, he set up a screen-printing business, which did very well. Not being too tech-savvy, he'd asked Wayne, whom he'd met through church, if he'd help with the computers now and then. Wayne was happy to do so, and the two men became close. Around 2012, Jerry sold his business and concentrated full-time on his hobby, selling antiques, mostly silver and gold coins. Wayne helped him out by listing items for sale on eBay. He didn't expect to be paid, but Jerry would give him a couple hundred dollars here and there to help with his rent, along with other items, like a camera, a toolbox, and a Garmin GPS. At this, the investigators pricked up their ears.

Jerry, who had no idea Wayne was in trouble, described him as a "true friend" who'd never let him down. "He's done some work around my house here and put the deck on the back porch. He's a very good handyman," he said. "When my wife passed, Wayne was there for me. I have nothing but good things to say about the man."

The detectives pushed him a little further. They asked him what he knew about the incident in Florida.

"I don't know much about it," said Jerry. "I'm trying to think of his friend's name, whose wife was murdered . . . I met him once, at the wedding."

"Can you describe him?"

"He looks like Wayne . . . he was just kind of the hit of the party . . . I wish I remember the gentleman's name . . . he was just very funny, just had people laughing and everything, doing things, and all that. Like I said, he looked almost exactly like Wayne."

Unlike Jerry Lubinski, Angie's family had always mistrusted Wayne. They were close to the Bolins, and were convinced Wayne was responsible for the preacher's disappearance. They were only too happy to share their suspicions about Angie's new husband.

On July 15, at 3:45 P.M., the two detectives interviewed Angie's brother, Robert Wideman. Robert confessed that he avoided Wayne whenever possible. "I'm scared of him," he admitted. Nobody knew what he did for a living. "Everybody is kind of clueless. I've heard he's a goat farmer. I hear he works on servers. But what does he actually do?" Even Angie didn't seem to know.

Robert Wideman told investigators he was surprised when a few days before the murder, Wayne, who was perennially broke, took him to lunch at Buffalo Wild Wings, then later picked up his bar tab. He told Robert he was "going to Florida to set up a server for a doctor's office" because "no one else knows how to fix it." He asked for some Adderall to help him keep awake during the drive. Robert gave him a single pill, advising him to take half on the way down, and the other half on the way back.

After the raid on his trailer, said Robert, Wayne had called him to say he didn't actually go to Florida that weekend as planned.

"He said that him and Angie got into a little bit of a dispute," Robert told the investigators. "And he basically told me that he just stayed around town and told her he was going to Florida just so he could have some time alone." If he needed someone to verify he was at home the weekend of Teresa's murder, asked Wayne, could Robert help him out? Robert didn't give him a direct answer. He found the question strange and suspicious.

The police were particularly interested in whether, since the raid on July 12, Angie had changed her story about the weekend Wayne was in Florida. Apparently, she had. On July 14, the detectives talked to her mother for a second time. The interview took place in a waiting room at the Cardinal Glennon Children's Hospital in St. Louis.

Kathy told the police that not long after the raid on her trailer, Angie had called her, sounding "a little hyper," and said that the weekend of Teresa's murder, she and Wayne had had "a misunderstanding" and he didn't go to Florida at all. He stayed home in the trailer while Angie was at her mom's, and she needed her mom to verify that to the police. "That kinda red-flagged me," said Kathy. She got angry with her daughter and hung up on her. When she felt calmer, she called Angie back. "I told her I loved her and that I was sorry she had problems, that I had my own problems. . . . And that was the end of it. She didn't say any more about Wayne, if he was home or if he wasn't home. . . . She didn't try to convince me after that, because I really didn't want to hear it."

"Did you get the impression she was trying to change your

mind? Was it the way she said it? Was it something specific she said?" asked Detective Lebid.

"First she says Wayne's gone one place, going to fix the computer. Then she said he was going to an auction. . . . Then he comes home Monday and turns around and tells her that he didn't go anywhere. Now, if he didn't go anywhere, why didn't he call his wife and say, 'Hey honey, I'm home.' That just doesn't make sense."

Everybody wondered: What did Angie know? Kathy was sure her daughter wouldn't help cover up a murder. Wayne must have convinced her he was being framed by the cops. "Angie will believe anything Wayne tells her," said Kathy. "She'll do anything for him. She'd even leave her children to be with him."

Her brother agreed: Angie was kindhearted but naïve. "My sister is head over heels in love with Wayne, and she's really proud to be married to him." Robert, too, said that Angie believed whatever Wayne told her. "Angie is a hundred percent certain in her mind that Wayne did not go to Florida," he told investigators. "She claims that she's talked to neighbors about where Wayne's whereabouts actually were, which was around the trailer." Detectives wondered whether Angie might have been trying to defend her husband. Robert didn't think that was possible. "Wayne has manipulated my sister to say the things that he wants her to say," said Robert. "But do I think she would lie to cover up a murder? No."

The hottest tip of all came from Angie's sister, Carrie Mertz, who, along with her husband, owned an auto repair shop. Carrie told investigators that, the week before Teresa's murder, Angie had rear-ended Wayne's Kia. It wasn't just a fender bender—she'd smashed into somebody with a trailer hitch, which went right through the front of the car. When Wayne dropped off the Kia at Carrie's repair shop on June 26, he said the accident was inconvenient, because he was about to go on a long trip out of town. Carrie recommended Enterprise Rent-a-Car, where Wayne picked up a white Hyundai Elantra.

Two days later, law enforcement had located the vehicle in Arizona and had it towed back to Florida. Sifting through the tubs of items they'd confiscated from Wayne's trailer, they found the Garmin GPS he'd borrowed from Jerry Lubinski and sent it down to Florida. Here, using state-of-the-art extraction software, the Lee County Police Department Digital Forensics Unit retrieved all deleted contents, and hit a gold mine.

Apparently, during the weekend Wayne rented the car, he put around 2,800 miles on the odometer. Even better, the GPS contained a trail of digital footprints leading from Wayne's trailer in Missouri all the way to the Sieverses' house in Florida and back, showing searches performed along the way for various gas stations, rest stops, and eateries.

Something else also grabbed the cops' attention. Before leaving for Florida in the early hours of Saturday, June 27, instead of heading straight for the highway, Wayne had taken a half-hour detour to a trailer park in Cadet, Missouri. When police checked on the address where he'd pulled up, they noted the property belonged to a convicted felon named Jimmy Ray Rodgers.

Better known as Jimmy the Hammer.

Chapter 11

Jimmy

South of the St. Louis suburbs lie the small towns of Jefferson County—Festus, De Soto, Potosi, Bonne Terre. Most are cut through by freight railway tracks, their main streets now dead and shuttered. Geographically, you're in the Ozarks, but the area is hilly rather than mountainous. Baptist churches, Dollar Stores, trailer parks, auto salvage. Twenty years ago, this was part of the Lead Belt, and although lead farming is long gone, the toxic detritus remains (an alarming number of children born and raised here have dangerous levels of lead in their blood). The mines are closed, too; even farms are few and far between. Ninety-eight percent of the population is white. Fewer than twenty percent have a college degree. Many are desperate and hard-pressed. Drug use is widespread. High rates of unemployment lead to poverty, which often leads to crime. The stigma of a prison sentence makes it even more difficult to get a job, steering ex-felons back into their former lives. The circle continues. What brings relief from the tedium? Drugs, alcohol, firearms. Making America Great Again. Finding Jesus. Getting clean, relapsing. Getting married, divorced, married again. Most of all: having kids.

Taylor Shomaker didn't finish high school and had never had

a job, but to her, none of that mattered. Overweight and baby-faced, all she wanted in life was to be a mom. By the time she was twenty-four, she had three children by different fathers: Oaklynn, Otis, and baby Ozzie. Taylor adored her kids and did everything she could to take care of them, but she struggled. She lived on food stamps and was fighting to get support payments from her babies' dads. In 2014, she was evicted from her home in Cadet, Missouri, for failure to pay rent.

It was definitely a setback, but not for long. Her boyfriend of three months, Jimmy Ray Rodgers, invited her and her kids to move into the trailer he rented from his boss. Taylor was relieved, but the trailer park where Jimmy lived, in Cadet, was hardly a great place to raise kids. Situated off Highway 21, between a trash haulage site and a landfill, the cluster of manufactured homes was surrounded by piles of abandoned construction materials overgrown with weeds. The only signs of life were a few satellite dishes and laundry hanging out on lines. Her new home might have seemed unwelcome on the outside, but Taylor tried to keep things cheery, moving in her children's toys and furniture. She covered some of the windows with blankets to block out the sun.

• • •

Jimmy Ray Rodgers was cursed from birth. Entering the world, he got tangled in his mother's umbilical cord. When he was two, in 1990, his mom was institutionalized, diagnosed with schizophrenia, and heavily medicated. After that, Jimmy and his older brother, Jackie Jr., had to fend for themselves. Their father was violent and abusive and would beat his sons, although Jimmy got the worst of it. Jackie Jr., older by five years, started lifting weights at the age of eight, building up his muscles so he could fight back and protect his little brother. But if Jimmy got it bad, their mother got it even worse—her husband would punch her in the stomach, then hold her down and smack her in the back of the head, leaving knots in her skull but no bruises on her face.

The family lived in Paris, Missouri, population 1,200. The Rodgers house was isolated, three and a half miles from town. Although it looked comfortable from the outside, there was almost no furniture—Jimmy and his brother slept on the floor, while their mother used the couch. Their father didn't see the point in furnishing the home because he was hardly ever there—he usually stayed in Sedalia, Missouri, a small town two hours south of Paris, where he worked at a manufacturing plant that produced wheels and brakes.

Jimmy's dad only bought groceries home once a month. If they ran out of food, Jimmy and his brother would have to go to school with no lunch. The boys had nothing—no birthday or Christmas presents, no new clothes, no haircuts, not even a toothbrush between them. Sometimes, Jimmy said, his mom would try to steal his dad's credit card so she could buy food and school clothes for the boys. But she soon gave up trying. Instead, she started hanging out at a neighbor's house, getting drunk. She got hold of street drugs, came on and off her meds. She died when Jimmy was nine. He believes she killed herself.

After his wife passed away, Jackie Sr. sent the two boys to live with their Grandma and Grandpa Rodgers (Jimmy thought it was so his old man could move his girlfriend into the house). Things weren't much better there—the elderly couple lived in a fifteen-by-eighteen-foot trailer whose living room contained a pair of La-Z-Boy recliners, an old wooden television set, and his grandmother's enormous collection of porcelain dolls. Jimmy said his grandparents were very traditional: Don't speak unless you're spoken to. Children should be seen and not heard. No eating between meals. Breakfast was at six A.M., lunch at noon, and supper at six P.M. Nobody could touch anything on their plate until Grandpa said a prayer and took his first bite.

Teresa Sievers was last seen alive at Southwest Florida International Airport, Sunday, June 28, 2015, 11:05 P.M. *Courtesy of Lee County Port Authority, Southwest Florida International Airport (RSW).*

Teresa practiced holistic medicine, but the media frequently downplayed her credentials as an MD after her murder. *Courtesy of Marie Hiller, Red Door Photography, Knoxville, TN.*

The Sieverses' home in Bonita Springs, Florida.
Courtesy of Lee County, FL, Sheriff's Office.

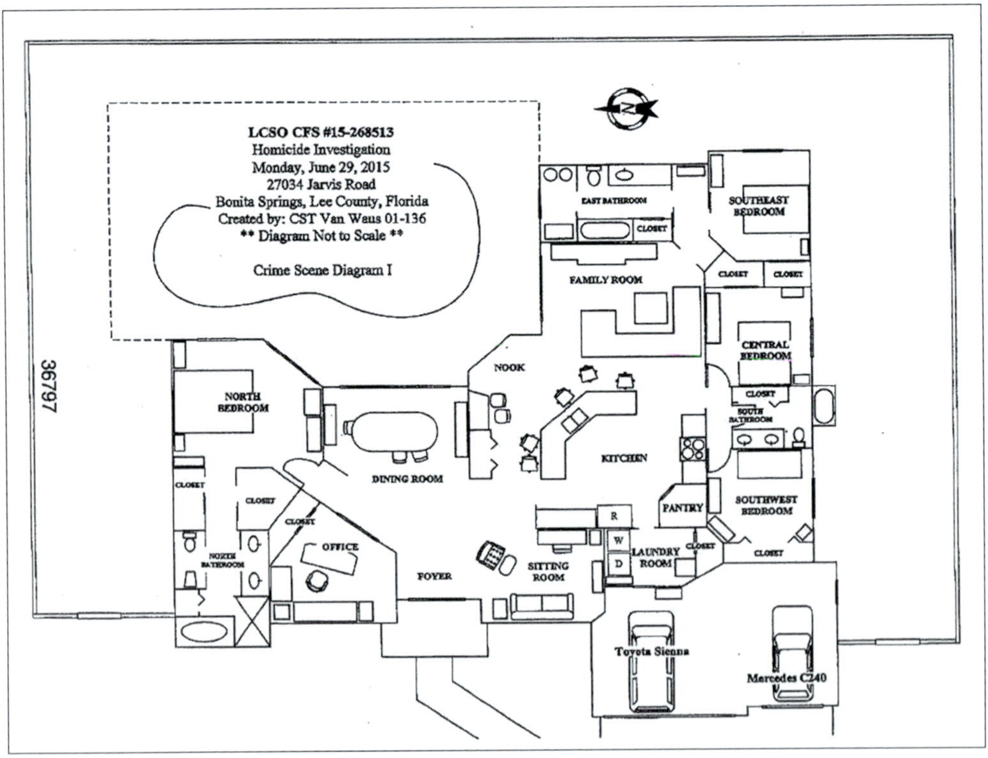

Police crime scene diagram. The intruder appeared to have pried open the side door to the garage.
Courtesy of Lee County, FL, Sheriff's Office.

The crime scene.
Courtesy of Lee County, FL, Sheriff's Office.

The hammer that shattered Teresa's skull with at least seventeen blows.
Courtesy of Lee County, FL, Sheriff's Office.

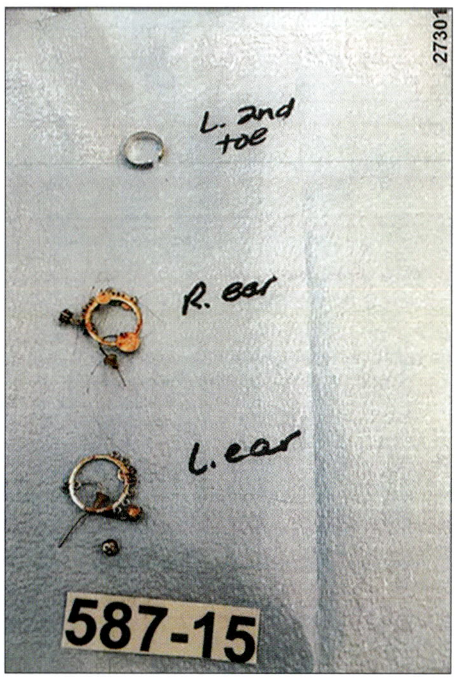

Bloodstained jewelry removed from Teresa's body during the autopsy.
Courtesy of Lee County, FL, Sheriff's Office.

Investigators noticed that Teresa had put down her purse after arriving in the kitchen, suggesting she was attacked from behind.
Courtesy of Lee County, FL, Sheriff's Office.

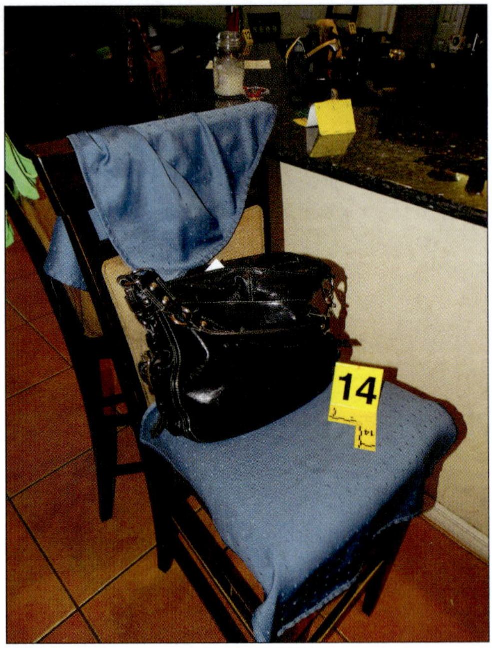

Items pulled out of Teresa's travel bag and suitcase in the garage, apparently by the perpetrators.
Courtesy of Lee County, FL, Sheriff's Office.

Part of Mark Sievers's extensive gun collection.
Courtesy of Lee County, FL, Sheriff's Office.

Mark had moved to Florida with his smart, talented wife. To his friends in Missouri, he had "made it."
Courtesy of Jennie Weckelman.

Mark and Teresa boasted a passionate marriage.
Courtesy of Jennie Weckelman.

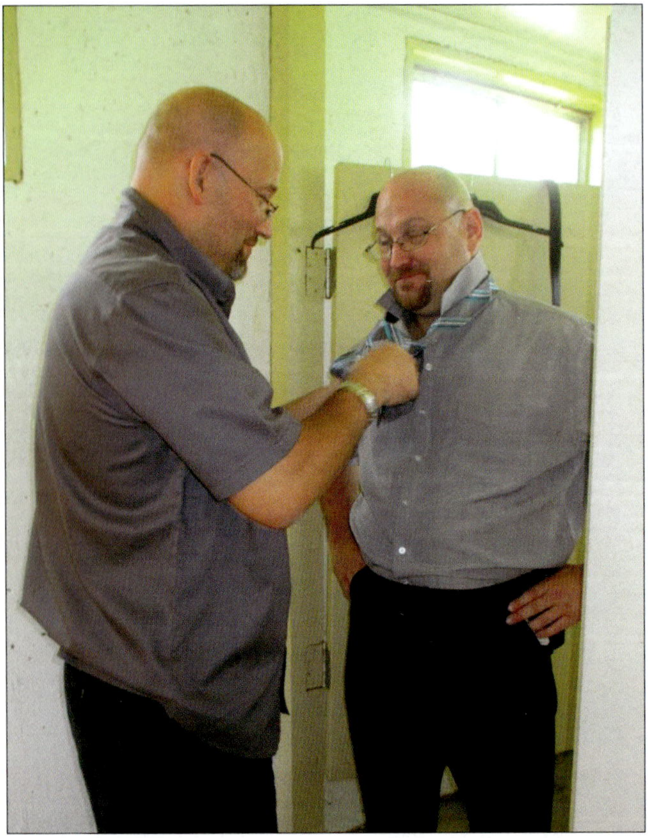

Mark (left) and his best friend, Wayne (right), getting dressed for Wayne's wedding. They enjoyed confusing guests with their resemblance. *Courtesy of Lee County, FL, Sheriff's Office.*

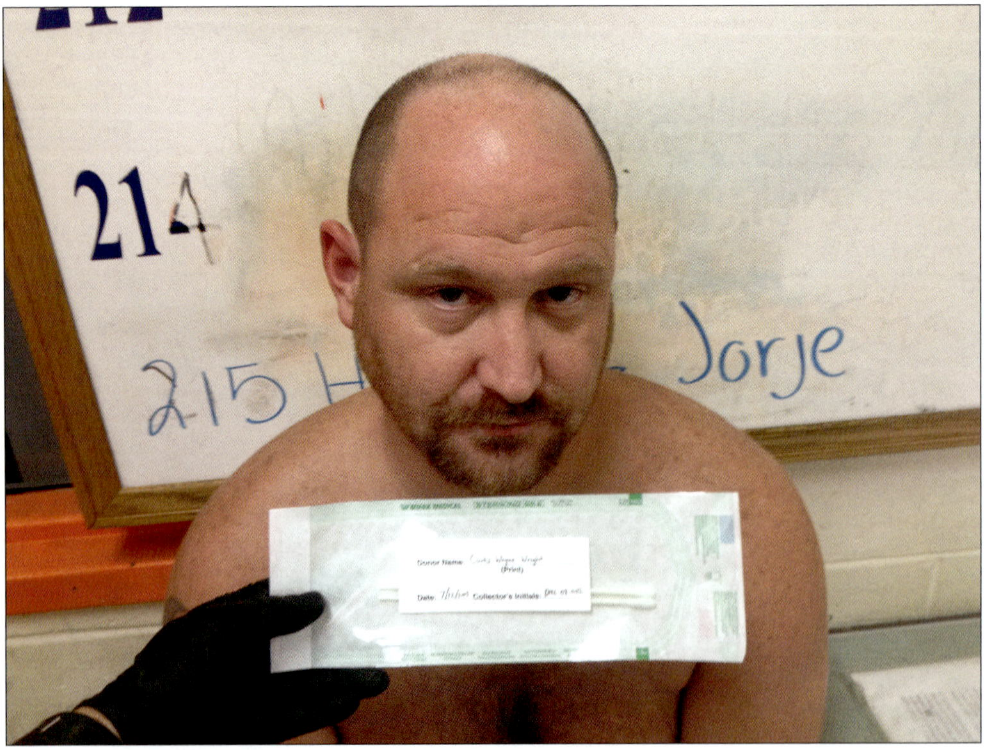

Wayne is arrested and booked into custody. *Courtesy of Lee County, FL, Sheriff's Office.*

Jimmy "the Hammer" is arrested and booked wearing a "#1 Dad" T-shirt.
Courtesy of Lee County, FL, Sheriff's Office.

Hammers and knives found in Jimmy and his girlfriend Taylor's bedroom.
Courtesy of Lee County, FL, Sheriff's Office.

Taylor led the police to Jimmy's discarded coveralls by the side of the road.
Courtesy of Lee County, FL, Sheriff's Office.

Jimmy and Wayne caught on a surveillance camera at a Walmart in Fort Myers the day of the murder. *Courtesy of Lee County, FL, Sheriff's Office.*

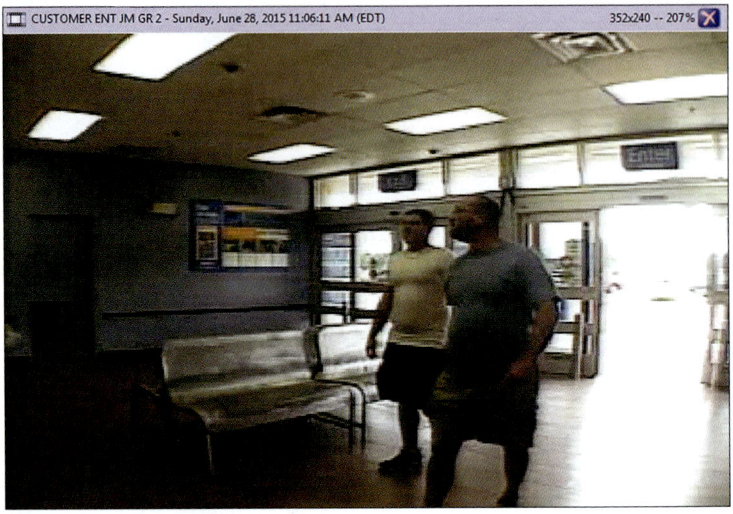

Jimmy caught on a surveillance camera at the Circle K/Shell gas station in Bushnell, Florida, a few hours after the murder. *Courtesy of Lee County, FL, Sheriff's Office.*

Wayne followed him in nearly ten minutes later, appearing distracted. *Courtesy of Lee County, FL, Sheriff's Office.*

In 2007, Jackie Sr. died—the brothers, relieved by his passing, left his grave unmarked—and since Grandma and Grandpa Rodgers had also passed away, there was no one to look after sixteen-year-old Jimmy. Jackie Jr., twenty-three, had joined the military, but he was released on grounds of family hardship. He tried to do his best for his younger brother, but he had emotional struggles of his own (he later said that "failing to be there for Jimmy" was the biggest regret of his life). Jimmy wasn't stupid, but he wasn't goal-oriented and had problems focusing. He was placed in special ed classes at school, and the other kids teased him for being "dumb."

Jimmy had a deep voice and talked tough. Tall, with dark hair, he might have been good-looking, except that his face had a kind of dopey expression. His eyes were a little too close together, and his jeans were always a couple of sizes too big. He could seem kind of a clown or he could seem threatening, depending on how you looked at it. He told people his dad murdered his mom and made it look like a suicide. He had a Chinese letter 9 tattooed on his chest, to memorialize his age at the time, along with the words DEATH MURDER DESTRUCTION.

Despite failing to provide for his family, Jimmy's dad had collected vintage cars, and Jimmy inherited his collection. At age seventeen, a few weeks after his father's death, he got caught driving a WS6 high-performance Trans Am at 160 miles per hour on a two-lane highway. He didn't see why it was such a big deal. "It was the middle of absolute nowhere," he said, later. "Kind of like looking at the ocean as far as I can see. Nothing but cornfields, bean fields, and cow pastures." He refused to pull over for the cops and was found guilty of resisting arrest and sentenced to five years' probation. Subsequently, as a convicted felon, he wasn't allowed to be around firearms. This was a problem. Jimmy Ray Rodgers loved guns.

In the family home he now shared with his brother, there was a case of vintage Remingtons that had never been fired, part of Jimmy's probate. When they came to check up on him, the cops found the guns and revoked his parole. Jimmy was outraged. "They were legal, registered, and under lock and key where I couldn't get to them," he complained. But the Feds didn't care. They arrested him, called him a danger to the community, charged him with unlawful possession of firearms, and, on August 20, 2010, booked him into the Ste. Genevieve County jail, an hour south of St. Louis.

Ste. Genevieve was a "federal holdover"—a county jail with a contract to hold federal inmates. Here, as in many prisons, the men were housed in separate sections known as pods, each containing between twelve and twenty inmates who shared a common area with metal tables and a line of phones. The prison gangs were race-based, and whites were in the minority. "If four or five black gang members go try to rob one white guy, we tried to stick up for each other," Jimmy explained.

One of the men in his pod was Wayne Wright, Jr., who was being held on meth charges. He was twenty-two years older than Jimmy, but the men got along, became friends. Wayne impressed Jimmy with his toughness. "Very dangerous," recalled Jimmy, admiringly. "A good guy to have on your side. A guy who used to be a professional cage fighter, who has a black belt in jitsu, who used to do kickboxing. I kind of gravitated towards him as far as just hanging out with him . . . I thought Wayne was a really good guy."

They spent a lot of time playing cards. Wayne liked Jimmy, too. He saw him as a nice kid who'd got a raw deal. "Jimmy's a character," he said. "He's always talking about something crazy. He made the time a little more enjoyable." But Jimmy was also a blowhard and a braggart, and Wayne suspected he was too volatile to have been involved in the deals he described—"high-level drug activity, Mafia stuff." When Jimmy showed Wayne a picture of himself with wads of cash in front of a fancy car, and another of himself in white suede tennis shoes with a briefcase handcuffed to his wrist, Wayne wasn't sure what to believe.

During his time in prison, Jimmy got a whole bunch of new tattoos. Above his left nipple was the anarchy symbol with a drug pipe. Beneath them was a golden crucifix. His lower back bore an image of a gun-toting devil alongside a semi-naked angel and the word BEWARE. Above this was his prison number, and across the back of his shoulders were the words FUCK THE FEDS in a sprawling Celtic font. A dragon curled around his left upper arm. On the right, a firebird sat beneath the words TRANS AM.

After Wayne left prison, he and Jimmy wrote to each other. Wayne gave Jimmy advice about defending himself behind bars. When Jimmy got out, he went into a halfway house, and Wayne would come and pick him up and take him to job interviews, then helped him to find a place to live. Wayne's ex-wife said he tried to get her to write to Jimmy in jail as a pen pal, but she wasn't comfortable with the idea. "I remember him saying he's a really nice kid and he was just transporting his dad's guns from the house and got caught," she said. Wayne also tried fixing Jimmy up with his cousin Chrissy, but that didn't work out. "She was batshit crazy," recalled Jimmy. Still, he continued to rely on Wayne for advice about girls, even after he'd got together with Taylor, texting him to ask, "What is a good fake reason to bring women to my house to fuck them?"

In 2014, Angie's daughter Chelsea moved in with Jimmy as a roommate, but she quickly moved out again, because he scared her. She said he was "different. And not in a good way." Like Wayne, Jimmy would boast about guys he'd beaten up, even killed. "He likes to talk about guns, weapons, things like that," his boss recalled. "Mainly his topic of conversation was his past criminal life, or guns." But as Wayne soon learned, Jimmy's "weapon of choice" wasn't a gun—it was a hammer. "He carried a ball-peen hammer with him pretty much wherever he went," said Wayne.

"He bragged about using a hammer all the time. He talked about how it worked really well for breaking joints and things like that." By the time he was twenty-two, he was calling himself "Jimmy the Hammer."

A neighbor told the police, "He always talked about how his favorite weapon was a hammer. He said it to me multiple times." Another neighbor said once Jimmy gave her husband a ride home from Walmart and showed him a hammer he kept under the seat of his car. He was "Jimmy the Hammer" on his Facebook page, too, where he posted nothing but racist, anti-government memes.

> You are entering a RED NECK AREA. You may encounter American Flags, Armed Citizens, and the Lord's Prayer.
>
> Are you going to listen to me in English? Or do I have to speak to you in 12 Gauge?
>
> If my guns were your problem, you'd already be dead.
>
> ONE FREE MURDER. This voucher entitles you to commit One Murder without social, legal, or financial consequences.
>
> Never rat on your friends and always keep your mouth shut.
>
> They aren't bullets, they are freedom seeds.
>
> I came into this world kicking and screaming while covered in someone else's blood. I have no problem going out the same way.

After getting out of prison, Jimmy earned a professional welding certificate, and became qualified in Hazardous Waste Operations. In early 2015, he started work at JV Contracting, a large company that employed around a hundred general laborers at different job sites. According to his boss, Jimmy, who did mostly painting and industrial cleaning, was a first-rate employee. He never missed work and was always on time. His only problem was his "mouth," in that he bragged constantly, but it didn't get in the way of his productivity. Most weeks, he worked between forty and sixty hours, at twelve dollars an hour.

Jimmy was the hardest worker Taylor had ever met. He'd work sixteen-hour shifts, then come home, and if she needed help with anything, or if she needed the trash taken out, he'd do that, too. She fell hard for Jimmy, and he seemed to feel the same way about her. He made sure to let her know that she mattered.

Most of all, she loved the way he treated her kids as his own. He spent hours in the yard, chasing them, rolling them around in a shopping cart, tickling them until they peed. When he got home from work, Oaklynn would run across the room shouting "Daddy! Daddy!" and hug his leg. The little girl even got jealous of her mother, trying to push Taylor off the couch so she could cuddle with her new dad.

Jimmy taught the kids to swim at the lake. He rocked Ozzie to sleep. He cooked candlelight dinners. He drove Taylor into town when she got the craving for ice cream. She knew he'd been in prison a couple of times and people said he could be violent, but around her, he was always gentle. She knew he had a thing for hammers. There were three on a shelf under the bedside table. Sure, it was weird. But Taylor didn't care. "Jimmy was really nice to me," she said. "He let me stay home and take care of my babies while he went out and worked. And then he would give me spending money to go grocery shopping. Jimmy's goofy and funny and loving. He treated me like a queen."

With three kids to feed and rent to pay, despite Jimmy's hard work, he and Taylor often found themselves in debt. When Jimmy told her that his prison buddy, Wayne Wright, had invited him to "do a job" out of town for 10,000 dollars, she didn't ask questions. He didn't tell her where he was going, but he said it had something to do with "stealing high dollar antiques." She knew Jimmy hung out with people like Wayne, on the wrong side of the law. She didn't like it, but the cash would be a godsend.

On Saturday, June 27, Wayne came to pick Jimmy up early, around 7:30 A.M. Taylor was annoyed to be woken up—she didn't do mornings—but she got out of bed to say goodbye and give Jimmy the lunch she'd packed for him. Wayne was driving a new-looking white car, she noticed—obviously a rental. Jimmy put a couple of things in the trunk—a black backpack, and the white cooler he always took to work with him. After they left, she took the kids and went to stay at her mom's in Bonne Terre. Cadet, where she lived, was a high-crime area, and she didn't like being alone.

While he was away, Jimmy texted her a few times, but he didn't say anything about what was going on, it was just "hey, how you doing?" and to tell her he loved her. He got back on June 29, exhausted. The job was a success, he told Taylor. He wouldn't get the 10,000 dollars for a while, but he showed her some new clothes he'd bought while he was out of town—a pair of lace-up dress shoes, and a short-sleeve jersey. He'd also bought two gifts for her: a T-shirt, and a wall plaque that read, "Don't Mind the Mess—My Kids are Making Memories."

But Taylor had an even better gift for Jimmy.

She'd just found out—she was pregnant with his baby.

Chapter 12

Accessory Before the Fact

Two and a half weeks after Jimmy's trip to Florida, while he was at home eating dinner with Taylor and the kids, his phone buzzed. Jimmy looked down. It was Wayne.

He took the phone into the kitchen. The kids were laughing and fooling around, but despite the noise, Taylor could hear Wayne's voice on the other end of the line. He sounded frantic. After a while, Jimmy took the phone and went outside. Taylor heard his raised voice outside the trailer.

He came back inside twenty minutes later, jumpy and on edge. Taylor, doing the dishes, asked him what was going on, but he wouldn't answer any questions, and she didn't push. She stood and watched as he gathered together everything he'd bought back from his trip with Wayne—the shoes, the T-shirt, the jersey, and the plaque—wrapped them in a towel, and left the trailer. Taylor started to get scared.

The following afternoon, around 3:30 P.M., there was a knock on the trailer door. Outside stood two men who identified themselves as detectives Mike Downs and David Lebid. They were looking for Jimmy. Taylor told the men he was at work, and she wasn't sure when he'd be back. Soon, probably.

"That's okay. We'll wait," said Downs.

Taylor knew how her boyfriend felt about cops. She told them she couldn't let them in without Jimmy's permission.

"That's okay," said Lebid. "We'll just wait outside."

The cops were young and friendly. Good-looking, too. After she'd put the baby to sleep, Taylor went outside to talk to them. At first, they were pretty sociable, chatting and asking questions about the kids. Then things took a turn. Detective Downs mentioned they'd come to Missouri because they were investigating the murder of a doctor in Florida. Teresa Sievers. The wife of Mark Sievers. Wayne's best friend. They had evidence, apparently, that suggested Wayne and Jimmy were hit men. Taylor was terrified. She stopped talking.

When Jimmy pulled up and saw the detectives, he was on edge and evasive. He wouldn't let them inside. Curtly, out on the deck, he answered a few questions. Yes, he knew Wayne Wright, but hadn't seen him for three or four weeks. He'd never heard of Mark Sievers. He'd never been to Florida and couldn't go even if he wanted to—he was on federal probation and wasn't allowed to leave the state.

The detectives asked whether he'd be willing to give them a sworn statement. Jimmy pretty much shut down.

When the cops left—they didn't have a search warrant—Jimmy looked grim and pale. He turned to Taylor. "We're taking a ride," he said.

Taylor kept quiet. She did what Jimmy told her. She didn't even have time to change out of her pink flip-flops.

First, they drove to Jimmy's workplace, the Doe Run company in Viburnum, Missouri, half an hour away. When they got there, Jimmy went to his locker, took out a cell phone, went over to a drinking fountain, soaked it in water, then stomped on it, broke it into pieces, then gave the pieces to Taylor.

"Get back in the car," he said.

She obeyed without asking questions. As they headed down Highway 47 East, Jimmy turned to her.

"Roll down your window and throw everything out," he instructed. She did what he said. Then he told her to turn around and get the blue coveralls that were bunched up on the back seat. When they came to an isolated, heavily forested part of the road with a bridge, he told her to toss those out of the window, too. "Throw them into the river," commanded Jimmy.

Taylor's head was all messed up. Her mind was racing. She threw out the coveralls. Jimmy didn't notice, but they missed the river and landed in a muddy ditch.

Cadet was a small town. People talked. Taylor was naïve, but she wasn't stupid. She knew the murdered doctor was the wife of Wayne's best friend. She'd met Mark briefly at Wayne's wedding. They looked so similar, she kept getting the two of them mixed up. She found it a little strange.

That night, she lay in bed in Jimmy's arms. The conversation was brief. Taylor got straight to the point. She asked him whether he and Wayne had been in Florida.

Jimmy admitted they had.

She asked him why he went down there.

"To make money," he said.

"I know you had something to do with this, Jimmy," she said. "Did you and Wayne go down there to kill Mark's wife?"

Again, Jimmy admitted she was right.

"Did you shoot her?" asked Taylor.

"No."

"Then how did you kill her?"

"With a hammer," he said, with what Taylor later characterized as "a stupid little chuckle."

She didn't sleep much that night.

• • •

The next day—Sunday, July 19—Jimmy got a call from Wayne, asking him to meet him and Angie at Hub's Pub and Grill, a restaurant, bar, and karaoke joint on the east side of Bonne Terre—their usual watering hole. Specifically, he told Jimmy to bring Taylor along, which made her very nervous. She'd met Wayne a handful of times, and thought he was "a little crazy." Inside the bar, Jimmy gave her some money and said he was going out to talk to Wayne out on the deck. He told her to stay inside with Angie and buy some beers—he wouldn't be long.

The two men were outside for more than half an hour. Taylor got a round of beers and sat down to wait. Angie could barely sit still—she was completely distraught. Describing the early-morning raid on their trailer, she told Taylor the cops were trying to frame Wayne for Teresa's murder.

"They know Mark didn't do it, because he was in New York," said Angie. "So they're going after his best friend. They've been trying to get something on Wayne ever since that preacher went missing."

Taylor said nothing. She knew Jimmy could be violent. He once told her he'd worked as a hit man in the past. The more she thought about it, the more frightened she got. What if he got angry with her? Was she in danger? Should she go to the cops? What would happen to the baby?

Occasionally, one of them would glance outside to see if they could find out what was going on. Wayne and Jimmy were huddled over on the deck, deep in conversation. When they finally came back inside, both men seemed uneasy, and Wayne started "bombarding" Taylor with questions about detectives Downs and Lebid. How long did they stay? What did they say to her? What did she tell them?

"Mostly, we just talked about the kids," she said. "When they said they'd come from Florida about the doctor's murder, I stopped talking."

"Did they offer you any money?"

Taylor shook her head. From the expression on Wayne's face, she could tell he didn't believe her.

"They've got no right to be bothering you." He handed her an attorney's business card. "If they come back, call this guy and tell him to get a restraining order."

For a month and a half after that, nothing happened. Tentatively, everybody began to breathe more easily.

• • •

In 2015, the Lee County Sheriff's Office in Florida was presided over by Mike Scott, a third-generation Fort Myers native who'd spent twenty-seven years in law enforcement, the last ten as sheriff—he'd been elected four times. Loud, tanned, bald, and burly, Scott was popular for being tough on crime, though he wasn't so well-loved by the media. He liked to grandstand and could be scathing when reporters—as he saw it—stuck their noses into critical investigations.

On Jarvis Road, neighbors were nervous—was there a killer on the loose? Did the police have any leads? The cops were tight-lipped. As often happens when official sources are unforthcoming, some journalists began doing their own investigations, going door to door, asking residents for their theories and opinions. On the one hand, reporters' investigations can be invaluable to law enforcement, because people will talk more readily to a reporter than a cop. On the other hand, the press can spread misinformation, destroy delicate relationships, and potentially contaminate the jury pool.

Scott didn't give out information readily and had little to say beyond the usual clichés. "Authorities are actively pursuing leads in this ongoing investigation," he announced, which meant very little. Everybody was getting frustrated. Eventually, tired of public criticism, Scott released a statement to show "how tenacious we've been with this." Instead of waiting for FedEx to deliver evidence to the lab, he said, "we physically got in the car and drove it there." It hardly inspired confidence.

WINK-TV, the CBS affiliate for Southwest Florida, pushed the sheriff's office for something more substantial. "We asked important questions, like if they have any leads on who the killer is, or if the public is in danger," announced WINK News on July 7. "They refused to answer any of our questions." The news team asked Scott whether they had any suspects. "I'm not going to speak to that," replied the sheriff. By now, although the autopsy report hadn't been released, word had leaked out that Teresa was killed with a hammer. But Mike Scott gave nothing away. "The sheriff's office cannot play this thing out play-by-play with each piece of information we get," he told reporters, impatiently. "We will share information as we think it will benefit the case. We are not going to share information simply to solve someone's curiosity."

Behind the scenes, however, things were moving fast. Forensic specialists had been working twenty-four hours a day retrieving deleted data from Wayne's GPS. Time-stamped searches for gas stations and fast-food outlets had led investigators to some damning surveillance tapes, including footage from the 6 Mile Cypress Parkway Walmart in Fort Myers, half an hour from the Sievers residence, where Jimmy and Wayne apparently enjoyed an impromptu shopping trip.

CCTV cameras caught them entering the store casually, side by side. Wayne, the stockier of the two, is wearing a blue T-shirt with beige shorts and beat-up water shoes. Jimmy, slightly taller and a little gawky, is dressed in a white T-shirt, black shorts, and sneakers. Wayne grabs a cart, and they walk out of frame. Ten minutes later, they're caught by another camera, walking down an aisle, Wayne in front checking out the shelves, Jimmy sloping behind.

According to a receipt later obtained from store security, they picked up some beach wear for Jimmy and a few extra supplies, just in case: wet wipes and a pack of seven thirty-gallon trash bags. Wayne bought a new pair of water shoes. Jimmy, too, picked up a few fashion items along the way. A pair of black Faded Glory lace-up dress shoes, a red Budweiser T-shirt, and an "SS Top" ("a set of two T-shirts that can be worn alone or layered to create four distinct looks"). A third camera captured a clear shot of Jimmy coming out of the store in his brand-new lace-up shoes.

Surveillance cameras at the RaceTrac in Brooksville, Florida, at 2:39 A.M. on June 29, caught a faint image of Jimmy banging on the window of a closed gas station, trying to attract attention. But the clearest images came from a Circle K/Shell station in Bushnell, an hour west of Orlando, where the men apparently stopped in the early hours of Sunday morning, when it was still dark.

At 2:53 A.M., a white Hyundai Elantra can be seen pulling up to a gas pump. Jimmy, still wearing his black dress shoes, enters the store and prepays. He leaves to pump gas, then returns to the cashier and collects his change. At 3:01 A.M., Wayne, wearing his new water shoes, enters the store—the video is so distinct you can see his facial expression. He heads to the left, perhaps to use the bathroom. He seems a little distracted, lost in thought, while Jimmy seems more at ease. They leave the store together at 3:05 A.M., and drive off into the night.

On August 24, law enforcement officers met with Jimmy's parole officer, Jennifer Jelinski, who, learning about his trip to Florida, registered a parole violation. This, along with the surveillance footage and the information from the GPS, gave the cops enough evidence to file for an arrest warrant. The next morning, a team of law enforcement officers, all dressed in black, banged on the door of Jimmy's trailer. Taylor and the kids were home alone—they were terrified. The cops made them wait outside on the back steps while they searched the home.

From the master bedroom, detectives confiscated:

"One (1) metal sledge hammer with wooden handle"

"One (1) metal claw hammer with yellow/black synthetic handle"

"One (1) metal claw hammer with black handle, missing claw located on end table near bed"

None of these tools connected him with Teresa's death. Still, things were looking bleak for Jimmy.

He was arrested during a traffic stop by cops from the Washington County Sheriff's Office, who'd tracked down his Kia. The vehicle held more damning evidence: "One (1) black rubber mallet with wooden handle located in the rear right floorboard."

Jimmy, in anticipation of his child's birth, was wearing a MAJOR AWARD #1 DAD T-shirt that Taylor had bought him for Father's Day. He was arrested for the parole violation, and on September 2, 2015, sentenced to six months in federal prison. He wasn't charged with murder—there was still a lot of evidence to amass. But with Jimmy behind bars, the cops had plenty of time.

Now, detectives turned to the weakest link: Taylor Shomaker.

• • •

While the cops were searching Jimmy's trailer, Taylor was growing more and more upset. The baby was crying, and the two older children were scared and confused. After half an hour or so, Detective Downs came out of the trailer and told Taylor she should call her mom to come and pick up the kids—they were taking her downtown. They didn't even let her change out of her flip-flops and sweatpants. She grabbed her cigarettes and a scrunchie, pulled her hair in a ponytail, followed Downs to the cop car, and was driven to the sheriff's office.

It wasn't a long ride, but it gave Taylor enough time to think. She knew Jimmy had killed the doctor. The right thing to do would be to tell the investigators everything he'd said. But what about the baby she was carrying? Jimmy had always wanted to be a dad. When she'd told him she was pregnant, he'd jumped up and down for joy, calling everybody he knew. If he went to prison, the baby would never know his or her father. She loved Jimmy to death. The more she thought, the more anxious she grew.

Then things got even worse. At the Washington County Sheriff's Office, Mike Downs took Taylor to an interview room and told her to sit down. It was cold in there. She pulled down her Missouri Tigers T-shirt as far as it would go.

Detective Downs sat opposite her, on the other side of a table. She glanced up and noticed a camera on the wall.

Downs told her flat-out that her boyfriend was a hit man. Jimmy and Wayne killed Teresa Sievers, he said. If she'd done anything to help them out, even just by keeping quiet about it, she could be charged as "an accessory before the fact."

Taylor didn't know what that meant.

"It means you're just as guilty as Jimmy," Downs told her. "We could take your kids away and put them in foster care, including your unborn baby. You could go to prison for life. You could even face the death penalty."

That's when Taylor realized—it was her life or Jimmy's, and she had three kids to think about. Make that four.

"I'll tell you everything I know," she said.

She described Jimmy's weekend trip with Wayne, how they were supposed to be "stealing high-end antiques," and that Jimmy had been promised 10,000 dollars. She described the panicky phone call from Wayne. She told the detective about Jimmy tossing the shoes and T-shirt in the dumpster. Destroying the cell phone at Doe Run. Jimmy's midnight confession. How he killed Mark's wife with a hammer.

Here, Downs interrupted her. "And why do you think he would use a hammer?"

Taylor shrugged. "That's Jimmy."

"Is that his weapon of choice?"

"Yes."

"Do they call him The Hammer? Does he call himself The Hammer?"

"Everybody calls him Jimmy the Hammer. All of his friends back home."

She also gave them a crucial lead.

"I just remembered something," she said. "The night before Wayne's wedding, when Jimmy met Mark, Wayne and Mark had went into the bedroom and talked privately for about an hour to two hours."

"So Jimmy and Mark knew each other?"

"They just met that night for the first time."

They also asked her about Angie. How well did Taylor know her? Had she spoken to her since the raid on Wayne's trailer? Did Taylor think she might be involved?

"She's hysterical about it," said Taylor.

"About what?" asked Downs.

"About the whole situation. She's like, 'I can't believe this is happening to us. I never thought that this would ever happen to us,' and stuff like that. The way she talked, it didn't sound like she knew anything about it."

When Taylor told the investigators about throwing Jimmy's coveralls into a ditch, Detective Downs asked if she'd take them to the place—maybe they were still there?

The pair set off east, down Highway 47. Just the sun was going down, they pulled over by the ditch where Taylor had thrown the coveralls a month ago. The blue bundle was lying by the side of the road. It had apparently been run over by lawnmowers at some point in the previous week, because it was covered in dry grass. Pieces of the cell phone were also found nearby. She then took the detective to Doe Run and showed him Jimmy's locker, where he'd kept the cell phone he'd destroyed. There was nothing there except a pair of shower shoes and a cigarette butt.

After that, thank God, they let her go.

• • •

Taylor was safe. Her kids were safe. She wasn't going to prison.

Then the situation sank in. She was alone, with no job, no income, three kids to feed, and another on the way. She hadn't been successful in claiming child support. She couldn't pay her rent. Jimmy's landlord had given her three days to pack up and move on. Taylor set up a GoFundMe page. "Me and my children have to move out of our home due to a very horrible situation and only have 72 hours to find a new one," she wrote. "All money I raise will be used to get all set up so that I can start looking for a job and return to School for me and my babys. We will be completely grateful for every donation."

The GoFundMe page brought in enough money to pay the landlord, but things were still tight, and her babies were going hungry. "I didn't know who to call or what to do," she said, later. Detective Downs had left her his card, in case she wanted to talk. Desperate, alone, and with nowhere to turn, Taylor wondered whether the cops might be able to help. She picked up the phone.

While it's officially illegal to pay witnesses and informants, as with many legal rules, there are workarounds. Payments can be classified as "expenses," for example, or "money to assist with witness protection." In Taylor's case, the Lee County Sheriff's Office agreed to add her to the payroll, putting down the deposit and first month's rent on a new trailer, giving her 1,050 dollars to move, and a monthly 400-dollar check for living expenses. After snitching on Jimmy, they argued, Taylor obviously couldn't go on living in his trailer in Cadet. Detective Downs told Taylor the payments had come from a 50,000-dollar "Witness Assistance Fund," and she'd keep on getting the money every month until Jimmy's case went to trial.

Taylor had turned Jimmy over to the cops. Currently, he

was in prison for the probation violation, but in all likelihood, he'd be extradited to Florida to face murder charges. By giving Taylor a monthly check, investigators were obviously hoping she'd testify against him at trial, when the time came. What the detectives didn't anticipate was the couple's illogical and self-defeating codependence.

After his arrest, Jimmy was taken to the St. Francois County Jail, half an hour away from Cadet. He and Taylor talked on the phone every day. He didn't blame her for turning him in to the cops—he assumed they must have taken advantage of her stupidity to feed her a false story. "Taylor does not even have the understanding of a 5th grader about how courts work," he wrote to her mother. "The detectives took tottal advantage of the fact that Taylor is slow and they compleatly manipulated the shit out of her."

Taylor certainly seemed gullible. She told the police Jimmy had probably killed Mark's wife with a hammer. When interviewed by the media, she agreed that Jimmy was a dangerous murderer. But she kept going to see him, told him she loved him, and even promised to marry him when he got out. When she told him about her conversation with Mike Downs, he wanted to smack her head against the wall. Your boyfriend's arrested for murder, so you call the cops and ask them to compensate for the loss of his salary? What was she thinking? "I thought that the prosecutors helping me out with the rent and stuff was nice of them," she said.

Jimmy couldn't believe the Lee County Sheriff's Office had actually put her on the payroll. It was clearly a smokescreen. How could they claim they were "helping her relocate" when she lived in the same town, mixed with the same people, even had the same Facebook page and phone number? "Don't you get it? They're trying to buy you off," he told her. "They're paying you to give evidence against me." But the more he thought about it, the more he realized this could work in his favor. What better way to expose police corruption? The scheme would surely backfire. If Taylor was stupid enough to testify against him, once people knew about the payments, anything she said would be completely inadmissible. Meantime, since he was sure to be getting out soon, maybe she could use the money to buy him a new car.

Chapter 13

"Love Is Patient, Love Is Kind"

People grieve in different ways, but the text exchange between Mark and Lenka Spiska two days after Teresa's murder was oddly casual and clear-headed given the fact that, in his police interview the following morning, Mark seemed to be having a nervous breakdown. At eleven A.M. on Tuesday, he asked her, "can we come over around 130 for a play date/swim with the girls? . . . i am going to funeral home w mimi & mom @ 230." Lenka said that was perfect. At 4:30 P.M., Mark asked her what time he should pick them up. "I miss my girls," he told her, "but I'm sure they're having a blast and this is probably very therapeutic for them."

Two days after Teresa's death, Mark and Lenka set up a GoFundMe account, linked to Mark's Facebook page, requesting donations to help support the Sievers family, now that the wage-earner was gone. Lenka wrote the introduction.

> As my best friend and colleague, Dr. Teresa Sievers was a visionary in her field. . . . She was referred to by many as "Mother Teresa" . . . I ask you and anyone you know to donate what you are able to help her family deal with the financial burdens they will be faced with, including

the education of her two young daughters who are only 11 and 8.

Money came pouring in. Given that Mark was set to collect a significant amount of life insurance from Teresa's death (later estimated at 4.4 million dollars), he can't seriously have been worried about "financial burdens." Even if it took a while for the insurance to pay out, he had 40,000 dollars in cash in his safe upstairs, plus plenty of collateral; the house on Jarvis Road, although mortgaged, was worth at least 300,000 dollars. He also owned two cars, a motorcycle, five units in Teresa's office complex, and a condo in Missouri. According to Wayne, there was probably a lot more squirreled away. "I know Mark," he said. "He's always got money hidden somewhere. He's one of those people that digs holes in his backyard."

Daniele Berardinelli grew up in Teresa's Connecticut hometown; they'd known each other since their teens, bonding over their love of animals. "I considered Teresa my very best friend," said Daniele, who thought of Mark as family, too. After learning about the murder, Daniele flew directly to Bonita Springs.

She checked into the Holiday Inn on Tuesday, June 30. Mark came by to see her that evening, knocking on her door at midnight. They hugged and wept; then, according to Daniele, her friend did something strange. "He . . . started talking about money, and how he was very concerned about how he was going to make money to raise the girls. . . . He said he didn't have a job; he hadn't worked for years. He thought maybe he could go back to nursing at some point and get recertified, but that would be a lot of time away from the girls."

Daniele was baffled. She reminded him Teresa had a substantial life insurance policy, and he and the girls would be well taken care of. "He immediately had a look of relief on his face," Daniele recalled. "He put his head in his hands, and he said, 'Oh,

I totally forgot, I completely forgot.'" At the time, she thought it was strange. But Annie reminded her, "Mark is weird. Don't overthink it."

When Mark's brother texted Wayne about the murder, Wayne immediately contacted Mark. His was one of a flurry of messages from friends and family expressing their horror, offering condolences, and asking about funeral arrangements. "Angie and I are going to leave today and come down to be with you and the girls," texted Wayne. "I can only imagine what you are going through and want to be there for you. . . . Love you brother."

After a grueling all-night drive to Southwest Florida, the couple arrived early the next morning. They weren't alone. Teresa and Mark's friends and family had been flocking to Bonita Springs from all over the country, and where they would stay was up in the air. Obviously, 27034 Jarvis Road was a crime scene. Mark and the children were staying with Bonnie and Melanie. Some were disconcerted that Wayne and Angie were asked to stay there, too, while everyone else had to make do with the Holiday Inn.

Teresa's family had learned of her death on the day of the murder, but had no idea what had happened until they saw, on the news, what Annie later described as "a gurney with a black body bag on top rolled out of my sister's house," and heard a commentator refer to a "gruesome scene." It was horrifying. Nobody wanted Emma and Olivia to go through a similar trauma, so the family sheltered them from the details. They knew their mother was dead, but no one had told them how or why.

On July 5, the day before the funeral, Mark gently broke the news that Teresa had been murdered. "There are bad people in the world who do terrible things," he explained to the girls, "but Mommy will always be with us in spirit." (In fact, after having her fingerprints taken by the police two days earlier, Emma had already worked out what happened.) After breakfast, Mark spent a couple of hours walking on the beach with Michele Petrites,

Teresa's closest friend in Bonita Springs. She'd just been accepted into law school at Indiana University and was leaving for Bloomington that fall. Now she didn't want to go. Wouldn't Mark need her to look after the girls? Mark convinced her: Don't lose this opportunity. Teresa would have wanted it that way.

The funeral, described as a "Celebration of Life," was held at the Unity Church of Naples on Monday, July 6, with over 450 people in attendance. All week, media trucks had been surrounding 27034 Jarvis Road, even though the house was empty—in fact, police had restored the crime scene tape surrounding the house to keep the press away—but Mark had asked for restraint and privacy at the church, and his wishes were respected. Before the ceremony, two hours were dedicated to visitation. Mark reunited and grieved with friends, family, colleagues, and patients.

The two pastors who led the service were a married couple, Reverend Dr. Judy Lee, and Pastor Judy Beaumont. Both had known Teresa well, partly through the church, and partly through their connection with Our Mother's Home. The readings they chose for the ceremony included 1 Corinthians 13, a scripture celebrating love ("Love is patient, love is kind. It does not envy, it does not boast, it is not proud"). Reverend Lee explained to the mourners that although the scripture was normally used at weddings, rather than funerals, she found it appropriate in this case because "the love established between Teresa and Mark in their marriage is the kind that fulfills this text, and so it lives forever."

Reverend Lee shared her most cherished memories of Teresa—how she cared for the homeless and destitute without expecting to be paid, found shelter for those who'd been evicted, filled out urgent paperwork for the disabled to help them get housing, advocated to judges on their behalf. When Reverend Lee had a rare form of stomach cancer years earlier, she recalled, Teresa had stayed with her in the hospital, sleeping in a chair by the bed. "What kind of a doctor does this, especially these days?" asked Reverend Lee, rhetorically. "She gave herself in love."

After the service, a distraught Mark walked down the aisle, clasping his daughters' hands. Emma, admirably stoic, read a moving eulogy and said a prayer, bringing everyone to tears, including her father, who joked that his daughter was stronger than he was. Mark's own speech was brief and clichéd. He was the luckiest man alive, he said, to have had a woman like Teresa. His memories would last forever.

A funeral mass was to follow, but first, Mark, Bonnie, and Mary Ann had compiled a slideshow featuring photographs of Teresa over the years, along with video clips from her nascent TV show, *Pathways 2 Healing*. As the sideshow began, the equipment malfunctioned. Wayne, the tech guru, stepped up to the plate and solved the problem. But after the slideshow, the DVD player also had problems. Awkwardly, the disc refused to play, while the audio got stuck on a loop of Teresa introducing herself. The words resonated uncomfortably again and again throughout the church. "Hello, I'm Dr. Teresa Sievers. Hello, I'm Dr. Teresa Sievers. Hello, I'm Dr. Teresa Sievers." It was haunting and unsettling. This time, Wayne couldn't fix the equipment. Later, during the mass, his asthma was apparently triggered by the incense, and he dashed from the church, sweating profusely.

After the funeral, family and friends got together to grieve and mourn. Annie, who'd rented a nearby condo, recalled meeting Wayne for the first time. She remembered that he looked "exhausted," and "spent most of the night trying not to fall asleep on the sofa." She embraced and consoled him. "Thank you for being there for Mark and the kids," she said.

Immediately after the murder, a line search of almost thirty detectives had slowly walked up and down Jarvis Road, searching for bloodstains or any other evidence. Crime scene personnel had remained in the vicinity of the Sievers home, still surrounded by yellow tape, for almost a week after the murder, but since then, apparently, nothing had been done. Teresa's friends, family, and neighbors were growing increasingly frustrated with the police and the press.

To appease the public, Sheriff Mike Scott began making announcements about the case suggesting they were following important leads, but at this stage, they couldn't release any information to the public. He announced this wasn't a random murder—there was, he hinted, a "connection" between the killer and victim. He implied the case had all kinds of bizarre twists and turns, anticipating that "books and movies" would be made about it. "We are vigorously—that's an understatement—looking through a multitude of leads and evidence. A great volume and body of work is at play here," he announced, on July 26.

Although the sheriff didn't announce it to the public, Jimmy Ray Rodgers was already behind bars, convicted of parole violation. Wayne Wright was facing arrest at any moment.

But when it came to Mark, they had nothing.

PART THREE

Chapter 14

The Reid Technique

On August 27, 2015, at 4:40 P.M., Curtis Wayne Wright, Jr. was arrested by Jefferson Country Police based on the probable cause that he "was involved in the intentional murder of Teresa Sievers by way of blunt force trauma utilizing a hammer." As during the dawn raid, Wayne was in bed when the cops came to pick him up; he arrived at the sheriff's office in Hillsboro in green cargo shorts, white socks, and blue Nike sneakers. Brought into the interview room shirtless, in handcuffs, he was a sorry-looking figure, his "ninja" body now soft, with a chubby paunch and a yin-yang tattoo on his left shoulder (allegedly, Mark had one, too). He was booked into jail, then put through a series of grueling interrogations by Detective David Lebid.

Lebid, who'd been assigned to the Lee County Sheriff's Office's Violent Crimes Unit in 2013, had a lot at stake. Like most young cops, he was fiercely ambitious, and this was a career-making case. Known for his sterling work in capturing and arresting those whom the sheriff's department referred to as "thugs" and "thieves," he'd also been reprimanded more than once for "bossiness, insubordination, and disrespect." He and Wayne were well-matched in the sense that they both had their own way of doing things, and seemed impervious to outside influence.

In his descriptive work on tactics used by the Baltimore Police Department, author David Simon explains how the setup of the "private" interview room—"four yellow cinderblock walls, a dirty tin ashtray on a plain table, a small, mirrored window and a series of stained acoustic tiles on the ceiling"—is calculatingly designed to elicit confession. These days, although the ashtrays are gone and the mirrored window has been replaced by a camera, the deliberate illusion of privacy remains, distorting "the natural hostility between hunter and hunted, transforming it until it resembles a relationship more symbiotic than adversarial."

It's been shown that more than eighty percent of suspects waive their right to silence, and most such interviews yield incriminating statements (whether or not the suspect is guilty), even with adequate Miranda warnings. This seems baffling. Why do so many people agree to be interviewed by the police without an attorney present, even when they know their words could be used against them?

The answer is simple: in tense and frightening situations, it's very difficult to resist the pressure of an apparently sympathetic authority figure. Beyond this, innocent suspects usually waive their rights because they believe they've got nothing to worry about, whereas guilty ones, like Wayne, mostly assume that refusing to talk would make them seem suspicious. Generally speaking, guilty suspects appear to believe, having rehearsed their alibis and excuses, they'll be able to come through the interview successfully.

During his interrogation, Lebid, as he later explained, used a "modified version" of the Reid Technique, an interview method widely used by law enforcement that applies psychological tactics to elicit confessions. The first premise of the technique is to engage in a "direct positive confrontation," which involves building rapport with the subject. Lebid, in plain clothes—a casual blue T-shirt and jeans—kicks things off by sympathizing with Wayne's fibromyalgia, which has reportedly been making him feel uncomfortable in the holding cell. Lebid tells Wayne that he, too, has "a right knee thing going on."

As he speaks, he stretches, yawns, then puts his arms behind his head and casually swings backward in his chair, giving the impression that, even though Wayne has been sworn in and read his Miranda rights, this isn't really an "official" police interview—it's more of a casual chat. Lebid sits close to Wayne, sometimes leaning in, occasionally touching him on the shoulder. Reducing the distance between interviewer and subject is another important part of the Reid Technique: "physical gestures of sincerity" should be used "to establish an attitude of understanding and concern." You're more likely to share a story with a friend than answer questions from a uniformed official.

Once rapport has been established, Lebid moves on to the next stage of the Reid Technique: "the subject should be confronted bluntly with evidence of their guilt." It's perfectly acceptable for police to lie at this stage, if necessary, but Lebid doesn't need to use deception. He's got a warrant in front of him formally charging Wayne with murder. Still, a charge isn't proof, and a confession would be crucial to the case. Lebid tells Wayne they've spoken to his landlord, studied the surveillance footage from the trailer park, and interviewed witnesses, and there's no evidence to show Wayne was home in Missouri the weekend of Teresa's murder, as he claimed.

"I know you weren't there," Lebid insists. "I have you physically documented with photographs. Where you went, where you shopped, where you spent time." At this point, the investigator takes out his phone and shows Wayne the CCTV camera footage from the Walmart in Fort Myers, and the Circle K gas station in Bushnell, Florida.

Wayne, no doubt severely rattled by the images, pretends to be unfazed. "It doesn't look like me," he mumbles, reiterating that he was sick the weekend of Teresa's murder, and spent most of the time in bed.

"I was hurting real bad, and I didn't really do a lot," he tells Lebid. "And that Sunday I was feeling better, and went over to the neighbors. . . . I was there. I was home." But he's clearly getting nervous, twisting in his seat, looking at the ceiling, twitching his thumbs, tapping his feet. He turns his head to one side, avoids eye contact, takes off his glasses and tries to clean them on his shorts (as much as his handcuffs allow). A "behavioral observation of the suspect" is crucial throughout the interview, and Wayne's demeanor suggests that he might be close, even if unconsciously, to relieving himself of guilt.

Lebid next moves to the second stage of the Reid Technique: transitioning from confrontation to sympathy via face-saving minimization. This is the longest portion of the interview. By means of a "sympathetic monologue," the interrogator should "propose reasons that will justify or excuse the commission of the crime," such as "placing the moral blame on someone else or outside circumstances," downplaying the ethical consequences without mentioning the legal ones.

Lebid moves closer to Wayne. "I don't think you're a bad person," he says, gently. "I think you made a bad choice, and now's the time to rectify that bad choice." Plausible motives are suggested. "I want to hear it from your perspective . . . was Teresa about to do something that you needed to protect your family from? . . . Did you maybe go there to talk to Teresa about the choices she was making?" He tries appealing to Wayne's conscience. "Here's your pass. Here's your forgiveness. I understand you attend church, you're a Christian. . . ."

It can help the "sympathetic monologue" for the interviewer to give the impression he knows more than he does about the situation, and the people concerned. "Teresa was a firecracker," insists Lebid. "She was going to take the kids away from him, and the kids are Mark's world. . . . She told her sister they were getting a divorce, that Mark was going to hit the road. . . ."

"You're telling me that they had marital problems. I was close, and I've never heard that. He never talked to me about that," Wayne responds.

Lebid then tries appealing to Wayne's vanity: "You are probably like fifty IQ points above Mark, at least," he says. Wayne demurs. "You have that extremely intricate technical coding know-how that's like another language," Lebid cajoles him. "You're intelligent, you're sophisticated."

When the smooth talk goes nowhere, the investigator offers a get-out clause: Maybe Jimmy killed Teresa while Wayne was merely the lookout? "We know what Jimmy did," he says. "That's why he calls himself 'The Hammer,' right?" At this, Wayne chuckles. He refutes Lebid with a lie that Jimmy's no doubt used many times before: his nickname doesn't refer to an actual hammer, but to his dick. "He talks about it all the time, taking it out in public, swinging it around and using it to chase girls," says Wayne. "He has no boundaries." He's never seen it erect, Wayne admits, but he's talked to girls who have. Apparently, it was impressive.

Talking about Jimmy's hammerlike dick allows Lebid to lead the discussion in a different direction. Maybe because he's seen the suggestive texts on Mark's phone about blindfolding Angie and wearing her panties, or maybe because he can't understand why Wayne would want to kill Teresa if he wasn't sexually involved with Mark, he starts to double down on Wayne and Mark's unusual bond.

"It's a special relationship," he affirms. "You two care about each other. You love each other. You're brothers. And that's special. It means a lot." Again, no doubt prompted by the texts on Mark's phone, Lebid suggests Mark might have asked Wayne to kill Teresa because she disrespected him, and "he wasn't appreciated enough." He then speculates that maybe Wayne and Jimmy killed Teresa without Mark's knowledge, possibly for some perverse sexual reason. He suggests that Mark, Wayne, and Jimmy have all been sexually involved in "threesomes and foursomes."

Wayne is indignant. To him, he says, being gay is wrong. "It's not my thing." Like Jimmy, in his banter, Wayne expresses a certain amount of homophobia. This might be a reaction formation—a person is quick to excoriate in others qualities they acknowledge (and repress) in themselves. When Lebid puts pressure on Wayne to admit he's "been with a guy," Wayne snickers and shakes his head.

"Okay," Lebid goes on. "What do you consider 'being with a guy'?"

Wayne smirks. "I believe in the three-inch rule," he says.

"The three-inch rule? What's that?" asks Lebid.

Wayne gives a dirty laugh and gestures toward his penis. "You've got to get more than three inches from them."

Later, when Lebid stresses that he's providing Wayne with an "awesome opportunity" to tell his story in this "special moment in time preserved for you and me" when "no one else is here," Wayne sniggers that Lebid makes it all sound kind of "gay."

For hours, Lebid attacks from all angles, but he hasn't been able to do what the Reid Technique is designed to do: "overcome the suspect's denials." Clearly, Wayne isn't going to budge. "You're asking me the same questions," he keeps insisting. "I can't tell you what happened, because I don't know." They're both exhausted. No confession is forthcoming. Still, Wayne is kept in jail on charges of second-degree murder.

• • •

The Reid Technique is outmoded—the first handbook was published by polygraph expert and former police officer John E.

Reid in 1962—which is why most investigators make it clear that they're using an "updated version." But almost all police interrogation techniques imitate the original Reid model, which rests on obsolete concepts of behavioral psychology, such as the idea that innocent people don't normally offer reasons why they didn't commit the crime, and that "tears positively indicate the suspect's guilt." Then, once they've concluded from body language and words that a suspect is lying, interrogating officers are taught to reject "denials of guilt."

Many psychologists believe the Reid Technique causes confirmation bias in the minds of investigators. They also see it inherently coercive, intimidating, and confrontational, overwhelming a suspect to such an extent that they feel hopeless, and the truth no longer seems like the best option. If you're put under immense pressure, especially if you've been kept in custody for hours or even days, you can easily resort to short-term thinking, so that even if you're innocent, confession becomes an escape hatch to get out of the situation—I'll say whatever they want me to say just so I can go home.

Another disadvantage of the Reid Technique is that it can lead strong-willed subjects to close down completely, giving no information whatsoever. This is what happened with Jimmy. As soon as Lebid read him his rights, Jimmy stopped talking. Obviously, opting out of questioning doesn't imply guilt, but it's usually taken that way.

Jimmy was photographed before being booked—the huge FUCK THE FEDS tattoo on his back can't have won him many friends.

Chapter 15

Hindsight Bias

When Sheriff Mike Scott, at a press conference, announced that two men in Missouri had been arrested in connection with Teresa's murder, people were baffled and disturbed. Everybody had assumed there'd be a single suspect, somebody local. Speculation was rife. When the two men's mugshots were shown on the news, Wayne's striking similarity to Mark was bewildering. It got people wondering. Why did they look so much alike? Some speculated that they were related, perhaps real brothers by blood, possibly even true twins.

The police said nothing about Mark, and released no information about any potential connection to the murder. This left everyone baffled. If Mark wasn't involved, why would his best friend want to kill his wife? Was Wayne in love with Mark? Had Teresa rejected Wayne's advances? Plus: who the hell was Jimmy Ray Rodgers? When a reporter from NBC2 News asked Annie whether she was surprised that Wayne had been arrested in connection with Teresa's murder, she replied, "I was surprised my sister was bludgeoned to death. At this point, nothing else would surprise me."

Mark was adamant: it was all a frame-up. Ever since he'd

learned about the raid on Wayne's trailer, he insisted that his best buddy had become a patsy. The cops weren't going to solve the case, concluded Mark, so to satisfy the press and public, they'd simply found someone convenient to blame it on: an old friend who just happened to be a convicted felon and who was the main suspect in a missing person case.

Teresa's close friend Bethany Mitchell, who lived in Tampa, said that, after learning about Wayne's arrest, Mark called her in a panic. "He was emphatic that Wayne had nothing to do with this," she recalled. "This was clearly the police fabricating a case. . . . He was worried that he was going to be arrested next." To Teresa's friend Daniele Berardinelli in El Paso, Mark expressed concern about what Wayne was saying to the police. He was anxious, according to Daniele, that "maybe, just out of fear of the situation . . . Wayne could implicate him." Daniele told him that was "ridiculous."

• • •

At the time of Teresa's murder, Mark was well-loved in the community—people saw him as kind and polite, decent and respectful, a fun dad, devoted to his girls, utterly devastated by the loss of his wife. But after Mike Scott announced the arrest of his look-alike best friend, everything changed. There was, as yet, no evidence connecting Mark to the murder, but everybody was convinced he must have been involved. Friends and neighbors who'd formerly liked and respected him, enjoying his company, now said they'd found something "off" about him all along.

If you start to suspect a close friend might have been involved in a murder, it's natural to look back, reconsider their behavior, and go over things that seemed innocuous at the time. You start to wonder: Did I ever truly know this person? What if they weren't the person I thought they were, but somebody else in disguise? Hindsight bias—our tendency to see events as being much more predictable than they are, and our opinions as more accurate—is a normal part of human thinking. Some psychologists even believe it's adaptive, helping us to make better predictions in the future.

Carrie Kain was an ex-girlfriend of Wayne's and an old friend of Mark's. On July 28, twelve days after the raid on Wayne's trailer, Carrie started to rethink Mark's behavior at the funeral. Concerned, she called the Crimestoppers hotline; they put her in touch with the Florida homicide team, who enlisted her to work as a police informant. In a sworn statement on August 24, Carrie told police some of the things that, in hindsight, she found suspicious. Her misgivings were minor, but in Carrie's mind, they added up.

The day before the funeral, she told police, she found it strange that Mark went for a "long walk" on the beach with "a local woman," and came back "looking sunburned." She recalled him telling her in a "creepy" way that "Teresa was hit on the back of the head seventeen times." She thought it strange that, unlike the families of most homicide victims, Mark didn't have the obsessive interest in the police search for the killer that usually supersedes all else in the wake of such a tragedy, noting that at one point, Mark said to her, "I'm not praying for justice, I'm praying to be free and cleared."

At the funeral, she noticed, he looked very sharp, and was wearing an expensive suit (she also noticed, as did others, that he appeared to be carrying a gun). He and Wayne "acted like businessmen" during the ceremony, she said. ". . . Their demeanor seemed not somebody at a funeral, but more of a transaction. . . ." Carrie also thought it was rude that Bonnie Sievers invited Wayne and Angie to stay at her house, while Mark's sister Jaemea had to stay in a hotel.

Carrie wasn't the only person to have retrospective misgivings about Mark, although she was the first to go to the police. Teresa's friend Daniele Berardinelli recalled that when she first saw Mark after Teresa's murder, they hugged, and "Mark sounded as though he was crying, his body was quaking as if he was crying, but when I searched his face there were no tears, no red eyes, no runny nose." Carrie Kain mentioned the same thing. "At the funeral, I started thinking that his tears are fake."

A friend of Annie's named Rebecca claimed, improbably, that right before the ceremony, Mark put his arms around her waist, slid his hand down to her ass, then kissed her on the lips. Annie, after realizing Mark was a suspect in the murder, decided he "gave her the creeps," and recalled an incident before he married Teresa, in which he apparently spied on her while she was trying on a new dress.

Rose Grunert said she met Mark for the first time at Wayne's wedding, and she didn't think he was behaving like a married man. "I do know that my friend said he was really flirting with her," she said. "He was flirting with everybody, especially her." Taylor Shomaker, who'd never met Mark before the wedding, said she found him "creepy" and "kind of a perv."

The Sieverses' next-door neighbor, Kimberly Torres, was interviewed by Detective Nolen shortly after Teresa's murder, and didn't mention anything about Mark apart from overhearing arguments from the Sieverses' house in the past, in which, she said, Teresa was clearly the aggressor. She said the same thing when she was interviewed by law enforcement in June 2015, and repeated the story to WINK News, NBC, and ABC7. But after Wayne was implicated in the murder, she suddenly started to "remember" finding Mark sneaking around her backyard and threatening her family. Apparently, she once came across him on her lanai—later, she said this happened "several, several times"—and another time she saw him "just standing in one place staring at his house."

On February 27, in an interview with 10 Tampa Bay, her "recollections" were even more expansive. "We had to change our locks three times in the seven years we've lived here, and each time was because of him," she said. "He'd show up in our yard, near our pool, or on our porch out of nowhere." Torres gave approximately eight interviews to various news outlets. In an interview for *Gulfshore Life* in April 2019, Torres "remembered" that, a few weeks before the murder, she heard Teresa yelling, "I'm fucking leaving you! I'm tired of this crap!" Mark had allegedly replied, "Fine, if that's what you want, but we will see about that!"

For eight years, Wendy Wilson and her husband had the office across the hall from Teresa's in the Estero Medical Center. Although neither she nor anyone in the building had mentioned their suspicions to the police, according to Wendy, "everybody in the building was ducking him thinking, 'you had to have something to do with this,'" while Mark was "just whistling along like he was this happy-go-lucky guy." To reporters from Fox 4 News, she described a highly improbable encounter with Mark that she'd never revealed before, certainly not to the police. "I walked up the back stairs, which we have access to and only the owners have access to," said Wendy. "As I opened up the door, there's Mark, two guns pointed right at my face. . . . I thought, 'oh my God, he could have shot me!'"

More hindsight bias: Teresa's friend Bethany Mitchell contacted the state's attorney's office long after the crime, telling them she'd always mistrusted Mark. She said she'd spoken to an "intuitive friend" who was in contact with Teresa's spirit, who told her she should contact the police. "Stone-faced is pretty much the word to use for him," said one of Mark's neighbors. "He just always gave me that funny, funny feeling," said another.

After Wayne's arrest, whatever was going through Mark's mind, he knew he needed a lawyer. The next time Detective Nolen asked to speak to him, on July 7, Mark referred him to Lee Hollander, a top-notch criminal defense attorney who told investigators that his client would no longer be cooperating with the police. This, of course, was something Mark had every right to do: when investigating domestic murders, cops can sometimes leap to judgment, arresting husbands or partners who have nothing to do with the crime. But everybody agreed: it didn't look good.

• • •

From the sheriff's office, there was no official recognition of Mark's involvement, but given Wayne's arrest, everyone assumed that Mark would be next. People wondered whether his daughters were in danger. News trucks hung around his house, filming the children's tutor as she arrived for their lessons. Mark was under siege. Whenever he walked to his car, he put his hand up to cover his face, waving the news cameras away.

This kind of harassment incensed Sheriff Scott, who had a long history of strongly worded battles with the media, and publicly criticized them for their speculation and second-guessing. He called them "half-baked people," and refused to give out any information relating to the case. When asked at a press conference if they'd established a connection between Jimmy and Mark, Scott said, simply, "We have established many connections between many people in this investigation." He then warned the press he'd deal with them "aggressively and professionally," which he did by keeping investigative documents sealed.

Regardless, the speculation continued. Neighbors reported that, two days after the murder, Mark was seen throwing computer equipment out of both the family home and Teresa's office. This raised a hunch: Had Mark been committing Medicare fraud, or similar shady dealings? Had Mark asked Wayne to kill Teresa because she'd found out, and threatened to go to the FBI?

Websleuths, the amateur crime-solving site, opened a special forum for the case, including a "Jarvis Road Stakeout," where Teresa's neighbors could update fellow armchair detectives on local activities. One of Dr. Sievers's former patients posted a copy of a suspicious email she'd received from Mark three days after Teresa's death, letting her patients know they could continue to order their Xymogen online through a colleague named "Dr. Roy." The letter gave them a Boca Raton cell phone number and told them they could order under the account name "HEILR." Patients found it suspicious that "Dr. Roy" didn't give his last name, and was encouraging them to use Xymogen without even meeting them. They found it even more suspicious that, in an email purportedly from Mark, Teresa's name was spelled "Theresa."

One savvy sleuth, by tracking down his license plate, connected "Dr. Roy" with the owner of a purple van that was seen outside the Sievers house shortly after the murder, which Mark had been filling up with computer equipment. When dodgy healer Roy Heilbron was indicted on health care fraud three days after Teresa's murder, the whispered hunch about Medicare fraud became a widespread conviction. "With indictment of dr Roy just a few days after TS' death," observed one Websleuths member, "there's got to be some connection."

On Monday, December 7, a little more than three months after Wayne's and Jimmy's arrests, there was a huge development in the case. At last, the Lee County State Attorney's office gave the media something substantial to chew on. They released thousands of pages of discovery documents relating to the charges against Wayne and Jimmy, including Mark's phone journal and many of his salacious texts, finally revealing the State's allegations that Mark had orchestrated the killing.

After Mark's phone logs were made publicly available, many people refused to believe they were real. By this time, to fans of *Nancy Grace* and similar crime shows, Teresa had become a martyred angel: beautiful, saintly, generous, and compassionate. It was difficult to square this image of her with Mark's explicit descriptions of the couple's over-the-top sex life. Especially unpalatable was the fact that she might have been sexually involved with Wayne. "TS does not seem to be the type of person who would have engaged in the swinging world," pronounced one Websleuth. Another concurred: "I believe none of the comments made by Mark—especially comments relative to their marriage or Dr. Sievers."

Some suggested that Wayne, with his tech wizardry and access to the couple's electronics, might have plotted with Mark to "spoof Teresa's phone" and fake the texts. Possibly Mark and Wayne had imagined that making Teresa look sexually voracious could lead law enforcement to believe she had been killed in a kinky sex game, or by a jealous husband or wife. One Websleuths commenter inferred that, if the texts were real, Teresa must have been suffering from Stockholm Syndrome. "I think sometimes intelligence and education is trumped by longstanding, deep emotional needs," opined another.

As soon as the documents were released, the Florida Department of Children and Families asked a judge to remove Mark's two daughters from his home, alleging that, based on the State's allegations about Mark's involvement in the murder, there was an "impending danger" to the children. Surely an arrest was imminent. On Jarvis Road, neighbors were excited. "Everyone . . . is watching out their windows right now!!" posted one, on Websleuths. "NBC is doing a live update . . . they have been there since this afternoon in a car . . . FOX van is also there. They have certainly been coming and going . . . probably looking for Mark." But although he was, according to the sheriff, "in the window of suspicion," Mark wasn't arrested. He wasn't indicted. He wasn't even charged. That night, the "grieving spouse" set off a bunch of fireworks, symbolically giving the finger to his neighbors.

• • •

At the hearing initiated by the Florida Department of Children and Families, Mark entered the courtroom looking defiant, in a smart black suit, yellow shirt, and brown tie. He won the case easily—the judge found "no probable cause" to remove the girls from their father's custody based on allegations and suspicions. His attorney, Lee Hollander, didn't even bother reading the documents. "They're just trying to screw with him," he told the press, adding that if detectives were alleging Mark orchestrated his wife's murder, then why hadn't they arrested him?

Hollander had a point. The State's Attorney's document dump was embarrassing, to be sure, but there was still no evidence of Mark's involvement in the crime. Sure, he and Teresa fought a lot, had money problems, and an unconventional sex life, but his alibi was intact. Meanwhile, Mark continued to defend his doppelgänger, even inquiring whether Wayne might be allowed to work remotely on the clinic's servers from behind bars. His allegiance to Wayne was still tight.

But tight enough for Wayne to die for him?

And then there was Jimmy. The wild card. He was a young guy—if he flipped and took a plea, he could be out by the time he was forty. On the other hand, if he and Wayne kept quiet, there might not be enough evidence to convict either of them. Plus, Jimmy loathed the government. It was hard to imagine him taking a deal.

• • •

Mark, Wayne, and Jimmy: three chess pieces, hazardously poised. Who would make the first move, and in what direction?

Chapter 16

State's Evidence

The drive to conceal and the impulse to confess are two sides of the same coin: they can't be separated. Anyone who talks to a reporter, journalist, or investigator knows—or surely must suspect—that anything you say could be used against you. Still, something compels us to speak. It feels unnatural to keep things to ourselves; sometimes we simply can't do it. Keeping a secret requires constant effort, even if that effort is unconscious. As Freud writes, "He that has eyes to see and ears to hear may convince himself that no mortal can keep a secret. If his lips are silent, he chatters with his fingertips; betrayal oozes out of him at every pore."

When two people are equally responsible for a crime—especially if they're close friends or lovers—they often make a pact: if both protest their innocence, neither can be convicted. They may pledge themselves to solemn oaths never to speak about what they've done, under any circumstances. They may promise to stick together even unto death. Perhaps some hold out. But in most cases, long separation causes the loosening of bonds, splitting off, and mental fragmentation.

The grim experience of prison life, too, can lead to desperate measures. The more serious the charges, the more likely that the weaker of the pair will crack and spill the secret. They may tell themselves they're confessing for moral reasons, following the dictates of their conscience, or coming clean before God, but for the most part, this is self-justification. It's the gradual realization that they can't possibly beat the rap that leads someone to cut their losses and make a deal.

After his arrest, Wayne was taken to Jefferson County Jail in Missouri. At first, he couldn't imagine being kept inside for long. On the phone, he told Angie and his family the cops were trying to frame him. He claimed, like Mark, that since they hadn't been able to solve the murder, law enforcement were going with the obvious suspect: the husband. But Mark had been out of town when the murder occurred. Who better to blame than his longtime best friend—a convicted felon and prime suspect in an unsolved murder?

The cops had no evidence against him, Wayne insisted—they were bound to release him soon. Meanwhile, he spent a lot of time with other inmates playing spades, and made a few friends. Angie and his parents sent him money, wrote to him, and visited, both remotely and in person. Teresa's murder was still in the news. Angie complained that reporters from Florida had been knocking on her door. Wayne was blasé. "Tell them if they want to report something, how about reporting the truth."

But months passed, and things started to weigh on him. He missed Angie—when he was arrested, they'd been married for less than four months. Prison officers wouldn't let him have his Xanax. Sometimes he didn't get his other medications, either. He suffered from constant headaches. He missed his younger daughter, and was devastated when her mother told him she didn't want the girl to talk to him anymore—didn't even want her to write. A friend told him his mother-in-law, Kathy Moran, had been talking to the press, apparently implicating him in the murder.

"Every time you dig into some of this stuff, it leads you to a scary place," said Wayne's friend, ominously.

Then things took a sharp swerve. Wayne's lawyer told him why the cops had revoked Jimmy's parole—it was because they had evidence from the CCTV videos that proved Jimmy had been in Florida the weekend of Teresa's murder. Wayne was alarmed. Lamely, he tried to bluff that, for whatever reason, Jimmy must have gone down to kill Teresa of his own volition. On the phone to his mother, he wondered whether Jimmy might have overheard Mark complaining about his marriage, and as a result, driven down to Florida to kill Teresa on his behalf. If that were the case, he said, it definitely wouldn't have been because Mark asked him to. Now, Wayne was fearful. "If Jimmy had something to do with this, they're going to try and link it back to Mark," he told his mother. "And I'm in the middle."

A few weeks later, still insisting he was innocent, he raised the possibility that he might be open to taking a plea. Clearly, the cops were going to frame him. Rather than go to trial, he told his mother, he might be prepared to plead "guilty to something," depending on what he was offered. "I'd consider some small charge just to get it over with," he resolved. Voluntary manslaughter was a Class B felony, which meant they couldn't sentence you to more than fifteen years. Wayne thought maybe they'd offer him seven to ten. In Missouri, the amount of time you serve depends on the parole board, and if he stayed clean, he might get out in four or five. On the other hand, if he went to trial and lost, they could extradite him to Florida, where you had to serve eighty-five percent of your sentence—minimum.

Down in Bonita Springs, the press and public were baying for Mark's blood, and Sheriff Mike Scott was trying to keep them at arm's length. After releasing documents that alleged Mark was involved in the murder, they still hadn't arrested him, and they hadn't given out any information about the connections between Wayne, Mark, and Jimmy.

The sheriff's attitude to the media was paradoxical. Sometimes he censured them; at other times, he pandered and preened. In his next press conference, he tantalized them, acknowledging that "people are very curious. They are captivated." But it was too early to release any information except how marvelous his deputies had been. "We're very proud of our body of work in this case. Our involvement has been nothing short of stellar, textbook. I want to tell that story."

Nonetheless, for the sheriff, things were looking better and better. In Ste. Genevieve County Jail, Wayne was gradually starting to realize no deal was forthcoming. Then came the last straw. They were extraditing him anyway, trial or no trial. At the news, Angie broke down completely. According to Wayne, "She was a mess." He even suggested to his sister that "you might delicately suggest that maybe she go check in somewhere."

To Wayne, too, the shock was devastating. Clearly, the Florida State's attorney had enough evidence to charge him with murder. His friends and family wouldn't be able to afford to visit him down there. Nor would Angie. But she consoled herself that God moves in mysterious ways, and must have a divine purpose in sending Wayne to Florida. "I'm sure he has a reason for this," she said, sobbing. "There's somebody down there who needs you to talk to them, or help them."

Angie was right. Four months after his arrest, Wayne told his attorneys he was ready to confess.

• • •

Mark and Wayne hadn't had any contact for almost a year. Had their time apart been enough to sever their special bond? But even if they were no longer "brothers," you can't separate yourself from your shadow. By telling the truth, Wayne was about to destroy them both.

• • •

Adam Dalgliesh, the fictional detective invented by crime writer P. D. James, says that all the motives for murder are covered by four Ls: Love, Lust, Lucre, and Loathing. He adds, "They'll tell you that the most dangerous emotion is hatred. Don't believe them. The most dangerous emotion is love." Only six to ten percent of female murder victims are chosen at random; the rest are killed by someone they know. A domestic homicide with deliberate overkill and no evidence of a robbery (or a vague attempt to suggest one) always points to the most obvious suspect: the husband.

Yet by all accounts, Mark adored his wife to the point of obsession. The photo on his Facebook profile was a picture not of himself, but of Teresa. He was immensely proud of her—her intelligence, her passion, her beauty. Sexually, he couldn't get enough of her. He'd devoted himself to supporting her and caring for their daughters. If he was about to lose his family, wouldn't suicide seem a more likely option than murder? How could someone kill a person they loved so much?

In fact, such crimes are surprisingly common. It's not a question of love turning to hate; it's rather that when a man sees his wife as his whole world, the threat of separation entails a loss of his own identity. Mark was a man in conflict with himself. If his texts are anything to go by, he suffered a long series of little deaths and indignities over the course of his marriage, leading him to feel embittered, deserted, and alone. Too, his lack of an independent career meant that, without Teresa, not only would his life become meaningless, but he'd have no source of income.

And the macho element also came into play. Although Mark was happy to be "Mr. Mom," he had a very traditional perception of manhood. He rode a motorcycle, collected firearms, spent his free time at the shooting range, often bringing friends along and teaching them how to use a gun. Others saw him as a "protector" who was well-known for "safeguarding" his family. If Teresa already made this tough guy feel emasculated, her desertion would be an even more humiliating affront—a kind of castration. Under such conditions, killing is basically an attempt at self-preservation.

Investigators had fingered Mark from day one. When they got hold of his phone, their suspicions were confirmed. A collapsing marriage. A wife who yelled, nagged, and treated him like her personal valet. There were financial motives, too. Police would later discover that there were five separate insurance policies on Teresa's life, totaling 4.4 million dollars.

Most domestic murders are impulsive—committed in a flash of anger triggered by a minor insult or a quarrel over money, love, or sex. This one was premeditated. What the cops needed to know was when, where, and how the murder was planned.

On January 6, Curtis Wayne Wright, Jr. signed a proffer agreement with the State of Florida. In criminal law, a proffer is an arrangement between a defendant and the State whereby the defendant promises to tell the full truth about a crime with the understanding that they won't face any additional charges. If the State finds the information credible, they'll usually offer a reduced sentence in exchange.

Wayne was currently looking at life in prison—possibly even a death sentence. His confession was crucial, in that it would allow the prosecutors to finally arrest Mark, but Wayne had been too closely involved in the crime to expect a sweetheart deal. In the end, he was offered twenty-five years for second-degree murder charges. It wasn't much comfort. Even with four years' shuffle room for good time, he'd be at least seventy when he got out. Still, if he stayed healthy, he'd probably see the light of day.

Wayne officially passed his burden of guilt over to Mark

on February 19, 2016, in an interview room in the Lee County Courthouse. His attorney, Joe Sconzo, was in attendance, along with Sconzo's partner, Elizabeth Parker. Also present were the two assistant state's attorneys who'd been assigned to the case, Hamid Hunter and Cynthia Ross; Investigator Anthony Vasquez from the State Attorney's Office; Sergeant Lebid, and Mike Downs, now also a sergeant. Wayne was brought into the room by a prison guard in a long-sleeved white T-shirt under red prison scrubs. He asked if his handcuffs could be removed, and they were. He seemed nervous, twitchy, ill at ease.

Confession, especially if self-incriminating, is always performative: an intoxicating display of guilt, exposure, and the specter of forthcoming retribution. To confess, we believe, is to open the window to the soul. From the Catholic confessional to the therapy room, we place a high price on personal unburdening; we generally believe it offers a promise of truth and a solution to a problem. Everybody wants to believe confessions—police, prosecutors, judges, and juries alike—because they seem plausible and self-authenticating. In fact, it's been shown that confessions have a persuasive force so enduring that, to people who hear them, they outweigh even scientific evidence.

In books, movies, and the popular imagination, confessions tend to unfold neatly, as chronological narratives, but in real life, they rarely happen this way. Legal scholars have shown that "shapely confessions—statements that advance the government's case in court, or strengthen its hand at plea bargaining—rarely, if ever, spring full-blown from the mouths of criminal suspects." In other words, confessions must be nudged, pulled, wrenched, and wrestled into shape.

This was certainly the case with Wayne. He came to the truth only reluctantly, after hours of evasion, distortion, and self-serving prevarication—a slowly unwinding spool of lies. As during his interrogation with David Lebid five months earlier, he squirmed restlessly as he spoke, shirking eye contact, looking up at the ceiling and down at the floor. Most of the time, he sat with his arms folded in front of his belly, intermittently clenching his hands, fidgeting, and twiddling his thumbs. He recounted events falteringly, in fragments, and out of chronological order. The story he had to tell was dismal, depraved, and abhorrent.

Chapter 17

Double-Cross

"Mark and I have been friends for most of our lives," Wayne began. "Mark and Teresa had—I guess a—I don't exactly know what to call it, but an open relationship . . . Mark had showed me pictures, you know, of him and Teresa with other people. So—I knew that that was going on." He described how, about six months before the wedding, Mark had mentioned a friend who was having "marital issues." He'd been vague with the details—"it was something to do with the spouse cheating," recalled Wayne. "There was some child abuse going on as well." This friend had apparently asked Mark if he knew someone who could "pay a visit" to his wife's lover. Mark had asked Wayne whether he'd be willing to help. Wayne assumed his friend was looking for somebody to run the guy out of town. "He started asking me if I knew anybody or if I could find somebody," said Wayne, who told Mark he'd consider it. "Mark used the word 'hypothetical' a lot. . . . I didn't think too much about it. I wasn't paying that much attention." The "friend" hadn't been mentioned again. Until the wedding.

• • •

After the cookout at Wayne's trailer, when the heat of the day was receding, Mark took Wayne aside and asked him if they could speak in private.

Wayne led his friend up the shaky wooden steps into the manufactured home. They entered the bedroom and closed the door. Voices and music were drowned out by the hum of the air-conditioner. Outside, the sun gleamed through the cottonwood trees.

In the swampy trailer bedroom, shadows lengthening outside, Mark returned to the subject. But this time he spoke frankly: there was no "friend." "He mentioned that Teresa and him were having problems. He talked to me about her having an affair. He said they were also having financial problems and that he was considering filing for bankruptcy." Wayne could tell his friend was on edge. He sympathized. He knew what it was like to lose your children. He'd lost his own son in a custody battle with his ex-wife. The boy was now a grown man, a virtual stranger.

Wayne wondered: did Mark want him to harm Teresa's lover? If so, he'd do what he could to help. But before Mark could give him further details, their conversation was cut short. There were people in the trailer, laughing and talking. Someone turned on the music. "So that was the end of that," said Wayne. "We were kind of partying after that, and drinking."

A second conversation on the subject took place in the public bathroom, when the men were getting dressed for the wedding. Mark didn't have time to go into detail, but he reiterated that "he was concerned about the kids, that Teresa was going to take the kids from him." Again, they were interrupted. Identically dressed, the two men returned to Walther Park in De Soto, where people were setting up food for the cookout. Wayne had gotten a nice deal on the hamburgers and hot dogs—his friend T.K., who owned a small deli, had a wholesale account at a restaurant supply company, and he'd let Wayne use his account so they could buy everything at wholesale prices. "He let me leave it in his walk-in cooler at the store," he recalled. A couple of hours before the ceremony, Wayne drove over to T.K.'s in nearby Crystal City and picked up the meat, but once they were back in the park and setting up the grills, he realized there was a box of hot dogs missing. Mark volunteered to drive back to T.K.'s with him to pick it up. It was twenty minutes each way.

Two bald men in tuxedos with a car full of meat. Now, they had time to talk.

While they were driving, Mark returned to the subject of his marriage. He told Wayne that Teresa was planning to ditch him, take the kids, and move out of state. "He said, there's no way he could allow that to happen," said Wayne. "He was emphatic: a divorce would destroy him emotionally and financially."

Wayne could tell Mark was sincere. "Mark doesn't joke around with things like that, especially when it comes to his girls." Wayne knew Teresa could be fiery and aggressive, but he'd always thought that was what made her such a great partner for Mark. "It took somebody like her to keep Mark in line," he said, later, "and make him become the Mr. Mom, which is a role I would never have seen him in." But more recently, Wayne had observed, Teresa had become "a wild person . . . she tended to be verbally abusive to Mark. Also, the kids. They acted like they were kind of afraid of her." He knew about Teresa's friendship with Nick Delgado, but he didn't realize she was planning to leave Mark for the doctor. Had they tried counseling? A trial separation? Could Mark fight legally for custody? After all, he'd done most of the parenting.

Unfortunately, said Mark, he wasn't in a place financially where he could afford a legal battle. As for counseling, they'd tried everything and were at the end of the line. A divorce was unacceptable. He couldn't let a stranger bring up his girls. They started talking about how to handle the situation, recalled Wayne. "And he said the only option that he had was to have her killed."

There was a financial incentive, too, added Mark. Teresa had a 4.4-million-dollar life insurance policy, and while Mark would be needing most of it (as the family's wage earner would be gone), he could promise his buddy 100,000 dollars minimum. And if things worked out, maybe he'd move back to Missouri.

As Wayne pulled up at Walther Park, he had one last question. "I asked him what kind of time frame he was looking at."

As soon as possible, said Mark.

He'd just agreed to murder his best man's wife. Now, Wayne took his marriage vows.

• • •

Yes, he agreed to be involved, Wayne told the investigators, but he did so for a noble reason—the safety of the children. "When Mark talked to me about it . . . this whole thing was really brought to me as about the kids, about their safety," he said. According to Mark, Teresa was about to take the girls and move out of state with "this doctor," someone Mark didn't trust around his daughters. "In any other situation, other than it being the kids, I wouldn't have even had anything to do with it at all." It certainly wasn't about money, Wayne lied. "When Mark talked to me about it . . . he didn't bring it to me as it was about money. He knows how I am with kids and especially those two, I'm extended family. They call me Uncle Wayne. . . . It wasn't just something that was like, Hey, you want to make some money. And really, I didn't really have any plans of getting any of it."

Wayne's account of his conversation with Mark was specious, deceptive, and self-serving. As he surely knew, Teresa and Nick had barely touched; their relationship was flirtatious, yes, but they'd set boundaries, mostly to appease Mark, although Nick, too, was in a committed relationship. But even if Nick had been single, there's no way a court would have let Teresa take the girls to his home in California. In fact, if Mark and Teresa had divorced, Mark would probably have been their daughters' primary caregiver. He noted as much on his phone on March 17. "if the worse comes to the worse and we do not stay together, she will have visitation and i custody!!"

After a divorce, true, their lifestyle would have been considerably different. No more whirlwind dreams of celebrity—Teresa would have to settle for her workaday office routine. Maybe she'd bring in a little extra money from laser treatment and supplement sales, but the house would probably have to be sold, and there'd be no more expensive vacations, private chefs, spa days, haircuts at the Ritz-Carlton, or 500-dollar trips to Whole Foods. She might have to pay child support until Mark could reactivate his nursing credentials, or find some other work. But they'd still have their daughters, their health, supportive friends and family, the Florida sunshine, trips to the beach. Whether or not they found new partners, their lives might have been more stable and settled. Less stressful. More emotionally secure. And relatively speaking, they'd still be immensely privileged.

Another lie: when investigators asked Wayne how close the two men were, Wayne backtracked. "As much as we talked about so many things, it was mostly about the computers," he said. "There really wasn't that much personal stuff."

• • •

In Patricia Highsmith's 1950 novel *Strangers on a Train*, the psychopathic Charles Bruno suggests to a man he's never met before, Guy Haines, that they exchange murders, each killing someone the other man wants dead. The novel is about the transference of guilt: one man commits a crime, and another pays for it. Bruno believes that, if he kills Guy's wife when Guy is out of town, no one could ever possibly find out. He's delighted by his own devious ingenuity. "A pure murder, without personal motives!"

Did Mark, like Bruno, believe his plan to be foolproof? According to Wayne, he certainly seemed blasé. The day after the wedding, Mark flew home to his family in Bonita Springs. Wayne texted him at 2:20 P.M. "It was really good to see you again. Hopefully we will talk again soon. We will talk soon about business things in detail." An hour later, Mark replied: "do not really want to use 'secure txts' as i believe nothing is really secure once its out there."

At the wedding, he'd told Wayne they shouldn't discuss the murder on their regular cell phones—they weren't safe. They should buy burner phones, he said, and send each other their numbers. "When I get my new information I will mail it to you at your home address," he texted Wayne on May 5. "if you could do the same and only use it for each other that would be great." Two days later, Mark had activated his burner phone, and sent Wayne the number. "mailing out today!!!! Call me, its very simple."

With burner phones, you can choose your own number. Mark picked a California prefix; Wayne chose one from Atlanta. Their plan was that if either of them wanted to talk about the murder, they'd send a text on their regular phone containing the word "other," which was an indication they'd shortly be calling on the burner phone. "hello brother from an 'other' mother," Mark texted Wayne on May 17. Sometimes their subterfuge was straightforward ("check other"), sometimes more complicated.

Clearly, Mark and Wayne had read too many detective stories. Their schemes were adolescent games, James Bond fantasies, with their secret phones, code words, and special language. Like teenagers, when they were together, the men seemed to regress, bringing out the worst in each other. The murder plot was a *folie à deux*—a shared delusion. It's safe to say Mark would never have had Teresa killed if he hadn't known Wayne—Mark had no criminal record and no history of violent tendencies. Wayne, even if he'd killed before, would surely never have murdered an innocent woman if Mark hadn't asked him to.

Wayne and Angie could barely pay their rent; Wayne certainly couldn't afford a trip to Florida. His credit cards were all maxed out. To cover his friend's expenses, Mark sent him a check for 600 dollars under the guise of payment for his computer work. He also gave him the garage code for 27034 Jarvis Road and the code to disable the house alarm, which were the same—1313, the number of the Munsters' house on Mockingbird Lane, in the old TV show. They'd been having trouble with the alarm anyway, he told Wayne, so it wouldn't seem strange if it hadn't gone off during the "break-in." Before Mark left for New York, he destroyed his "other" phone and told Wayne to do the same. On their "real" phones, the two man's regular playful texts continued daily until the day before the murder.

Wayne knew he couldn't fly to Florida—airline tickets could be easily traced—but his aches and pains would make it difficult for him to drive. Plus, he didn't know if he could handle the murder alone. He needed a sidekick. Jimmy was his first choice for three reasons. One, he was reliable. Two, he needed money. Three, he'd committed murders in the past. Or so he claimed. "Jimmy is always bragging about his past, and his criminal history, and how he used to be a hit man," recalled Wayne, cynically. "He was always trying to find ways to make money fast. He said his dad murdered his mom, and he had something to do with his dad being killed. He said he stabbed somebody multiple times with a pocketknife. He was always looking for ways to get rich quick and make money."

One afternoon, a couple of weeks after the wedding, Wayne

called Jimmy at work. "I told him I might know a way he could make some ready cash if he was interested." Jimmy was on board right away—he didn't even know what he was agreeing to. That night, they met up at Hub's Pub in Bonne Terre. "I asked him what he was willing to do," said Wayne. "He said, 'anything.' So, I brought up what Mark wanted to have happen. Jimmy was gung-ho about it." Wayne hadn't told Mark he was planning to bring a partner. "Mark didn't want to know the details," said Wayne. "The less he knew the better, is kind of the way he looked at it."

Although he claimed it was a secondary motive, Wayne also had a financial interest in Teresa's murder. But Jimmy had no connection with Mark. "For Jimmy, it was all about money," said Wayne. And that was a problem. Mark estimated that after Teresa's death, it would take at least four months for the insurance to pay out, and Jimmy didn't want to wait. Wayne came up with a solution. Mark, who wanted the murder to look like an interrupted robbery, had told Wayne to take all the valuables from the house. There was cash in the safe upstairs, he reminded Wayne, as well as some rare silver dollars, one of which was worth around 10,000 dollars. Wayne figured Jimmy would be happy with the immediate spoils, while he and Mark waited for the big payout.

Unlike Wayne, Jimmy didn't have a large circle of friends and family who might have been curious about an unplanned trip to Florida. The only person who'd notice his absence, apart from Taylor, was his boss, Tyler Juliette. Jimmy told Tyler he was heading to Florida to see his brother, Jackie Jr., who'd just graduated from law school. To celebrate his graduation, said Jimmy, his brother had promised to pay for his trip, and buy him a fancy suit.

• • •

After a short break, Hamid Hunter asked Wayne to describe exactly what happened during the murder. "Don't minimize your role in any way, shape, or form—everything is off the table right now," he warned.

Wayne said he understood. But when it came to describing what happened that night in the kitchen at Jarvis Road, he prevaricated. He went on tangents, talked in circles, moved closer to the crime, then backed off again, getting into some unrelated incident. Finally, he told a flat-out lie. It was Jimmy, he said, who killed Teresa. He was on the scene, he admitted, but he wasn't in the house. His role, he said, had been to stand lookout "in a wooded area near the apartment complex" where they'd parked the car.

His story was absurd, and everyone knew it. How could Wayne possibly have alerted Jimmy if he was standing in the woods? If he was merely a lookout, why would he have taken protective clothing? Was Jimmy really going to be answering his phone and checking his texts while committing a brutal murder?

Assistant State's Attorney Hamid Hunter reminded Wayne the proffer was only good if he told the truth. If the prosecutors found out he'd been lying, the deal was off. Plus, according to the Florida law of felony murder, as Hunter reminded Wayne, "if you have two guys that come to an area for a murder to be committed, and one guy . . . provides access to a home, and the second guy actually goes and does the killing, they're both just as guilty of the crime." Wayne said he was aware of the law; nonetheless, he repeated: he was only the lookout. Jimmy alone killed Teresa.

Unsurprisingly, the investigators didn't believe him. "When you talk about standing outside and not being in the house, your demeanor changes a little bit," observed Sergeant Downs, perceptively. "That would indicate to me that you're somehow trying to dissociate yourself with being inside the house. Not so much to be deceptive to us, but I think that you also have an emotional attachment. . . . Is that correct?"

Wayne said nothing.

"The scene holds a different story," Downs continued. "If I had to bet money, I would say that you were in that house. For sure. This is uncomfortable to you. It's very uncomfortable. But that's where we're at."

Wayne began to sweat. He asked for a break. Accompanied by a guard, he and his attorneys returned to the holding cell to hold a short, private meeting. They conferred—Wayne said later that he prayed—then, after twenty minutes, returned to the interview room. The questioning continued. Despite his brief communion with God, Wayne continued to lie, although each lie brought him progressively closer to the truth. Now he admitted that he was in the house. He even went into the kitchen while the murder was in progress, he said, but added, risibly, that it was "really kind of after she had already been attacked." He had nothing to do with killing Teresa, he repeated. But he was ready to admit—"yes, I was in the house."

As before, his story made no sense. Why would he go to Teresa's house to kill her, then fail to help Jimmy with the murder? Why get dressed up in protective gear? Wayne's initial lies did him no favors. The prosecutors were aware: he was crying wolf. Deception—misleading statements, wishful thinking, exaggerations, concealment—are bad enough, but deception during a purported confession is more pernicious.

The officers already knew Wayne and Jimmy had committed the crime together—they just needed Wayne to admit it. Instead of intimidating him, Sergeant Downs tried a new tactic: speaking gently. "It's important that we're honest," he said. "No matter what you did . . . we need to know what happened so that we can move on. We're not here to pass judgment." Wayne's reluctance to confess was natural, said the officer, but it "wasn't helping anyone."

Downs had hit the right note. Sensing Wayne was about to break, he minimized even further, speaking to him softly, like a kind father. "I understand, because you're a human being," he said, reducing Wayne's culpability to such a degree that the horrible crime became no more than an awkward blunder. "People have done far worse," he cajoled. "Everybody makes mistakes."

Wayne sighed deeply and lowered his head for a moment. Then he looked up and gave a brief, barely discernable nod. Weak, drained, and exhausted, he was ready tell the truth.

Chapter 18

The Hit

Wayne and Jimmy were reckless would-be tough guys who'd both done time in prison and were both perennially broke. Both claimed they'd killed before, but nothing had ever been proven. Sure, Wayne was the lead suspect in the Ronnie Bolin case, but all he'd ever actually been charged with was manufacturing meth. Jimmy's record was equally unglamorous—he'd been locked up for possessing his dad's guns.

The wannabe hit men took on the job with little hesitation, and while in some respects they took precautions, in others, they were stupendously rash. Their biggest mistake: telling people they were going to Florida. Wayne's friend and landlord, Christian Taylor, was envious ("What part of Florida? Possibly need company? . . . Probably couldn't anyway but just got me daydreaming"). Their second mistake: having no plan other than to hit the beach. Their third mistake: having no weapon.

But when it came to things like avoiding contact with blood and not leaving fingerprints, they'd prepared obsessively. At the time, Jimmy was working on a job that involved close contact with battery acid. Every day, his boss gave him a fresh navy blue, acid-resistant, heavy-duty jumpsuit, thick rubber boots, blue booties to wear over them, and a pair of blue latex gloves that extended beyond the wrist. It wasn't difficult for him to pick up some extra sets of protective clothing after leaving work. Wayne also bought a heavy-duty wide-brimmed safari hat with a perforated back—the kind Mark sometimes wore to protect himself from the sun.

Mark wanted Wayne to use a gun, to make the crime look more like an interrupted burglary, but Wayne was reluctant—he and Jimmy were both convicted felons, and if they got pulled over by the cops with firearms in the car, they'd be in serious trouble (which, in the light of what they were about to do, seems absurd). But there was no Plan B. The men talked vaguely about hitting Teresa over the head and throwing her in the swimming pool to make it look as if she'd drowned, but that didn't seem feasible.

In the end, Wayne came up with the arbitrary idea that, despite his fibromyalgia, he'd knock Teresa out with a martial arts maneuver. "My intention was to put her in a chokehold, which cuts the blood off, so the person passes out within five seconds," he recalled. That way, "she wouldn't be fighting and yelling." Then, presumably, he'd strangle her—which, Wayne boasted, was how he'd killed before.

Successful murders involve careful planning, and are very specific with respect to weapon, attack location, time, and manner of death. How many interrupted burglars kill by strangulation? This was less a murder than a murder fantasy, sordid and pathetic. To Wayne and Jimmy, the crime was a boys' adventure, a daydream. Imagining themselves as skilled assassins, they hadn't thought seriously about the crime. Had they done so, they wouldn't have gone to Florida at all. "We weren't very good at it, obviously," Wayne sheepishly acknowledged.

They hadn't even decided where the murder would take place, although during their burner-phone tête-à-têtes, Wayne and Mark had narrowed it down to one of two scenarios. The first was to attack Teresa at home; the second was to target her when she was leaving the clinic. She always stayed late on Monday. She'd leave work when it was starting to get dark, exiting down the building's back stairs. To get to the parking lot, she had to walk down a secluded path at the side of the clinic, past a large outdoor air-conditioning unit with barricades around it that Wayne could hide behind. Ironically, in the past, Mark had expressed concern about her walking there ("don't walk out alone baby . . . don't forget to call me when walking to car . . . keeping u safe!") Just four weeks before the murder, he'd texted her anxiously after she left her office without calling him, as she normally did. "i'm a big girl," Teresa scoffed.

What if Teresa wasn't alone? Mark was prepared for that. Anyone with her would be "collateral damage," he said. Things might even be better that way—it would seem less like a targeted hit.

The wannabe hit men planned to make the eighteen-hour trip to Florida in a single day. Wayne, in his rented Hyundai Elantra, picked Jimmy up on Saturday, June 27, around 7:30 A.M. Jimmy was hauling a cooler, a backpack, and a fake Florida license plate he'd picked up somewhere, which he stuck on the back of the car so it didn't attract attention in Bonita Springs.

Wayne drove the first leg of the journey. They switched over somewhere in Kentucky, during a bathroom break. On the way, they kept weighing the options. Jimmy had his phone with him. Whoever wasn't driving would use it to pull up Google Maps and study aerial views of both the Jarvis Road house and Teresa's office in Estero.

With gas, restroom, and food breaks along the way, a few traffic snarls and the change of time zones, the trip took around twenty hours, and the men didn't reach Bonita Springs until the early hours of Sunday morning. On the way to Jarvis Road, they passed Teresa's office and stopped briefly to check it out, but Wayne was uncomfortable with the layout—anyone hiding behind the air-conditioner would be pretty exposed. Better the hit take place at home.

• • •

At 6:09 A.M. on Sunday, June 28, using the code Mark gave him, Wayne deactivates the alarm at 27034 Jarvis Road. He knows Mark's mom is coming by twice a day to feed the pets, but he's pretty sure they're early enough that they won't run into her. Still, to play it safe, they park in the lot of an apartment complex across the street. Wayne isn't too worried about the neighbors' security cameras. "If somebody were to see me, they'd think it was Mark anyway, so nobody would really pay any attention," he said, later. "We really didn't want to spend much time in the house . . . we really didn't want to disturb anything that morning. It was really just scouting it out." Mostly, the brief recon mission is for Jimmy, who's never been there, to see the layout of the rooms, but also to see whether the dogs, who are contained in an area behind the kitchen, will react to him. They know Wayne; Jimmy's a stranger. But they're both old and docile. They simply love on him.

Wayne knows there are weapons in the house—Mark collects guns, the kitchen's full of knives, and a pair of ornamental samurai swords hang on the living room wall—but Wayne and Jimmy aren't interested. They've decided to stick to Wayne's plan: strangulation. After scoping the layout, they decide to attack Teresa just after she gets out of her car, as she walks from the garage into the house. That way, she won't have time to grab a weapon or reach the alarm. They'll hide behind her Mercedes, they figure, then assault her as she passes through the utility room into the house.

As they're about to leave, Jimmy sees a claw hammer lying on top of Mark's toolbox. He picks it up. Grinning, he makes a hammering motion.

"Teresa's destiny," he says.

• • •

Exhausted after their all-night drive, the two would-be hit men then drive to Bonita Beach, park in a busy lot by the bathrooms and showers, and take a three-hour nap. After that, they head for the ocean. Wayne, ready for his Florida vacation, has brought swimming trunks, water shoes, and a towel, but Jimmy, who's never been outside rural Missouri, has nothing to wear. And so, around eleven A.M., the pair stop by the Walmart Supercenter on 6 Mile Cypress Parkway in Fort Myers, a two-minute drive from the Lee County Sheriff's Office. They pick up some beach wear for Jimmy and a few extra supplies. At the checkout, Wayne hands over one of the six hundred-dollar bills sent to him by Mark.

All set for lazing in the sun, the men drive up and down Estero Boulevard, checking out the beaches between Bonita Springs and Fort Myers. They walk on the pier, browse the stores, stop for lunch at a hole-in-the-wall taco shack, grab cocktails at a beachside bar, and visit the souvenir stands, where Jimmy picks up his gifts for Taylor: the Fort Myers T-shirt and the decorative plaque.

Teresa will be getting into Fort Myers at 11:25 P.M., according to Mark. Around 10:30 P.M., leaving plenty of time to prepare, Wayne and Jimmy drive back to Jarvis Road and park in the same spot outside the condo complex. Then, with their protective gear in Jimmy's backpack, they clamber through a tree-lined ditch that separates the complex from Jarvis Road, then head over to the Sieverses' residence, entering through the garage and closing the door immediately after them. Wayne checks the alarm, but Mark's mom doesn't appear to have reset it. They stay in the garage as planned, but for obvious reasons, they don't turn on the light. It's dark, stuffy, and hot in there—they open the side door to the yard and go outside from time to time to get some air. Jimmy's never seen so many stars.

At 11:03 P.M., Wayne gets a final text from Mark. "no need to call me. Hope ur having a nice day."

The two men spend the next twenty minutes helping each other into their protective clothing—they tape their wrists and ankles with some silver duct tape Jimmy's brought along, to fasten their jumpsuits more securely. Wayne puts on his safari hat; Jimmy's wearing a baseball cap. They're sticking with the plan to hide in the garage until Teresa comes home, and decide to just "wing it." Wayne finds a twelve-inch flat bar and uses it to pry open the garage side door, trying to make it look like a break-in. By the time they've finished, it's around 11:15 P.M. Teresa's flight will just have landed. The drive from Fort Myers airport to Bonita Springs is no more than twenty minutes. Plenty of time to loot and trash the house.

But unbeknownst to Wayne and Jimmy, Teresa's already on the ground. When Mark said she'd be there at 11:25 P.M., he'd already factored in the twenty-minute drive to the house. On top of that, her flight lands early. At 10:43 P.M., she's caught on the surveillance camera at the terminal concourse. At 10:51 P.M., she pays her parking ticket at the airport lot. At 10:53 P.M., she texts Mark in New York to let him know she's arrived safely. At 11:20 P.M., she turns into the driveway at 27034 Jarvis Road.

In the garage, Jimmy's sniffing around, checking out a toolbox. Wayne's admiring Mark's motorcycle. Headlights sweep up the drive. There's a rumbling sound. Lights come on. The garage door starts to lift.

Murder can be a spontaneous act, occurring in the heat of the moment, or it can be premeditated, taking place with prior intent. Teresa's killing, in a way, was both—the crime was intentional, but when the time came, it was spur-of-the-moment, nasty, and slipshod. Even when things go as planned, murder is a messy business. When botched, it's often more violent and horrifying than the perpetrator could ever imagine. People don't die easily, especially young, healthy people who fight for their life. Even if Wayne and Jimmy had killed before, neither was prepared for what was about to happen. The sheer stupidity and brutality of the crime was beyond imagination. It was cruel, atrocious, and unspeakably futile.

When he hears the garage door lifting, Wayne dives down behind a pile of boxes so the headlights don't hit him. He's not positive where Jimmy goes: is he still in the garage, or has he run into the house?

Teresa gets out of the car, walks around to the back, and pops open the trunk. She pulls out her wheeled suitcase, rolls it a little way toward the utility room, then leaves it there, at the bottom of the short flight of steps leading into the house. Wayne is crouched behind the stack of boxes in the threshold of the doorway. He's next to the chest freezer, where Mark keeps the dog food. On top of the freezer, there's a ball-peen hammer. In a panic, he grabs it and follows Teresa into the house, planning to use the hammer to knock her out. She enters the kitchen and puts down her purse on the countertop.

Then Wayne steps in the dog dish.

A loud clatter. The bowl upends and skitters across the floor. As Teresa swings around, Wayne smashes the hammer into the back of her head. He assumes the blow will knock her out, but it does nothing. She puts up her arms to defend herself. Wayne hits her twice more, but strikes her arms, not her head.

The safari hat covers most of his face, but at one point, as Teresa tries to ward off the blows, she looks him directly in the eye. She's shocked and confused, but there's something else there, too. Recognition.

She says only one word: "Why?"

At that moment, Wayne realizes: she thinks he's Mark.

Suddenly, Jimmy appears out of nowhere, and starts smacking Teresa over and over, holding the hammer with both hands. Still, she doesn't go down: she fights back violently. She lurches, stumbles, but stays on her feet. She won't give in. It's horrifying. Jimmy keeps hitting her head with the hammer, but the blows seem to have no effect. She staggers but stays conscious. The struggle goes on and on. Finally, she puts one hand on the countertop and leans forward. Another blow from Jimmy knocks her over, and she slumps slowly to the floor, face down. Jimmy keeps bashing her head in. He must have killed her, but no, she's still alive. She keeps moving, making noises as if she's trying to say something. Then there's a kind of snoring, gurgling sound. Wayne drops his hammer. Teresa is dead.

But Jimmy doesn't care. He's not done. He goes berserk, hitting her over and over again. She's lying motionless on the floor, and he keeps smashing his hammer into her brain. Wayne tells him to stop, but he won't. It sounds like somebody smashing a watermelon or a pumpkin. Wayne finally gets Jimmy to leave the kitchen—but he goes back for more. "He was laughing about it," said Wayne, later. "He said he used the claw side of the hammer."

They leave her face down on the floor, beside the refrigerator. Affixed to its side, beside a picture of Mark's mother and her partner, is a framed photograph of Mark, wearing black-framed glasses, smiling handsomely against a blue background. But take a closer look. It isn't Mark. It's Wayne.

As they leave the crime scene, Jimmy takes out the wet wipes. Even though they've been wearing gloves, he rubs down all the door handles to get rid of possible DNA. In the garage, the men help each other out of their protective clothing, which they stuff into the black backpack, along with the duct tape and the rests of the wipes. They're surprised how little blood there is. Apart from a few stray droplets, there was no blood splatter at all during the attack, just a large pool that was seeping out from under Teresa's head as they were leaving. Detective Nolen, when he reviewed the crime scene the following morning, said that in light of the crime's violence, he was surprised there wasn't blood on the ceiling.

They'd planned to ransack the house, stealing Mark's cash and rare coins, but they're so shaken by the murder, they just want to get away. Half-heartedly, as they exit the garage, Jimmy pulls a few things out of Teresa's luggage, but it's a feeble gesture. They creep through the neighborhood back to their car and hit the road. The beachgoing, holiday mood has suddenly turned somber. Before leaving Lee County, they pull over at a rest stop and clean out the car. Wayne takes a pile of trash over to a dumpster and discards his jumpsuit, the duct tape, and the used wet wipes. He tells Jimmy to use a different trash can—it would be better, he thinks, if everything isn't in the same place.

They're both in shock. Wayne is frozen and numb. Jimmy's even worse, freaked out and panicking. Wayne's taken aback—Jimmy claimed to be a contract killer. He said he does this kind of thing all the time. Now, no longer laughing, he's bug-eyed and babbling.

Three hours north of Bonita Springs, in a town called Brooksville, the men stop for gas at a RaceTrac. It's 2:30 A.M. The pumps are turned off, but the place is clearly open: eerily, there are people inside, and the lights are on. Jimmy and Wayne go over to the window. They wave. They bang on the door. Nobody pays attention. They're two dead souls walking on earth, invisible to the outside world.

• • •

In the interview room, Wayne told his story hesitantly, using vague terms ("while it was going on," "when it was over," "when it happened") or using the passive voice ("she was hit from behind"). Due to his memory problems, he told the investigators, he'd blanked out a lot of the murder scene. But when it came to peripheral, incidental details, his memory seemed perfectly intact. He clearly recalled the place he and Jimmy got lunch in Fort Myers. "I can't remember the name of it, but it's a little bitty place. . . . I think it's like a Mexican taco place or something. . . . If you're starting there on the pier . . . I think that road makes a ninety-degree turn there . . . and you're on that road going south, it was just a couple of buildings down. There's a hotel that has a bar on the roof of it. . . . We parked in that little parking lot across from there. And that's where the little taco place was at."

However peripheral they seemed, these incidental details were useful. The prosecutors needed Wayne to give them specifics, such as where and when he spent the money Mark gave him, what gas stations they went to, what they bought, where they stopped to eat, what sites they visited on Jimmy's phone. To charge someone with murder, you need more than circumstantial evidence. To find them guilty beyond a reasonable doubt, you need confirmed proof and verifiable facts.

And finally, the state had what they needed. It was time to arrest Mark Sievers.

• • •

In the eight months since Teresa's murder, Mark's world had become a living hell. He was under siege. As he must have known, the cops had been watching him closely. So, more conspicuously, had the media. Often, there were trucks and cameramen camped outside his house. He couldn't even take out the trash without being filmed. So persistent was the scrutiny, Mark had to isolate himself and his children. By this point, even Teresa's family had turned against him.

A neighbor of Mark's told Jeff Giordano, a member of Mark's legal team, that at one point during the media siege, Mark started to behave very oddly. Apparently, he would back up his car in front of her window and move forward. "He would do this twenty, thirty times—back up, put on the brake, go forward. Sit in his car and go back and forth, back and forth." While the neighbor was puzzled and alarmed, Giordano, an ex-cop and private investigator, had a different interpretation. "He's trying to lay the ground for an insanity defense," he speculated. "He knows what's coming."

Those who supported Mark also knew what was coming, although they believed him when he said he'd been framed. "We were expecting it for a long time," said his stepmother, Jennie Weckelman. "You could see the trajectory, the way everything was pointing. And of course it was Mark's best friend."

At last, on February 26, 2016, eight months after Teresa's murder and shortly after Wayne's confession, Mark Sievers was handcuffed and taken from his home to the Lee County Sheriff's Office. His neighbors watched and celebrated. "It's a great feeling for everybody in the neighborhood. People were cheering," said one. Later, dressed in a red jumpsuit and still handcuffed, Mark was perp-walked from the sheriff's office, past the waiting media, and into a patrol car, flanked by Detective Mike Downs and Sheriff Mike Scott.

Scott, who'd been critical of what he saw as the media's interference in the case, was happy to speak to them now. "He's a killer. He did the unthinkable," he told WINK News. "I'm not a hundred percent sure he's got blood in his veins. I think he might have ice." Emma and Olivia were taken to the Florida Department of Children and Families to await a shelter hearing. In May, Mark was indicted and charged with first-degree premeditated murder and conspiracy to commit first-degree premeditated murder. He was held without bond. The District Attorney announced he'd be seeking the death penalty.

• • •

The union between Mark and Wayne was broken. The brothers were now enemies. It was ironic, then, that after Mark's arrest, at least one media outlet published a photograph of Wayne identifying him as Mark, and vice versa.

PART FOUR

Chapter 19

Murder-for-Hire

In February 2016, Jimmy Ray Rodgers was extradited from St. Francois County Jail in Missouri to Collier County Jail in Naples, Florida. He was pissed that he didn't have his glasses, but otherwise, he wasn't too concerned. The cops, he believed, had nothing on him. They wouldn't keep him for long. Sure, his mugshot had been on television, along with those of Mark and Wayne, but all they had against him was Taylor's statement.

By now, he'd managed to convince Taylor that the cops had lied to her. After threatening to take her kids away and send her to jail for life—which, according to Jimmy, they had no authority to do—they'd fed her the "hit man" story and were now paying her to say things that weren't true. Swayed by Jimmy's revised version of events (despite his midnight confession), Taylor promised that, if necessary, she'd swear under oath she'd been manipulated by law enforcement. As soon as that happened, Jimmy thought they'd have to drop the charges. "hopfully i will be going home soon," he emailed his brother, Jack.

He was especially irritated that Taylor had told investigators he was known as "Jimmy the Hammer." Now, he complained, "the media is using my nick name against me." He instructed Taylor to backtrack and give them a different story. She suggested she could say that people called him Jimmy the Hammer because he was "always fixing stuff." Jimmy found that laughable. He told her to say "the hammer" referred to his dick. Taylor agreed, and added that, if anyone asked her, she'd tell them it was his childhood nickname. Jimmy was exasperated by her idiocy. "I pointed out that people would not be talking about the size of a young kid's dick."

The couple's relationship was tangled and confusing. Taylor still loved Jimmy and hoped to marry him one day, but her confession had caused him to be charged with murder. She was constantly being seduced by the media. "i know you love me but considering the position im in i would like an explaination as to why your lieing? i just want you to tell the truth tayler. my life is on the line here," he wrote.

He was furious with her but told himself she was too stupid to know any better. More fundamentally, perhaps, the couple stayed together out of necessity. Taylor was Jimmy's main contact in the outside world. His brother, Jack, helped him by putting money on his books but was too busy to give him the support he needed. Plus, Taylor was the mother of his only child. In March 2016, she'd given birth to a seven-pound, six-ounce daughter, Jazlyn Paislee Rose ("She's definitely got your chubby rosey cheeks," Taylor wrote).

Because Jimmy's was such a high-profile case, he was assigned a team of three attorneys from the public defender's office: Chief Assistant Public Defender Kathleen Fitzgeorge, and Assistant Public Defenders Donald McFarlane and Rexford Darrow II. Jimmy was conspicuously unimpressed. He was particularly dismissive of Ms. Fitzgeorge, who, he believed, had taken his case merely "to have her name on the news." He begged McFarlane to get a sworn statement from Taylor that she'd been lying to the police, but McFarlane, according to Jimmy, said "he would of loved to do that but being that he is a assistant public defender they can't spend the money . . ." He couldn't even speak to his lawyers on the phone from prison, he complained, because they couldn't afford to take collect calls.

Still, he continued to believe his case would be dropped. The only thing keeping him in jail, he assumed, was Taylor's statement to the cops, and he could easily prove not only that the police had pressured her to lie, but they were even paying her to do so. He was shocked, then, in early April 2016, when Donald McFarlane told him the state was going to take the case to trial, and it would probably take "a year or two" before that happened. Jimmy couldn't believe it. Two more years in a Florida jail? "i pointed out that speedy trial act is 180 days. he just roled his eyes at me," he wrote his brother. Still, he tried to stay upbeat. "there is not a dout in my mind that we will win," he told Taylor, reminding her again to send him his glasses ("i cannot see shit and am blind").

On April 11, Jimmy turned twenty-six. It was a gloomy birthday. Conditions in the jail were starting to get him down. He'd lost so much weight, they'd put him on a special protein diet, but it wasn't helping. "i got to bed with hunger pains in here almost every night," he told Taylor. She had news that made things even worse: she'd been brought down to Florida to be questioned by a Grand Jury, and while she was there, she'd been seduced once more by the media.

In a television interview, she'd referred to him yet again by his nickname. Jimmy was incensed. He saw the TV interview in prison, and told Jack to watch the clip on YouTube. "you will not like it and you will see she is lieing to the press during it," he wrote. Taylor's Grand Jury testimony must have been equally damning, because on May 6, Jimmy was indicted on charges of first-degree murder. He didn't hear from Taylor for a while after that. Jack told him that she'd been given a "no contact" order. Jimmy didn't think it was legit. "its just a scare tacktick," he told his brother. "she is so dumb that she believes them."

It wasn't until June that Jimmy learned how and why Wayne had been arrested—that he'd been "turned in" by his mother- and father-in-law "because he had told them he was going to teresa house to do computer work the weekend she was murdered." Now, Jimmy could understand why Wayne didn't want to go to trial. "wayne is compleatly fucked," he wrote Taylor, who'd already broken the "no contact" order with apparent impunity. "we no longer got to worry about him killing you or me or our kids." He didn't realize Wayne had implicated him in the crime. He still thought the only thing that tied him to the murder was Taylor's confession—or, as he characterized it, "the detective's sworn statement with taylers name on it."

But he was finding it hard to look on the bright side. He'd been in jail for over four months, and his attorneys still hadn't sent him a copy of his discovery material. Prison conditions were miserable. Jack was too busy to answer his emails. Jimmy couldn't afford to call anyone, and he was suffering from hunger and lack of sunlight. "im broke as a joke and look like a tooth pick. i look like im dieing of cansear. im peal white and thin as a pole," he emailed Taylor. Then, in June, he had more bad news. "the prosicuter has anounced that he is asking for the death sentence. he wants to kill me and have me put to death tayler. dispite wayne already admitteing to being the one who killed this woman."

His attorneys, when they visited, were worse than useless, in Jimmy's opinion. "one of my lawyers 'kathleen' told me that she knew nothing about my case other than what she has seen on tv," he emailed Jack. When he complained to "rex one of my other lawyers," the attorney's response was even more dispiriting. "rex said that kathleen is a head of him on the case that he hadn't even watched the case on tv . . . he told me that he didnt know shit about my case ither other than what he heard me say in the 10 or so minet than he has spent in a room with me talking."

During their visits, Jimmy complained, all his attorneys wanted to do was talk about themselves and their own problems. When it came to the murder charges, "my lawyers tell me they are not going even to look clousely at my case until clouse to trial which they say will be in the winter of next year." To Taylor, he summed things up. "im 140lbs starved, pale, and facing the death sentance for a crime i didn't do." And he still didn't have his glasses.

Throughout 2016, Taylor kept him up to date on Jazlyn's progress, how she was growing and crawling. She sent him pictures of her other children, too—Jimmy thought of them as his own, and didn't want them to forget him. She told him about Jazlyn's first Easter ("My Uncle Randy grilled for the holiday. It was really good pulled pork, tater salad, and deviled eggs"). Jimmy, nostalgic, began to grow excited about his upcoming release. "im glade Ozzie is big for his age like Oaklyn. i cant wait to teach him foot ball, buy him a bb gun, and to take all the kids fishing."

But Taylor had her own life to lead. She got a job at Proffer Produce, a grocery wholesaler, and started to make new friends. By spring 2017, their relationship was starting to fall apart. They hadn't seen each other face-to-face in over a year. "I loved you but now I feel that we don't no one another any more," Taylor emailed him on March 3.

Jimmy tried to make her see reason. "don't thank that just because im in jail now that im a different person than the loving caring boyfriend i was all the way up until the very day i was arrested and took away from you." But his sweet talk didn't work. Taylor's messages got briefer and briefer. When she stopped writing altogether, Jimmy, in denial, assumed she'd got another "no contact" order, but he was wrong. By the time his case came to trial in October 2019, almost four years after his arrest, Taylor had remarried, and was raising Jazlyn with another man.

Equally disturbing: he'd learned Taylor's testimony wasn't the only evidence against him. His attorneys had shown him Wayne's proffer statement, as well as the security camera footage of the two of them shopping in Walmart. Even if Taylor recanted her statements under oath, Jimmy, too, it seemed, was "compleatly fucked." He'd been charged with first-degree homicide in what was potentially a capital case, and unlike Wayne, he'd turned down the deal put forward by the prosecution. (It wasn't much of a deal—they'd offered him life without parole.)

Jury selection for Jimmy's trial began on October 1, 2019. Both his and Mark's attorneys requested a change of venue—Teresa's murder had received so much media attention that many felt it would be tough to find people who hadn't already heard about the crime. But the judge refused. News channels have a very short memory, and in the years since Teresa's death, there'd been plenty more attention-grabbing murders, scandals, and outrages. In January 2017, for example, police in Fort Myers arrested twenty-one members of a notorious criminal gang known as the "Lake Boyz," whose trials were a riveting saga that went on for years. Also, a week into jury selection, two women were murdered in Cape Coral on the same night: one strangled to death as she slept in her bed; the second strangled, beaten, pushed out of a car, and run over repeatedly. Media coverage of these crimes, and the search for the perpetrator, redirected much attention from the Jimmy's trial.

Of course, some potential jurors had to be dismissed for other reasons—they had been Teresa's patients, for example, or they knew the Sievers children, or they had moral or religious convictions against the death penalty. A few had followed the case closely at the time it was unfolding, and these had to be eliminated, but they were in the minority. Most people in the jury pool were unaware Jimmy's trial was such a big deal.

For the most part, those who recalled the case did so only vaguely: "I thought it was a doctor—somebody died, and allegedly there was a friend involved." "I know there was a doctor that was killed." "I just know that somebody, unfortunately, lost their life, allegedly." "I can't remember anything except the people accused of the crime . . . maybe extradition. Somebody was far away." Even those who recalled the murder more fully thought they'd be able to weigh the evidence with an open mind.

Jury selection took four days—longer than usual, but this was a death-eligible crime. In the full glare of the media, things had to be done carefully, and by the book. The final jury contained seven women and five men. In keeping with the local demographics, they skewed older. Of the twelve jurors, five were retired; those still actively working included a pilot, a high-school teacher, a credit clerk, and two stay-at-home moms.

Trials, especially those involving capital murder, can take years to come to court. Attorneys must gather evidence, subpoena witnesses, scrutinize discovery material, and take depositions. As a result, by the time things kick off, the defendant might have spent years in prison—long enough for the initial shock to be over, and for them to get used to prison life. On the other hand, this extended stretch of time can lead them to build up irrational hopes, to become obsessed with their legal case, and to assume—often blindly—that when people finally hear their side of the story, their whole terrible ordeal will be over.

By the time Jimmy came to court, he'd spent more than four years behind bars, and was fully convinced he'd be home by Christmas. Despite Wayne's confession and the CCTV footage, he still believed that Taylor's statements were the only plausible evidence that he was involved in Teresa's murder. And even if Taylor testified against him, whatever she said would surely be thrown out once the jury learned she was being paid by the cops.

The judge in Jimmy's case had given permission for cameras to be present in the courtroom. The trial was filmed by a documentary production team who'd been following the case ever since Teresa's murder, and was also livestreamed by the Law and Crime Network. Many people think livestreaming trials makes them into public entertainment, reducing their seriousness—and it's true that making the trial publicly accessible stirred up visceral emotions in the online audience. At the same time, few people have direct experience with the criminal justice system. You could argue that watching real trials helps teach people how different they are from TV shows, which tend to break things into isolated, dramatic moments, resisting longer and more nuanced messages.

In general, the more family support a defendant has in court, the better the chance of a favorable verdict. If a jury sees someone as a real human being surrounded by people who know and love them, they're less likely to convict. Unfortunately, major trials are usually lengthy and tedious, and only the most devoted supporters manage to stick it out. In Jimmy's case, although thousands of people have since watched the trial online, there were perhaps five or six people on the public benches every day.

His only family support came from his brother, who, now working as an attorney himself, had a busy schedule and couldn't attend regularly. Mark's stepmother, Jennie Weckelman, was present every day, including during the jury *voir dire*. She didn't know Jimmy and certainly wasn't supporting him; she was there for Mark. If the jury found Jimmy innocent, the "hit man theory" would no longer stand, and there was a strong chance that Mark, too, would be found not guilty.

On the judge's bench was the genial, smiling Bruce Kyle, a Catholic Republican who'd served four terms in the Florida

House of Representatives before being elected to the 20th Circuit Court bench in 2006. Hamid Hunter, the lead prosecutor, resembled a young Fats Domino. "I didn't have any feeling about the assignment," he said later, "but it ended up being the most high-profile case of my career." Hunter's delivery was slow-paced and straightforward, with no rhetorical flourishes. He was assisted by Cynthia Ross, an older attorney with a gentler approach. Jimmy, scrubbed, polished, groomed, and civilized, wore a smart blazer, blue shirt, red tie, and glasses. His hair, cut short and neatly gelled, came down a short point in the middle of his forehead, like child werewolf Eddie Munster. His eyes were glazed over with boredom, or perhaps despair.

During the proceedings, some were surprised to see Jimmy, accompanied by a law enforcement officer, sporadically walking up to the judge's bench with his three public defenders (who'd now been joined by a fourth, Jay Brizel). In Florida, defendants have a right to be present at all material stages of the trial, including sidebar conferences. It did seem a little odd, however, when Jimmy approached the judge's bench. He was accompanied by his guard, four public defenders, plus the two prosecutors and the court reporter. Sidebars looked more like football huddles.

The defense's case was predicated on the theory that Wayne killed Teresa because he wanted Mark for himself. Jimmy, no doubt on the advice of his attorneys, didn't testify in court, but later expanded on this theory. "Think about it," he said. "You've got Mark Sievers, who's a male nurse, and Wayne Wright, who wears hot pink, and the two of them are talking to each other for three, four hours a day. Two grown men calling each other at two in the morning and this has been going on for years. Just think about it. They're both gay. That's just what it is."

The problem for the defense was that none of the salacious texts between Mark, Wayne, and Teresa had been allowed into evidence, on the basis that there's nothing illegal about having an unusual sex life. It was difficult, then, for them to prove that Wayne was in love with Mark, apart from oblique references here and there. In her opening statement, Kathleen Fitzgeorge said, of Wayne and Mark, "the evidence will show they had quite a bizarre relationship," but as it turned out, nothing about this "bizarre relationship" was ever brought into play. In fact, the matter was never mentioned again.

The air-conditioned courtroom was chilly—a couple of the jurors bought blankets to wrap themselves in. At least one was reprimanded by the judge for falling asleep during the testimony, which wasn't particularly surprising, although the attorneys certainly weren't to blame. Hamid Hunter's opening statement was striking and concise. "This case," he began, "was about the perfect marriage, the perfect friendship, the perfect alibi, and the perfect murder."

Yet once the opening statements were over, despite the high stakes—Jimmy was facing the possibility of the death penalty—the proceedings were, as with most long trials, dull and tedious. Most witnesses had a connection to the case that was professional, not personal. Their testimony dealt with facts, not feelings. They'd never known Teresa and had no emotional link to the crime.

The defense argued that Jimmy had been framed. After Teresa's murder, the police, announced Kathleen Fitzgeorge (who made the opening statement), found themselves "in a bit of a bind." She went on, describing Teresa dismissively, "It's the high-profile murder of a doctor, pretty young doctor, young mother, very sad, very tragic." Since the police had no suspects, claimed Fitzgeorge, they decided it must be the husband. She claimed that Wayne killed Teresa for reasons of his own; then he put half the weight of the murder on Jimmy. She reminded them that Wayne was a five-time convicted felon, and that he'd lied a number of times during his proffer, sending them down several "blind alleys." First, he claimed he wasn't at the crime scene and didn't do anything; then he finally admitted he beat Teresa to death with a hammer. "That's a big swing," said Fitzgeorge. "No pun intended."

Things kicked off with a steady flow of first responders, paramedics, and law enforcement officers, including Jamie Nolen, David Lebid, and Michael Downs, as well as detectives from Missouri and various other crime scene investigators. Over the next few days, witnesses included five digital forensics analysts, a DNA analyst, an FBI trace evidence analyst, a medical examiner, a document analyst, and fingerprint analyst, two telecommunications analysts, and security personnel from Walmart, RaceTrac, and Circle K.

Crime scene examiner Kimberly Van Waus spent two days going over photographs of Jarvis Road and describing items of evidence she'd collected, assessed, and catalogued, right down to hairs from the Sievers family pets. FBI trace evidence examiner Linda Otterstatter, who found microscopic fibers at the crime scene that contained Jimmy's DNA, reminded the jury of the Locard Principle: "Every contact leaves a trace."

However dull it may have been for the jury, the testimony of these witnesses allowed the state to bring in the physical evidence they needed to present: phone records, surveillance tapes, fibers, fingerprints, and GPS data. Even then, Jimmy's attorneys were undaunted. The evidence showed Jimmy was in Florida with Wayne—so what? According to the defense theory, he simply "helped a friend who had problems falling asleep while he drove, and in exchange for that, he got caught up in another man's madness." They argued that Wayne, "the puppet master," killed Teresa alone, spontaneously, in a fit of sudden anger. Jimmy's only crime was not going straight to the cops—but who could blame him? Wayne was a dangerous man.

Testimony from personal witnesses was more compelling. In a shaking voice, Sandra Hoskins recounted the morning Teresa didn't show up to work. Mark Petrites described his emotions upon discovering Teresa's dead body—"it was a very eerie feeling being inside the house with that atrocious finding." Jimmy's brother talked about their abusive upbringing. Wayne, for a day and a half, reprised the confession made during his proffer. Jimmy's defense attorneys, of course, used Wayne's earlier lies against him. They claimed his story was fabricated. The only evidence to tie Mark to Teresa's murder, argued defense attorney Donald McFarlane, was the uncorroborated words of a five-time convicted felon. "Curtis Wright is the only person that hit that woman," he yelled. "And he's lying, to save his own worthless skin!"

But it was Taylor Shomaker who dug Jimmy's grave.

• • •

Taylor hadn't seen her ex-boyfriend for more than four years. She'd moved on. Her new husband was bringing up Jimmy's daughter, Jazlyn, now three years old. Further, she was testifying against a man she'd betrayed, given up to the cops, and now was possibly sending to the death chamber. She was so frightened of having to face Jimmy that she was actually scared to enter the courtroom—Cynthia Ross had to ask the judge's permission to go out into the hallway and guide her through the doors.

Taylor, who'd put on even more weight in the last four years, wore a short-sleeved gray dress, a draped sleeveless cardigan, and a nose ring. Although physically sturdy, she was obviously emotionally fragile, and avoided looking at Jimmy as she passed through the room. On the stand, to calm her down, Cynthia Ross suggested she drink some water. When Taylor lifted the glass to her lips, her hand was visibly trembling. Ross told her to "take a deep breath" and answer the questions as best she could. Judge Kyle kept reminding her to raise her voice.

Hiding her pale face behind long, thick hair, Taylor recalled how she'd first met Jimmy a few months before Wayne's wedding, and how she'd moved into his trailer shortly thereafter, when she got evicted for not paying her rent. She described Jimmy getting back from Florida with his new clothes and gifts for her, and how she'd greeted him with the news she was pregnant. With tears in her eyes—Ms. Ross handed her a Kleenex—she told the jury about Jimmy asking her to throw his jumpsuit into the ditch, and how, in bed that night, he confessed to killing Mark's wife, boasting that he'd used a hammer.

"And did Mr. Rodgers have a nickname?" asked Ms. Ross.

"Yes," admitted Taylor.

"And what was that?"

"Jimmy the Hammer."

At one point, during a break during Taylor's testimony, Jimmy approached the judge's bench for a sidebar with his attorneys; as he did so, Taylor became even more distraught, putting up her right hand against her face so she wouldn't have to see him. After the sidebar, Ms. Ross showed Taylor a photograph taken at Wayne's wedding at Walther Park in De Soto. When asked what she was wearing, she replied, with a brief smile, "My black polka dot dress." In the picture, Jimmy stood beside her, grinning proudly.

Taylor described how difficult it had been for her to go to the cops, how painful it was for her to be in the courtroom, and how torn she'd felt about asking the sheriff's office for financial assistance. Finally, she was asked to identify Jimmy by describing an item of clothing he was wearing ("red tie," she said, after a quick glance). Jimmy remained stoic as Taylor testified, but his breathing seemed shallow, and his face reddened. Occasionally he jotted something down, and once or twice, he leaned over to speak to Donald McFarlane, on his left.

Cynthia Ross finished her questioning, but Taylor's ordeal was far from over. She now had to face a painful cross-examination from defense attorney Kathleen Fitzgeorge, whose argument echoed Jimmy's—that the cops had talked Taylor into turning him in, and had paid her to testify against him. "The police were aware of what they had in Ms. Shomaker," she proclaimed. "An unemployed, uneducated single mother." Her picture of Taylor echoed Jimmy's. "Mr. Rodgers was her protector physically, financially, and emotionally until she hooked up with the police."

Fitzgeorge had a patronizing, nagging manner. She was disorganized and repetitive, insinuating the police had blackmailed Taylor into testifying against Jimmy by threatening to take her kids away and put her in prison. She got Taylor to admit she'd given a lot of media interviews about the case, and that the documentary team that was following the story had flown her and her new husband out to California, put her up in a fancy hotel, and introduced her to George Clooney.

Ultimately, none of this came to anything, but Fitzgeorge did make one significant strike against Taylor's testimony: that she was being paid by the police, and was still receiving money at the time of trial. After an initial 1,050 dollars, she'd been getting 400 dollars a month for three years. "She's a grifter," proclaimed Fitzgeorge. "She's looking to make money. She'd do anything to get it."

But to Hamid Hunter, who gave the prosecution's closing arguments, Taylor's payments were neither here nor there. The police had made it very clear that the money was meant to help Taylor out with her expenses, and wasn't contingent on her testifying in court. Her statements, on top of Wayne's confession, made the facts irrefutable: this was a classic case of murder-for-hire.

After nearly two days of deliberation, on October 23, 2019, the jury returned with a verdict—a confusing one. Jimmy was acquitted of first-degree homicide and conspiracy, but was guilty of the lesser charge: second-degree murder *without* a weapon, in addition to trespassing. Presumably, the jury believed that Jimmy took part in the murder, but either he didn't strike any blows, or if he did, the two men shared one hammer between them. It was perplexing. "I have no explanation to give for the jury verdict, but I accept and respect it," said Hamid Hunter, complacently. But, as

Jimmy's defense attorney Donald McFarlane told the press afterward, you can't be found guilty of murder without a weapon when there's clear evidence the murder was committed *with* a weapon. Still, there's no law that says jury verdicts must be consistent, and to Jimmy, the outcome was the same: life without parole.

Chapter 20

Capital Crime

In the eight months between Teresa's death and his arrest, Mark had gone broke. Top-notch defense attorneys don't come cheap. By February 2016, he was living on worker's comp payments, plus the Social Security money he qualified for to care for his daughters. The house on Jarvis Road, Mark's condo in Missouri, his car, his beloved motorcycle—all had been seized by the state, and he'd been declared indigent. The 4.4 million dollars in life insurance payments had gone to Teresa's sister, Annie. She'd invested the money in a trust fund for Emma and Olivia, who were staying nearby with their grandmother in a rented condo. The girls could talk on the phone with their father, and exchange emails, but their contact was strictly monitored. They weren't allowed to talk about Teresa or discuss the case.

After his arrest, Mark was taken to the Lee County Jail, placed in solitary confinement, and kept there for almost four years. Inevitably, the ordeal wore him down. Over time, according to his mitigation expert, Jeff Giordano, he was so traumatized that he became virtually catatonic. "I'd visit him in jail and he'd sometimes sit there silently for hours," recalled Giordano. Mark's trial began on November 12, 2019, just twenty days after Jimmy's concluded.

His family and defense team were unhappy about this, arguing it left them inadequate time for preparation in the light of Jimmy's verdict.

They were also disappointed that, even though Mark and Jimmy were being charged with the same crime, their trials were separated (although the proceedings were bundled together: same courtroom, same judge, same prosecutors), which led to the loss of valuable attorney cooperation. Mark didn't get to see Jimmy's trial, but he knew the verdict didn't bode well. He also knew that his face was all over the media, and his trial would be livestreamed by Court TV and the Law and Crime Network. As an extrovert, Mark used to love publicity; after years of hounding by press and police, he'd no doubt changed his attitude. He was surely aware that the morbid fascination engendered by Jimmy's trial would be notched up exponentially when his own case came to court.

For prospective jurors, as with Jimmy's trial, the vetting process was far-reaching; potential candidates were questioned closely about their moral and ethical attitudes toward the death penalty. Again, as in Jimmy's case, the final jury consisted primarily of retired white women (there were nine women and three men). This may have been simply a reflection of the local demographic, but it might also have been a strategy on the part of the defense. Legal scholars have shown that older jurors are generally more tolerant of human frailty than younger ones. Then again, these kinds of studies are always contingent—others suggest older jurors are more certain of their verdict decisions than younger ones, and more likely to convict. And even if jurors empathize with the defendant, that might not always be a good thing: the type of person who feels deep sympathy might not be easily persuaded by the fact-oriented arguments of fellow jurors. Either way, empathy plays less of a part in jury decisions than it did a few decades ago—apparently, jurors these days are likely to have "reduced sensitivity for the emotions of others" because they're so used to seeing violence and emotional trauma in the media.

Mark had more family support in the courtroom than Jimmy, although only his stepmother was there every day of the trial. Bonnie's health issues limited her attendance, but she and Melanie were there most of the time. His brother, Scott, and his stepsister, Connie, came to court when they could, but they both lived a long way from Florida and had pressing work schedules.

Before his arrest, when news cameras had caught him taking out the trash and doing errands, Mark had seemed jaunty, defensive, even cocky. Striding to and from the courthouse with his attorneys, even during his perp walk, he'd held his head up high, as if he had nothing to be ashamed of. Four years in solitary must have ground him down; nonetheless, in the courtroom, he'd got his moxie back. Poised and self-satisfied, he looked clean and well-groomed, even handsome, in a neatly pressed dark blue suit with a lighter shirt and tie. The white handkerchief peeping from his breast pocket was presumably intended to wipe away tears; in fact, he took it out only once, to sneeze.

Throughout the proceedings, he sat with his head mostly lowered, occasionally pushing his stylish glasses up his nose (defense attorneys often encourage their clients to wear glasses, even if they're non-prescription, because it's been shown people associate glasses with intelligence, honesty, and decreased propensity to commit a violent crime). For the majority of the trial, he never showed the least sign of emotion, but sat making notes on a legal pad, contemplating them from time to time with the air of a satisfied author.

This seems like an odd way to behave throughout a capital murder trial, but Mark's demeanor was orchestrated by his defense team. Jurors in the courtroom (and observers at home, if the trial is being livestreamed) watch the defendant closely, cataloging their mannerisms and reactions, ready to pounce on smirks, smiles, grimaces, and tears. For this reason, defense attorneys often advise their clients to look down and make notes (or, at least, scribble on a legal pad) so they're not judged by their facial expressions and eye contact, or lack of it. Staying studious and attentive may make them appear more sympathetic, as well.

In some ways, Mark was in a stronger position than Jimmy. He clearly wasn't in Florida at the time Teresa was killed. On the other hand, as the purported initiator of the crime, the charges against him—first-degree murder and criminal conspiracy—were far more serious. Mark's family, short of money, had reached out to a few high-profile lawyers to see if any of them would take the case. No one seemed interested until, by a stroke of luck, they were approached by a prominent and charismatic attorney named Anthony Faga, who offered to take the case at a state salary—essentially, *pro bono*. Faga, who was based in Naples, Florida, had worked with some notorious clients. In 1981, he defended the two men responsible for a quadruple homicide known as the Tri-Willow Nursery Murders; in 1982, he represented John Lennon's killer, Mark David Chapman, in a right-to-die petition during his hunger strike at Attica. Unfortunately, halfway through trial preparations, Faga was diagnosed with cancer, and passed away, age sixty-seven, on October 3, 2018.

At that point, it was too late to appoint new counsel, so Mark was defended by one of Faga's associates, forty-three-year-old Michael Mummert, who, when it came to homicide, was a novice. Although he'd handled over thirty felony trials, this was only his third murder case, and only one of the previous two had gone to trial. Nor was he a "death-qualified attorney," which meant that, if Mark was found guilty and the death penalty was on the table, Mummert would have to be replaced by a more experienced colleague. Later, Mummert admitted he had been woefully underqualified to represent Mark. He hadn't been trained to deal with such a serious capital case, and made many mistakes, including failing to ask Wayne about his traumatic brain injury, or whether he'd been asked to take a polygraph.

"Mike was sincere and optimistic," conceded Mark's stepmother. But in the courtroom, Mummert resembled a ham actor, making theatrical arm movements, blustering, posturing, and smacking his tongue annoyingly. Rather than speaking off-the-cuff, like the prosecutor, he relied on notes, shuffling papers, glancing at them after every sentence, sometimes even in the middle. Incidentally, Mummert, like Mark, was completely bald, which brought a droll aspect to the proceedings, especially when Wayne's glowing dome also entered the room. Online, court-watchers were bemused. "Mark Sievers chose another doppelgänger as his attorney," observed one. "Did the attorney and the defendant coordinate the 'cue ball' look together?" wondered another.

In *Strangers on a Train*, suave, gullible Guy Haines, after having a few drinks, speaks openly to the sinister Charles Bruno about his unhappy marriage, unaware that Bruno is completely obsessed with him. Without Guy's knowledge, Bruno murders his wife, hoping it will bring the two men together. Of course, he's a deluded psychopath.

This scenario, in a nutshell, formed Mark's defense. In a letter to his mitigation specialist Jeffery Giordano, Mark, referring to himself in the third person and to Wayne by his first name, Curtis, wrote that "CW planned and carried out this horrific crime on his own." He speculated that Wayne may have been motivated by a longtime sexual fixation with Mark and his jealousy of Mark's lifestyle. Mark said he'd told Wayne about his open marriage, and how he and Teresa had sometimes fantasized about Wayne joining them in bed. But for Wayne, Mark suspected, fantasies weren't enough. He wrote, "CW was *obsessed* with Mark!"

The two men's relationship was the crux of the trial. The state needed to show that their childhood bond was strong and deep enough that Wayne would kill Mark's wife on his friend's behalf. But if they put too much weight on the men's relationship, they'd be ceding the ground to the defense, who hoped to prove that Wayne killed Teresa alone, because he was obsessed with Mark, and wanted him for himself. Mark's attorneys considered using the men's kinky sexual texts to demonstrate Wayne's deranged passion for their client. The State didn't want to open this Pandora's box, and in the end, Mummert agreed, speculating that if any members of the jury were homophobic, it would have damaged their case.

Moreover, entering the texts into evidence would inevitably bring up Teresa's aggressive temper and her unconventional sex life, which might lead some jurors, even unconsciously, to lose sympathy with her. As a result, when in his cross-examination Michael Mummert brought up the text Mark sent Wayne about "wearing Angie's panties" to the wedding, Hunter immediately objected. At a sidebar, Judge Kyle allowed the text to be entered into evidence but added a wry warning. "The further we go down the rabbit hole with people sleeping naked and wearing panties—when we're in, we're all the way in."

The same experts who spoke at Jimmy's trial were called to the stand again—cops, digital forensic experts, crime scene technicians, record custodians, trace evidence examiners. There were the same procedural detours, the same dull testimony. There was so little to report, in fact, that it made headline news when Mark, feeling ill, was speedily ushered out of the courtroom one morning to vomit loudly into a nearby trash can.

Things changed when Mark Petrites took the stand. A composed, slightly stiff-looking middle-aged man with a thin mustache, the doctor explained to the jury that he'd met Teresa in 1996, when they were both doing a surgical residency, and they'd reconnected after running into each other again in Florida. He had a professional relationship with Teresa, proclaimed Dr. Petrites.

"Her patients may have something like a gallbladder problem, or breast cancer, and she would refer them to me."

But, he added, they also had a close personal relationship. His wife Michele was one of Teresa's dearest friends. The couples socialized, went out to dinner, celebrated their children's birthdays together, and spent time at each other's homes. Dr. Petrites was formal and collected, which made it even more difficult to bear when, as he described entering the Sieverses' kitchen and finding Teresa dead on the floor, you could tell he was forcing back tears.

During his interview with Lieutenant Nolen, Mark had implied that, like Teresa, he was very close to Mark and Michele Petrites. He referred to Dr. Petrites as "Uncle Mark," the name his daughters used. But in the witness box, Petrites disavowed his association with "Mr. Sievers," saying he knew him only "through association with Dr. Sievers." Until Teresa's death, said Dr. Petrites, "I wasn't very close to him."

Petrites's testimony became highly significant after the trial, when Mark's legal team, as part of their appeal, claimed the surgeon hadn't told the truth about the men's friendship. In fact, as the defense later proved, the two Marks had been good friends. They went sailing and rode bikes together. They swapped restaurant recommendations, shared funny things their children had said, discussed what iPhone to buy. Mark Sievers gave Mark Petrites a dehumidifier and a shredder, and made him gluten-free sandwiches, soup, and French toast.

More significantly, Dr. Petrites had trusted and encouraged Mark to take his wife, Michele, to the range and teach her to shoot. When Petrites wanted to buy his wife a gun for Christmas in 2011, Mark gave him advice about what weapon to buy ("17 or glock 19"). The gift went over well—"she was absolutely tickled." The surgeon urged Mark to take Michele shooting as often as possible—he liked the fact that it made her "frisky" ("When r u taking my girl back to the range?") and asked him to look out for her ("Take care of MY girl 4 me!!!").

After the murder, when Dr. Petrites immediately distanced himself from "Mr. Sievers," he clearly downplayed the nature of their former relationship. Mark's legal team later tried to claim that, by doing so, Dr. Petrites had perjured himself at trial. Their argument was rejected.

A more composed Taylor Shomaker testified on the seventh day of trial, November 19, 2019. Gone was the mournful moon face. She'd lost a little weight and was sporting a new look—bouffant hair, fashion-forward glasses, and a black lace top. In demeanor, she was relaxed—after all, Jimmy wasn't in the courtroom, and she had nothing to fear from Mark, whom she'd met only very briefly, at Wayne's wedding (finding him, as she told the prosecutor, "kind of a perv"). Again, she described Jimmy's confession, although during questioning by the defense, she confirmed that Mark didn't know Jimmy was involved in the murder, which made the plan, as Hamid Hunter explained, "what the law textbooks call a line conspiracy; from A to B, from B to C. Jimmy Rodgers was C."

As the defense made clear, when it came to the case against Mark, the only real evidence against him was Wayne's confession, in which he claims, as Guy Haines puts it in *Strangers on a Train*, the murder "had not been his will. It had been the will of his double, working through him." Now, for the first time since their arrest four years earlier, the "doubles" were about to meet face to face. Mark's former "brother" was due to testify on the second day of the trial, December 3, 2019.

Court-watchers anticipated his entrance with fervent curiosity. In fact, even while they were in prison awaiting trial, there'd already been tension between the two men. In July 2018, Wayne had written a letter to the judge asking to be moved to a different facility after hearing a rumor that Mark was working to harm him, in cahoots with an inmate who used to be a Lee County Detective and still had connections in the sheriff's office. The rumors were never proven, but to be on the safe side, Mark's one-time doppelgänger had been moved to a different jail.

After a short break in the middle of the afternoon, a guard led Wayne into the courtroom from the holding facility. His wrists were shackled by handcuffs attached to a waist chain, which made it awkward for him to raise his hand to be sworn in by the judge (one of his cuffs was finally loosened). His demeanor was humble, a little sheepish, and he carefully kept his face averted from Mark. As his former doppelgänger crossed the room, Mark lowered his gaze, scowling momentarily, but there was no eye contact.

The men's bond was broken. Now, apart from their glistening domes, they were no longer alike. Four years in solitary may have left Mark psychologically devastated, but physically, he looked sleek and trim. Gussied up in his neatly pressed suit and tie, he could have been a smart young CEO. Wayne, in contrast, had gained weight in prison. He had a football-sized stomach, and his once-impressive muscles had turned to flab. With his hangdog demeanor and shuffling gait, he looked more like Mark's opposite than his double.

Boldly, Hamid Hunter got straight to the point. "Mr. Wright, who killed Teresa Sievers?"

"Jimmy Rodgers and I physically did it," said Wayne, his voice unexpectedly soft.

"Why did you do it?" asked Hunter.

"I was asked to do it," said Wayne.

"By who?" asked Hunter.

Looking directly at the prosecutor, Wayne raised his voice.

"Mr. Sievers," he said.

"Is Mr. Sievers in court today?"

"Yes, he is."

Looking directly at Mark, Wayne identified his former friend:

"He's the middle gentleman there at the table, in the darker colored jacket."

Although Wayne was a "many-time convicted felon," as Michael Mummert repeatedly reminded the jury, his testimony was innately credible. Once again, he described his long friendship with Mark, the planning of the crime itself, Jimmy's involvement, and the burner phones. The drive to Florida was recounted, along with the horrible, botched murder. His somber, deadpan tone faltered only once, when Hamid Hunter showed him photographs of his wedding, enlarged for the benefit of the jury, to remind him of when and how Mark first raised the question of killing his wife. On seeing the photographs, Wayne relaxed a little and smiled. "They bring back good memories," he said. (Ironically, when asked to identify himself, it took him a moment to work out which was him and which was Mark.)

Mark himself didn't take the stand—a disappointment for those following the trial, who were hoping to gain some insight into a mind many considered to be evil, or perhaps psychotic. According to his stepmother, Mark struggled with this decision. "He strongly wanted to tell his side of the story, point out lies and inconsistencies with what Wayne was telling, and allow people to see for themselves that he was no threat," she said.

In the end, however, his defense team decided the risks outweighed the reward. Having Mark testify would open the door for cross-examination about his extramarital affairs, his jealousy of Nick Delgado, and Teresa's threats of divorce. Moreover, during a tough cross-examination, even the most prepared defendant can display signs of fear or emotional discomfort. Also, in Mark's case, his size may have spoken against him. His bulk made him seem intimidating (especially in contrast with Teresa, who was petite).

The state's argument was simple. "The evidence has shown that Mark Sievers hired Curtis Wright, his best friend, to kill his wife, Dr. Teresa Sievers. An unconscionable act." The defense, too, was simple. Their case rested on a single question: whether Wayne was telling the truth. "When you weigh the evidence and you look at all these facts," argued Michael Mummert, "ultimately, the one question you all have to ask yourselves: Do you trust Curtis Wayne Wright? The only evidence that you actually have of an actual conspiracy came from Curtis Wayne Wright." His question was rhetorical. "Mr. Wright," he concluded, "is a five-time, bipolar convicted felon who lied repeatedly, murdered Dr. Sievers, manipulated his neighbors, and only came clean when given the choice to cooperate, or sit where Mark sits now."

The jury was out for only four hours and ten minutes—a very short time for a case of this magnitude; deliberation time in high-profile trials is usually twice that, at least. And while juries are notoriously unpredictable, short deliberation times tend to indicate a guilty verdict. An acquittal, which in a murder case is often controversial, usually involves more time spent in the jury room going over evidence and carefully rereading documents.

Judge Kyle had made it very clear he'd tolerate no outbursts of emotion when the verdict was read—a much-needed instruction, as feelings were running high. By this time, the courtroom was full. Most of Teresa's family were there: her mother, Mary Ann; her sister, Annie; and her brothers, Frank and Patrick. Waiting, they held hands, tense, red-faced, heads lowered, perhaps in prayer. The jury foreperson came forward and handed a piece of paper to the clerk, who stood and read it aloud.

Guilty on all counts.

Everyone restrained themselves, as the judge had commanded, but you could sense an enormous release of pressure. Mark remained expressionless in his seat, although, for the first time, his face colored slightly. As soon as judge and jury had left the room, Teresa's family hugged one another, embraced Hamid Hunter and Cynthia Ross, and wept. Mark's family sat in silence.

• • •

According to Florida statute, when a person's found guilty of a felony, there's a separate penalty phase shortly after the trial at which the same jury determines their sentence (to recommend death, the verdict must be unanimous). At this hearing, members of the victim's family are allowed to give impact statements describing the pain of their loss. This is sometimes seen as a sort of "payback" for the burdensome ordeal of sitting through the trial. But the defendant, too, is allowed to have mitigation witnesses who try to paint a fuller picture of the person whose fate hangs in the balance.

In Mark's case, the sentencing phase came two days after the trial, and there were only two options: death, or life without parole. For the prosecution, there was a single mitigation witness: Teresa's mother, Mary Ann Groves, who spoke for the family. It had been four years since her daughter's murder, and although her grief was still palpable, she managed to remain calm. She described Teresa's great achievements, her intelligence, beauty, and extraordinary compassion for the neglected and abandoned. She reminded the jury of the two motherless children Teresa had left behind.

"I have lost my dear Teresa," she lamented. "My precious girl who I loved beyond measure. . . . The light of our lives. The star of our family who loved us all so fiercely. . . . The void is unimaginable. She was our rock, our joy." She concluded her moving, eloquent speech by screening two video clips of Teresa, both from her nascent television show. Suddenly, her daughter came to life in the courtroom, a vibrant, lively, beautiful human being. In the clips, as in her infomercials, Teresa was lively, articulate, and full of energy—you can see how she could have been a celebrity.

Mary Ann's speech was a *tour de force*—a modern version of the execution sermons that were once preached before a public hanging. The intensity of the family's ongoing grief, and the vivid, living depiction of Teresa on screen, made it clear that, for them, closure would be achieved only by death: an eye for an eye.

Mark said later that he had no interest in having any mitigation witnesses. "Mitigation," he explained, "is for the guilty." But his legal team, hoping to save him from the death penalty, disagreed. His first mitigation witness was his mother, Bonnie. Unlike Mary Ann, Bonnie didn't have a pre-prepared speech, but responded to questions from Greg Messore, the "death-qualified" counsel who'd taken over from Michael Mummert in Mark's defense. Bonnie described Mark as a child, called him "my baby," and recounted anecdotes about how he helped other children, how he waited expectantly for Santa on Christmas morning, how he was "a protector who always wanted to take care of the underdog."

Next, his brother, Scott, talked about his relationship with Mark as they were growing up, the death of their father, and the disruption it caused to their family life. He said Mark adored his wife and daughters and was "always bragging on them."

Connie Reiss, Mark's stepsister, described how Mark had always embraced and encouraged her, especially during her recent battle with cancer, even though they weren't blood relatives. Finally, his stepmother, Jennie Weckelman, described Mark with enormous love and affection, showing pictures of him as a child, which were projected on a screen for the jury. She told the jury that his family members had been visiting Mark every week and talking on the phone whenever possible.

Greg Messore looked like a gangster, with slicked-back hair and a gravelly voice. He wanted to show that Mark's loved ones were supporting him and would suffer enormously from his incarceration. By implication, if he were given life without parole, he'd remain an active participant in family life, instead of wasting away in despair. As his family spoke about him, Mark's chin quivered; still, he remained stoic. No tears spilled.

After Mark's mitigation team had spoken, Judge Kyle summarized their findings, accepting that "Sievers had been a good, hands-on, devoted father who taught his children their faith. He had been a good family member, had taken care of sick relatives, helped people, and made charitable contributions. He had no disciplinary record in jail." The judge added that, in addition to his relatives who spoke in court, Mark's daughters had also made it known that they didn't want the death penalty to be imposed."

Mark's mitigation team no doubt wanted the jurors to see their client as a real person, not a vile monster. He'd been a sweet, lovable child; as an adult, he was kind, caring, and generous. Unfortunately, their strategy backfired. All it showed was that Mark had been born into a loving, supportive family. He didn't suffer any significant childhood trauma. He was well-liked by friends and acquaintances and had plenty of successful relationships. Rather than making Mark seem more relatable, this, in the eyes of the jury, made his crime even more heinous. Although they conceded that Mark's crime hadn't been committed for pecuniary gain (evidence substantiated at trial by an accountant), and he didn't have a history of violence, they took less than three hours to recommend a sentence of death. Their decision surprised no one. When the sentence was pronounced, Mark, for the first time in the entire trial, seemed anxious and shaken. As he was handcuffed and taken out of court, his mother blew him a kiss.

For the most part, those involved were gratified by the outcome of the case, while acknowledging its limitations. "While justice was served," said Detective Mike Downs, "it will never fully give back what was taken from the family. No amount of jail time could ever really pay retribution for what was taken."

The sentence didn't become official for another three weeks, when, on January 3, 2020, Mark stood once again before Judge

Kyle, who ratified the jury's decision. "I judge people's actions, not people's souls," said the judge, as he sentenced Mark to death. "That's for someone else to do." A last-ditch attempt from the defense attorneys to appeal the conviction was overturned. In court, Mark made a short statement. "Although a jury found me guilty, I'm innocent of all charges," he said. "I can't feel remorse for something I had nothing to do with. I'll fight this wrongful conviction."

Chapter 21

Death Row

Most people, when they hear the words *death row*, think of scenes from the movies: lines of barred cells from which, periodically, a repentant convict is led mournfully to the execution chamber. In reality, Florida's death row is more like a poorly funded assisted-living facility. There are currently over 300 men waiting to be executed, the majority convicted of first-degree premediated murder. They're housed at Union Correctional Institution (UCI) in Raiford, fifty miles west of Jacksonville, in a separate facility from the prison's 1,800 other inmates. Inside the razor wire fences, there's a small town: cement streets, cell blocks, visiting rooms, workshops, a hospital, and a chapel. Just outside the perimeter, in a large nearby field, sits the prison cemetery.

One block inside UCI does, in fact, resemble the popular image of death row, and that's the block that contains the "death watch cells" set aside for inmates whose death warrant has already been signed by the governor. Here, the evening before your execution, you can order a last meal, but it must cost less than forty dollars, and the food must be easily available (so no suckling pig or roast guinea fowl). You can still choose the electric chair rather than lethal injection, but nobody's done so since 1999. Unlike in the movies, last-minute commutations are virtually unknown.

Like most convicts on Florida's death row, Mark Sievers is far more likely to die of natural causes than to be executed. Once a death sentence has been imposed, decades can pass before it's carried out—assuming all appeals have failed. The amount of bureaucracy involved in putting someone to death is inconceivable. On average, those on Florida's death row have been there for twenty-three years.

Unsurprisingly, it's the less-notorious inmates who tend to escape lethal injection. Inmate-author Caryl Chessman wrote, of his fellow convicts on death row, that it's the weakest and most deteriorated inmates who are granted reprieve. "A man needs a measure of true life in order to be worth executing," explained Chessman. But even high-profile inmates don't stay famous for long. Shocking homicides are commonplace, especially in Florida, and once out of the limelight, even serial killers are soon forgotten. If they go back to court, there's generally little interest. When it comes to appeals, procedural issues seem stale, abstract, and complex, and are seldom read by anyone other than the attorneys involved in the case (and sometimes not even by them). Victims' families generally regard appeals as needlessly cruel delays, due to technical difficulties, in reaching execution. Some see them as an exploitative way of helping guilty people escape consequences for what everybody knows they've done.

Mark Sievers was forty-seven when he was arrested for murder; it's fair to say the second half of his life will be very different from the first. A death row cell at UCI is six feet by nine feet, around the size of an average bathroom, with no windows, and old-fashioned prison bars rather than solid steel doors. Due to the age of the building and lack of funding, there's no air-conditioning, only fans. Death row inmates get three meals a day, brought to their cell, served on a tray, and eaten with a plastic spork. Until

April 2022, they were completely isolated from other prisoners, excluded from prison educational and employment programs, and generally spent twenty-three hours a day alone in their cells.

This is no longer the case. In 2022, the judge in a federal civil rights lawsuit brought by eight Florida death row prisoners described their living conditions as "extreme, debilitating, and inhumane." Consequently, the Florida Department of Corrections agreed to make changes, and things have since improved. Now, death row prisoners can, if they so choose, spend up to twenty hours a week in a day room, where they can socialize, play cards, and watch television. They have more access to phones, tablets, and video visits, once-a-day showers, and six hours a week of outside activity. Some, depending on eligibility, are allowed to work—in the prison's wood or metal shops, on its cattle farm or abattoir, or, following age-old tradition, making license plates.

Ironically, according to mitigation expert Jeff Giordano, being sent to death row may have saved Mark's life. "The death penalty comes more quickly when you're amongst the general population," explained Giordano. "You'll probably be killed within the first ten years after committing a crime like Mark's. . . . There have actually been cases where people, through appeals, have been taken off death row, and they've actually ended up killing another inmate or a guard just to try to get back there." Mark, too, believes—given the circumstances—he's better off on death row than amongst the general population. "On death row, you're one of only 300 people, and, as a constitutional right, you're guaranteed the services of a state-appointed attorney to help with your appeal," he explained.

• • •

In December 2020, there was an odd development in the Sievers case. Mark's mother, Bonnie, received an envelope from Jimmy

Ray Rodgers at South Bay Correctional Facility, Florida ("I was terrified to open it," she said). Inside was a six-page handwritten letter beginning, "Your son Mark Sievers is an innocent man. What has happened to him is a tragedy and miscarriage of justice. Mark should never have been arrested. Mark had nothing to do with Teresa's murder."

In his letter, Jimmy made some bold claims. From the day of Teresa's murder, he wrote, the cops immediately assumed Mark, the husband, was responsible. It was lazy police work, he suggested. In such cases, the spouse is always the main suspect. But since Mark had an iron-clad alibi, they assumed he must have hired an assassin, and when they learned about Wayne's suspicious trip to Florida, they realized they had their man.

The cops fed Wayne the "hit man story," claimed Jimmy, then offered Wayne twenty-five years if he agreed to implicate Mark. Jimmy also happened to be in Florida with Wayne, and so he, too, had to be tied into the "hit man story." To do so, they paid Taylor to testify against him; she agreed because she'd resented the way Jimmy had treated her (he said he was sleeping with two or three different women every week until Taylor "tricked" him into getting her pregnant), and of course, she needed the money. In his indignant, semi-literate letter, Jimmy made some surprising allegations.

FACT: Taylor said she purposely got pregnant by me while we are not dating. Taylor testified the pregnancy was planned.

FACT: I used to make almost $1000 a week.

FACT: Taylor has 4 kids by 4 guys and no job. Taylor lived completely off government handouts, and needs money!

FACT: I was an ass hole to Taylor and she did all she could to put me in prison.

FACT: The detectives had no evidence of the [hit man story] they was telling and could not make an arrest until Taylor repeated it!

FACT: In 2015 Wayne told the detectives he is BIPOLAR to the point of being mentally unemployable.

FACT: Wayne testified that he was unarmed and randomly spontaneously grabed the hammer off the deep freezer because it was the only thing in arms reach . . .

FACT: . . . Wayne and Teresa got in to an argument by the deep freeze and BIPOLAR Wayne snaped.

As soon as this peculiar letter arrived, Bonnie turned it over to Mark's attorneys, who immediately filed for a re-hearing on the basis of "newly discovered evidence" which, they claimed, had it been presented to a jury, would likely have produced an acquittal. "Rodgers' version of the events on the night of the murder are equally, if not more plausible than Wright's uncorroborated murder-for-hire yarn which saved him from the death penalty or life in prison," argued Michael Mummert, adding that, "Jimmy Rodgers—unlike Curtis Wright—has nothing to gain by setting out the facts in his letter." This is clearly absurd: if the "hit man theory" was thrown out, Jimmy could no longer be tied to the murder.

• • •

Even though his conviction was affirmed by the Florida Supreme Court and his death row appeal denied, on the basis of this "newly discovered evidence" and claims of "ineffective assistance of counsel" (although not of "actual innocence"), Mark Sievers was granted an evidentiary hearing, which took place at the Lee County Courthouse on October 13 and 14, 2025. Mark, at fifty-eight, looked haggard and worn-down; he wore a short, graying beard, thick glasses, and an amplifying headset (which occasionally sent out annoying high-pitched squeaks) to compensate for his hearing loss. He was represented by a (bald) public defender, John LoBianco.

At the hearing, Mark's former attorney, Michael Mummert, acknowledged once again that, after Anthony Faga's death, he'd been completely unprepared for trial. He made some terrible mistakes, he admitted—not pushing for a change of venue, not admitting Wayne and Mark's salacious texts into evidence—and claimed that Greg Messore, the death-qualified attorney who'd come on board at the last minute, was "barely involved," and only attended one or two depositions.

Two crime scene investigators, who hadn't been called to testify at Mark's original trial, described how they'd found evidence at Jarvis Road that might have substantiated the claim that only one assailant was involved. The first, J. D. Thomas, admitted that "it could have been a single person"; the second, Bob Trussel, said that items from Teresa's purse appeared to have been placed on top of the bloodstains on the floor, and it was possible that "someone had tried to manipulate the scene."

Unlike Mark, Jimmy Ray Rodgers, now thirty-five, seemed to have thrived in prison—at a muscular 200 pounds, he was much stronger and healthier than when he'd appeared in the courtroom seven years earlier. During this time, he'd managed to concoct an even more laughable story. The reason he'd gone down to Florida with duct tape, boots, and protective coveralls wasn't to kill Teresa, he now claimed, but to help Wayne paint her house. He'd been excited about visiting Florida in July, he said, after watching YouTube videos of Miami Beach (he confessed to being extremely disappointed—"I didn't realize there were beaches in Florida that were full of old ladies"). He said Wayne had been on a "drug bender" when they'd set off from Missouri, and his marriage to

Angie had already "gone to shit." He reiterated his claims that Wayne was obsessed with Mark, and after confronting Teresa at the house, he allegedly "went crazy" and chased her around the kitchen with a hammer. Jimmy was horrified by what happened, he said, and not only because he had a "phobia of blood." He now had PTSD, and suffered from "night terrors."

The only plausible evidence introduced by Mark's defense attorney, John LoBianco, was that Mark received inadequate mitigation at his sentencing hearing. Apparently, two mitigation specialists had taken on the assignment but dropped out after realizing they'd wouldn't be given enough time to prepare, leaving Mark's attorneys to hire Jeff Giordano at the last minute. For some reason, Giordano's carefully prepared PowerPoint hadn't been used. Mark's mother and stepmother took the stand to describe how confused they'd been at the time they testified, and didn't really understand what they were doing. Bonnie, in particular, didn't even seem to know what the word *mitigation* meant, or what its purpose was. Finally, Michael Mummert admitted that he "cried many times" during Mark's conviction and sentencing. He even cried, apparently, during his deposition. "I still believe Mr. Sievers is innocent," he said. "I'll go to my grave believing that."

On February 24, 2026, Mark's request for a new trial was denied. There's an extremely high bar to receiving this kind of dispensation, especially in Florida; all reasonable inferences are drawn to support the validity of the jury's original verdict. And in the absence of further relief, it's difficult to believe Mark's death sentence will be overturned, partly due to the notoriety of the case, and partly due to the need, in regard to this terrible crime, for a symbolic sacrifice.

• • •

Most people serving time for murder claim they didn't get a fair trial. Others admit they committed the crime, but insist the full circumstances were never explained or considered. Many, like Mark, claim they're innocent; some, no doubt, have come to believe it.

According to Wayne, prior to the murder, Mark had described how he planned never to speak of his involvement in Teresa's death. He wouldn't talk about the crime, said Mark, because it would "change his thought pattern." Did he go so far with this exercise that he no longer recognized his guilt? Perhaps. There's also, surely, a level of self-justification at play. Mark might have wanted Teresa dead, but it's probably fair to say he didn't want anybody to beat out her brains with a hammer. It may only be a short stop from here to telling himself he had nothing to do with the murder. But another explanation seems more likely.

During a defendant's preparation for trial, which can take years, they begin to perceive the world differently. Often, they devote themselves to obsessively dismantling the prosecution's argument, searching out tiny holes and flaws. Every day is spent engrossed in legal paperwork, reconsidering arguments, meticulously analyzing details.

If convicted, like Mark, they may fill their empty days in prison obsessed with "due process," consistently planning their appeals, endlessly driven to find loopholes in the state's arguments, pushing, emphasizing, repeating, insisting to themselves that the prosecution didn't overcome the burden of doubt. Injustices breed; realities recede. It becomes natural, over time, for the truth to go on the back burner—for a person to stop thinking about what "really" happened and, instead, to start thinking of "my legal case." The prosecution was flawed, the trial unfair, the verdict false. It's a small step from thinking yourself deeply wronged to thinking yourself innocent.

Too, Mark has a constantly chipper, upbeat personality. He

stays thoughtful and polite even in the direst of circumstances, always looking on the bright side (referring to his "room," for example, rather than his "cell"). He's reluctant to look back at the past, driven to work toward what he believes will be his eventual exoneration.

His interactions with the outside world are limited. None of his friends or family live nearby, so his visitors and few and far between. He has no contact with his daughters, a decision made by Teresa's family, who felt it was in the best interests of the girls. Mark can use the telephone and a tablet, and speaks to his mother, stepmother, and friends every week. He can also send emails, which are limited and monitored.

He has visitors approximately once every couple of months: usually his mother, Bonnie, and her partner, Melanie, or his stepmother, Jennie Weckelman. Visits take place on Saturdays, and last up to six hours. In the visiting room, two or three guards stand sentry over fifteen to twenty death row inmates, who, at stainless steel picnic tables, spend time with their loved ones. You can talk, hug, even have lunch together. Reportedly, Mark remains upbeat and seldom complains.

Taylor Shomaker's husband, Gary James, lost his battle with kidney cancer at the age of thirty, in March 2022. Since then—perhaps surprisingly, perhaps not—she and Jimmy have reconnected. She still believes in Jimmy's guilt and admits he did a "monstrous thing," but insists he isn't a monster himself. "I don't judge anybody for anything they do, and I don't feel that it's my place because I'm a Christian," she said. "I believe it's for God to judge and not for me to judge. And I'm also a big believer in forgiveness." There's no option for video visits at South Bay, and Taylor can't afford to go to Florida, but Jimmy talks to his daughter Jazlyn on the phone as often as he can. In fact, he still claims all Taylor's children as his own. "He always wanted to be a dad," she said. "I've always loved him. I've never stopped loving him."

Angie divorced Wayne in 2020, and married for the third time in 2024, carrying a bouquet of white roses. Emma and Olivia live in Connecticut with their grandmother and aunts. Jimmy Ray Rodgers is serving a life sentence in South Bay Correctional Facility. Wayne Wright is currently incarcerated at an undisclosed location in Florida. Mark Sievers remains on death row at UCI. Currently, he has no execution date. He maintains his innocence to this day.

NOTES

Prologue

2 **"I'm at a friend's house":** Transcript of 911 call from Mark Petrites, Lee County, Florida Sheriff's Office, case #15-268513, June 29, 2015.

4 **with spinach leaves:** Teresa Sievers Autopsy Report, Office of the District Medical Examiner, Lee County Sheriff's Office, No. 00587, 6/29/2015.

4 **"pulverized":** Ibid.

PART ONE

Chapter 1: "Lord, It Is Night"

8 **Emma, eleven, and Olivia, eight:** All the names of children under the age of eighteen have been changed.

11 **"do not mention to passengers":** Mark was officially informed of Teresa's death by Detective Nolen at 7:12 P.M. that day.

13 **"the carrots":** During the crime scene investigation, the dogs were walking freely about the house. One of the crime scene technicians, Jason Brod, mentioned to investigators, "I did see the black dog, fuzzy dog,

looked a little older . . . the dog had come up and stepped on the hammer." Hastily, Nana and Lucy were herded to the lanai, along with Zoey, the family cat, then impounded by Animal Services until Mark could come and pick them up.

14 **Organic, of course:** Information in this chapter is from: interview transcripts Jason Brod, 6/29/15; Annie Lisa, 7/1/15; Mark Sievers, 7/1/15; crime scene photographs ("Scene Day #1"), Lee County Sheriff's Office, case #15-268513.

Chapter 2: "A Modern-Day Mother Teresa"

16 **"accused of such a serious crime":** See United States v. Martoma, 990 F. Supp. 2d 458 (S.D.N.Y. January 6, 2014) (the suspect was, in fact, found guilty).

17 **"emotional freedom technique":** The technique is apparently intended to "stimulate acupressure points by pressuring, tapping, or rubbing while focusing on situations that represent personal fear or trauma." See https://www.webmd.com/balance/what-is-eft-tapping accessed, March 18, 2025.

21 **"inclusive Catholic community":** see https://winknews.com/2015/07/10/good-shepherd-pastor-remembers-murdered-doctor-as-an-angel/, published July 10, 2015; updated January 19, 2016; accessed November 12, 2023.

21 **Mark's family was Jewish:** Bonnie identified herself as "Jewish reformed."

23 **"But not the way I thought":** Information in this chapter drawn from: transcript and police video of interviews with Mark Sievers, 7/1/15; Annie Lisa, 7/1/15; Bonnie

Sievers, 7/1/15; Mary Ann Groves, 7/2/15; Lee County Sheriff's Office, case #15-268513.

Chapter 3: Targeted, Stalked, and Slain

25 **"the body of Teresa Sievers?":** The *Nancy Grace* producer was Christo Taoushiani; emails sent Monday, July 27, 2015, 9:16 A.M.; Thursday, August 20, 2015, 1:32 P.M.; Thursday, August 20, 2015, 3:54 P.M. WINK-TV representative was Robin Wolf; email sent Tuesday, July 28, 3:30 P.M.

26 **seventy percent of murders:** Murder victims by weapon used in the US 2023, published by Statista Research Department; see https://www.statista.com/statistics/195325/murder-victims-in-the-us-by-weapon-used/; accessed February 8, 2024.

26 **"weapons of opportunity":** Murphy, GK. "Beaten to death": An autopsy series of homicidal blunt force injuries. *American Journal of Forensic Medical Pathology*. June 1991; 12 (2):98-101. PMID: 1882786.

26 **The type of object used:** Mohammad Rahim Kamaluddin, PhD, Azizah Othman, DPsych, Khaidzir Hj. Ismail, PhD and Geshina Ayu Mat Saat, PhD. Psychological markers underlying murder weapon profile: a quantitative study. *Malaysian Journal of Pathology*, 2017; 39 (3): p222.

27 **"neuropathic shock":** Trial transcript, State of Florida v. Jimmy Ray Rodgers, case no. 15-CF-000673 A, October 18, 2019, p3648.

27 **"They're textbook wounds":** Ibid., p3660.

27 **per thousand inhabitants:** Statistics drawn from Lee County Sheriff's Office. See https://www.sheriffleefl.org/crime-map-2-0/; accessed February 22, 2024.

29 **babies circumcised:** Melissa Montoya, "Local organization raises money for Teresa Sievers memorial," Fort Myers *News-Press*, July 22, 2015. https://www.news-press.com/story/news/local/estero/2015/07/22/local-organization-raises-money-teresa-sievers-memorial/30529751/; accessed December 8, 2023.

30 **"to see one girl make it":** Quote taken from page 4 of undated letter from Michele Petrites to "Teresa, Mark, Emma and Olivia," Lee County Sheriff's Office, case #15-268513.

30 **fabric class:** Texts from Mark Sievers's phone used in this chapter: 9836 (4/21/2012); 14647 (2/12/2013); 30069 (2/14/2014); 30108 (2/25/2014); 31928 (4/4/2014); 32788 (4/21/2014); 47002 (4/20/2015); 47011 (4/20/2015); 50018 (6/18/2005); 45768 (3/17/2015); 46010 (3/25/20150).

30 **charges of child neglect:** January 15, 2015, "Teen mother arrested on child neglect charges," Local10.com, https://www.local10.com/news/2015/01/06/teen-mother-arrested-on-child-neglect-charges/; accessed October 2, 2024.

32 **"It was devastating":** Interview with Kenny Cousins, NBC2 News, October 29, 2015. https://www.youtube.com/watch?v=KICgdJZmL2E&t=140s; accessed February 8, 2024.

32 **"loved to swear":** Annie Lisa, *What My Sister Told Me after She Was Murdered: A Shared Journey of Transformation*, Divining Your Life, LLC, 2025. P20. Hereafter, "Lisa."

32 **transitioning from male to female:** Kristine Gill and Dania Maxwell, "M to F: The story of a 12-year-old's transition," feature previewed at https://www.youtube

.com/watch?v=ByZrn-8j6AQ June 26, 2015. Accessed February 21, 2024.

32 **It seemed nuts:** Other information in this chapter drawn from transcript and police video of interviews with Mark Sievers, 7/1/15; Annie Lisa, 7/1/15; Bonnie Sievers, 7/1/15; Mary Ann Groves, 7/2/15; Lee County Sheriff's Office, case #15-268513.

33 **"the body count is now up to 10":** Email sent from John Christopher Hammell to Lee County Medical Examiner's Office, July 24, 2015, 4:45 P.M.

33 **twice-daily coffee enemas:** Vickers, A. (2004). "Alternative cancer cures: 'unproven' or 'disproven'?" *CA: A Cancer Journal for Clinicians*. 54 (2): 110–118.

34 **these doctors were all in their sixties:** See Jay Syrmopoulos, "Another Florida Doctor Murdered, Bringing Total to 8 Dead & 5 Missing in Just the Last Month," *The Free Thought Project*, July 24, 2015. https://thefreethoughtproject.com/health/florida-doctor-murdered-bringing-total-8-dead-5-missing-month; accessed October 29, 2023. Some believed over 100 doctors were mysteriously killed. See Erin Elizabeth, "Unintended Holistic Doctor Death Series: Over 100 Dead," *Health Nut News*, March 13, 2016. https://healthnutnews.com/recap/; accessed October 29, 2023.

Chapter 4: Bliss Oil

35 **"It wasn't a waiting room":** See "Colleague of murdered Bonita Springs doctor speaks out," NBC2 interview with Sandra Hoskins, https://www.youtube.com/watch?v=Rl3KrJG-K7A&list=PLFDGFHygGV12deNuUzSSTcCPTwVtXg3E6&index=5, July 6, 2015; accessed February 21, 2024.

36 **"wholesale and indiscriminate":** Bill Cornwell, "Anti-aging doctor practices what she preaches," Naples *Florida Weekly*, August 5, 2010 https://naples.floridaweekly.com/articles/anti-aging-doctor-practices-what-she-preaches/; accessed November 19, 2023.

38 **"reach the disease state":** Ibid.

40 **"Nemenhah Native American Church":** See https://normshealy.com/bliss-healers/; accessed July 11, 2023. Information about Bliss Oil drawn from https://normshealy.shop/products/dr-shealys-5-bliss-essential-oil-set; accessed January 23, 2024. See also Websleuths forum post regarding the connection between Dr. Sievers and Norm Shealy by dmac55, April 2, 2016. https://www.websleuths.com/forums/threads/owner-of-the-infamous-purple-truck-dr-roy-heilbron.304247/page-3. Apparently, the Bliss Oils were popular with Teresa's family. Annie also used them, and so did Olivia.

40 **Some argue this is simply a marketing technique:** For AMA position on in-office supplement sales, see https://code-medical-ethics.ama-assn.org/ethics-opinions/sale-health-related-products; accessed February 1, 2024.

40 **PureCapsPro:** All financial records are taken from State of Florida v. Mark D. Sievers, Case no. 15-CF-000673-B, Circuit Court of the Twentieth Judicial Circuit in and for Lee County, Florida Criminal Action, discovery materials.

41 **"a twenty-first-century wellness center":** Lisa, 108.

41 **"crystal healing bed":** Ibid., 141.

41 **"joint nutritional product":** Cision PR web announcement: Flexcin International, Inc. January 10, 2014, https://www.prweb.com/releases/the_doctor_is_

in_the_house_dr_dr_teresa_sievers_announced_as_new_spokesperson_for_flexcin_international_inc_/prweb11462185.htm. Accessed February 9, 2024.

42 **seven Flexcin "informational videos":** Dr. Sievers's Flexcin infomercials are all available on YouTube. See https://www.youtube.com/results?search_query=flexcin+sievers. All accessed December 26, 2023.

42 **"awesome motion lotion":** See https://www.youtube.com/watch?v=hKbhc9opz4g, 28.21.

42 **Lifetime Guarantee:** Tamer Elsafy directed and acted in the infomercials with Teresa, extolling the benefits of Flexcin (he also branched out into the animal market, successfully launching Flexpet and appearing in photographs holding two fluffy dogs). Either his ethics were not entirely above reproach, or he was simply careless, but on July 13, 2015, two weeks before Teresa's murder, a consumer rights organization complained to Florida's WINK News that Flexpet was selling expired supplements online. Investigators went to the Flexcon warehouse to speak to Elsafy, but "he refused to comment and instead slammed the door in the crew's face.""Local company caught selling expired pet supplements," WINK News, July 13, 2015, https://winknews.com/2015/07/13/local-company-caught-selling-expired-pet-supplements/; accessed February 9, 2024.

42 **glossy, smart, sparkling:** Clips from *Pathways 2 Healing* and Teresa's other television appearances can be seen here: https://www.youtube.com/@teresasieversmdmsmsfaarfma5197. All accessed February 9, 2024.

42 **"spiritual encounters":** Spookily, on May 28, 2014, exactly a year and a month before her murder, Teresa noted down a strange moment her daughter experienced. "Emma was asking for sign from God and thought she saw flashing light in bathroom, and she came to me and said I think it means you move on to a higher place."

43 **"Joy Negotiator":** Mary Lynn Ziemer, "The Joy Negotiator—Intro video," see https://www.youtube.com/watch?v=0OyUA5UQOzI, October 12, 2023; accessed February 9, 2024.

44 **"My lead's off the roof":** Mark Sievers, interview with detective David Lebid, July 1, 2015.

44 **remove heavy metals from the blood:** Jeff Bradstreet, another of the holistic doctors reported to have died mysteriously, was highly criticized for his use of chelation therapy on autistic children, believing autism to be associated with high levels of mercury in the blood.

44 **planned to reduce her office hours:** Mark's appointed mitigation specialist, Jeffrey Giordano, later wrote a self-published book about his experience, *The Mitigation of Mark Sievers—'Till Death do us Part* (April 2023). In it, he reproduces several documents from the case, including Michele Petrites's letter, and a fourteen-page letter from Mark to his attorneys in which he outlines information to be used in mitigation proving he is innocent of the crime (most of which was not used during the trial proceedings). Of this letter, Giordano writes, "He gave me a copy and requested I make this public so everyone can see his final thoughts that he wanted presented at his closing arguments at trial" (the book is unpaginated). This letter is hereafter referred to as Sievers Mitigation Letter.

44 **chelation is only FDA-approved:** "What is Chelation Therapy?" WebMD. Written by WebMD Editorial Contributors. Medically Reviewed by Melinda Ratini, MS, DO, on September 20, 2023. See https://www.webmd.com/balance/what-is-chelation-therapy accessed December 13, 2024.

44 **Norman Shealy:** C. Norman Shealy, MD, PhD, is a Harvard-trained neurosurgeon sometimes referred to as "the founder of organic medicine," although many other practitioners also claim this honor.

45 **constant, manic grin:** *Unleaded* trailer, produced by Adler & Associates Entertainment, is available at https://www.youtube.com/watch?v=Habw4URyFBk; accessed February 8, 2024.

45 **"Jim Healthy Publications":** For Dr. Heilbron's interview with "Jim Healthy," see https://www.youtube.com/watch?v=1pYnN85pkzQ&t=956s; accessed December 13, 2024. *The 30-Day Diabetes Cure Special Reports* (available from "Jim Healthy Publications") include "Deadly Diabetes Lies," "How to Heal Your Pancreas," and "Healing Diabetes with Yoga." Accessed December 13, 2024.

46 **Scrooge Collections:** Florida Department of State Division of Corporations, https://dos.fl.gov/sunbiz. Caring Cardiology: doc no. P98000106253; Hart-Heilbron Realty LLC: doc. no. M03000002621; Heilbron Baptist Church, Inc: doc no. N9500000580; A Well for Health Church (as Reverend Roy M. Heilbron): doc. no. N06000006044; Santa Fe Soul, Health and Healing Center, Ebenezer Financial Services, and Scrooge Collections: doc. no. M03000002620. Accessed February 9, 2024.

46 **studied under Babaji:** https://www.facebook.com/events/434593456655480/; accessed February 8, 2024.

47 **"holistic urologist":** Steve Terrell, *Santa Fe New Mexican*, "Ex-Santa Fe cardiologist sentenced to four years in fraud case," July 11, 2018, https://www.santafenewmexican.com/news/local_news/ex-santa-fe-cardiologist-sentenced-to-four-years-in-fraud-case/article_8c440615-7817-57a5-b022-dbea331871d8.html. Accessed October 27, 2023. See also February 2, 2018, United States Attorney's Office, District of New Mexico, "Santa Fe Cardiologist Pleads Guilty to Obstructing Justice While Awaiting Sentencing on Health Care Fraud Charge," https://www.justice.gov/usao-nm/pr/santa-fe-cardiologist-pleads-guilty-obstructing-justice-while-awaiting-sentencing-health. Accessed April 3, 2025.

Chapter 5: "The Dictionary Definition of a Happy Marriage"

48 **"key to any successful marriage":** Mark's texts taken from Florida v. Sievers, case #15-268513, State's exhibit #96B, p2589-2621. Texts used in this chapter: 306 (4/3/2010); 326 (4/5/2010); 392 (5/7/2010); 582 (6/28/2010); 603 (6/29/2010); 756 (7/7/2010); 1689 (9/29/2010); 1891 (10/16/2010); 2868 (1/31/2011); 2736-2742 (1/17/2011); 3360 (3/16/2011); 3480 (3/29/2011); 3645-3654 (4/9/2011); 3704 (4/10/2011); 3715 (4/11/2011); 5731 (9/3/2011); 5742 (9/5/2011); 5776 (9/5/2011); 6581 (10/16/2011); 6957 (10/30/2011); 7471 (11/13/2011); 17456 (5/4/2013).

48 **When selecting a romantic partner:** See, for example, Geher, G. "Perceived and actual characteristics of parents and partners: A test of a Freudian model of mate selection." *Current Psychology* 19, 194–214 (2000). https://

doi.org/10.1007/s12144-000-1015-7; Daly, M. & Wilson, M. (1990). "Is parent-offspring conflict sex-linked? Freudian and Darwinian models." *Journal of Personality*, 58(1), 163–189.

50 **"comic book guy":** Lisa, p109.

53 **statistically, most swingers:** See Jenks, R. J. "Swinging: a review of the literature." *Archives of Sexual Behavior*. 1998 Oct; 27 (5):507-21. doi: 10.1023/a:1018708730945. PMID: 9795730; See also Kimberly, C., McGinley, R. "Changes in the swinging lifestyle: a US national and historical comparison." *Culture, Health, and Sexuality*. 2019 February; 21(2): 219-232. doi: 10.1080/13691058.2018.1460692. Epub 2018 May 15. PMID: 29764311. Justin Wilt, Marissa A. Harrison & Cobi S. Michael (2018). "Attitudes and experiences of swinging couples," *Psychology & Sexuality*, 9:1, 38-53, DOI: 10.1080/19419899.2017.1419984.

54 **Swingers' parties take place everywhere:** Apparently, the image of an upside-down pineapple on someone's cabin door is a sign meaning "swingers' party in progress—come on in!" The pineapple doesn't necessarily have to be upside-down. For those in the know, pineapples (more usually, images of pineapples) displayed on someone's door indicate the person is part of the swinging community and interested in making friends. See Rachel Varina, "The Super-Sexy Meaning Behind the Upside-Down Pineapple may Surprise You." *Cosmopolitan*, April 12, 2024. https://www.cosmopolitan.com/sex-love/a60459870/upside-down-pineapple-meaning/.

54 **Here they met John and Julie:** Names of all "swingers" involved with Mark and Teresa have been changed.

55 **"wrong mama":** Other information in this chapter drawn from: Lee County Sheriff's Office, Affidavit of Kimberly Torres, 9/20/19, LCSO CFS #15-268513; Sievers, Mitigation; Sworn Statement of Crystal-Downs Afanador, June 29, 2015. Transcript and police video of interviews with Mark Sievers, 7/1/15; Annie Lisa, 7/1/15; Bonnie Sievers, 7/1/15; Mary Ann Groves, 7/2/15; Lenka Spiska, 7/2/15, Lee County Sheriff's Office, case #15-268513. All texts taken from Florida v. Sievers, case #15-268513, State's exhibit #96B, p2589-2621.

Chapter 6: Profit Margins

56 **"sacred contract":** Lisa, p113.

57 **didn't want to leave his kids in the car:** Mark's texts taken from Florida v. Sievers, case #15-268513, State's exhibit #96B, p2589-2621.Texts used in this chapter: 14329 (1/24/2013); 11418 (1/28/2013); 14524 (2/3/2013); 15239 (3/3/2013); 15257 (3/3/2013); 15266 (3/3/2013); 15422 (3/7/2013); 15492 (3/8/2013); 15587 (3/15/2013); 15805 (3/23/2013); 15868 (3/27/2013); 15939 (3/29/2013); 16069-16072 (4/4/2013); 16277 (4/12/2013); 16299 (4/12/2013); 16499-16506 (4/17/2023); 16568 (4/18/2013); 16858 (4/22/2013); 16771 (4/21/2013); 16681 (4/19/2013); 17972 (5/13/2013); 18242 (5/20/2013); 18332 (5/22/2013); 18399 (5/23/2013); 18411 (5/23/2013); 18475 (5/25/2013); 18679 (5/30/2013); 19670 (6/21/2013); 20095 (7/6/2013); 20170 (7/10/2013); 20299 (7/16/2013); 21545 (8/18/2013); 21730 (8/22/2013); 21792 (8/23/2013); 21804 (8/24/2103); 22162 (9/4/2013); 22281 (9/8/2013); 22498 (9/14/2013); 22533 (9/16/2013); 23146 (9/27/2013); 23455-23480 (10/3/2013); 23498 (10/4/2013); 23804

(10/14/2013); 23847 (10/15/2013); 23878 (10/17/2013); 24760 (11/06/2013); 24966 (11/11/2013); 25231 (11/18/2013); 25374 (11/21/2013); 26107-26107 (12/6/2013); 26367 (12/11/2013); 26668 (12/15/2013); 26732 (12/16/2013); 26857 (12/19/2013); 27087 (12/23/2013); 27106 (12/24/2013); 32788 (4/21/2014).

59 **"I'm wasting my fucking time":** Lisa, p20.

60 **Jennie Weckelman:** Personal communication, March 9, 2025.

62 **"back taxes":** Mark's texts taken from Florida v. Sievers, case #15-268513, State's exhibit #96B, p2589-2621. Texts used in this chapter: 8021 (12/24/2011); 8398 (1/15/2012); 9200 (3/3/2012); 9506 (3/23/2012); 9766 (4/13/2012); 9849. (4/23/2012); 10057 (5/4/2012); 10388-10487 (5/17/2012); 10565-10581 (5/18/2012); 11031 (6/14/2012); 11949 (8/13/2012); 12418 (9/2/2012); 12838 (10/5/2012); 13083 (10/29/2012); 13085 (10/29/2012); 13291 (11/7/2012); 13314 (11/8/2012); 13321 (11/9/2012); 14100 (12/30/14); 18432 (5/24/2013); 2868 (1/31/2011); 33062 (4/27/2014).

Chapter 7: Wayne

68 **"They morphed into each other":** "The Plot to Kill Dr. Sievers," CBS 48 Hours, January 3, 2023, 31.27; see https://www.youtube.com/watch?v=5tk4LwJXXT0&t=1687s; accessed 15 January 2024.

70 **introduced Mark to her best friend, Gloria:** Carrie Kain interview, Websleuths podcast, https://www.youtube.com/watch?v=JYemWNvgO34 February 12, 2020. Accessed 4/3/24.

70 **Wayne studied electrical engineering:** At trial, attorney Kathleen Fitzgeorge stated, erroneously, that Wayne had "a couple of degrees in engineering."

77 **"He was constantly on the phone":** Personal communication, March 19, 2025.

78 **"unsure of his true self":** Sigmund Freud, "The Uncanny," Translated by David McLintock, Penguin Classics, 2003, p35

78 With doppelgängers, you can never be sure: Information in this chapter taken from Jessica Lipscomb, "Tangled web surrounds suspects Curtis 'Wayne' Wright, Jimmy Rodgers in death of Dr. Teresa Sievers," *Naples Daily News*, October 31, 2015, https://archive.naplesnews.com/news/crime/tangled-web-surrounds-suspects-curtis-wayne-wright-jimmy-rodgers-in-death-of-dr-teresa-sievers--2345-339128031.html/; accessed March 24, 2023. Jefferson County Sheriff's Department, Police Report Number: 964440-3 (Ronnie Bolin case file); Missouri Public Records; Sievers mitigation; interview transcripts: Jerry Lubinski and Sundaye Harrison 7/14/15; Angela Marie Wright, 7/12/2015; Robert Wideman, 7/15/15; Carrie Kain, 8/24/15; Audio files: 15-268513-Wright Curtis-(Involvement Statement)-(1)-Downs-LCSO-4.WMA; 15-268513-Wright Curtis-(Confession)-(2)-Downs-LCSO-4.WMA; 15-268513-Wright Curtis-(Confession)-(3)-Downs-LCSO-4.mp3; 15-268513-Wright Curtis-(Confession)-(6)-Downs-LCSO-4.WMA; LCSO, Deputy Report for Incident, p56. Petrites deposition, p17; Gotham Investigations Podcast with Jeff Giordano, "The Mitigation of Mark Sievers: The Hidden Chapters: Marks stepmother reveals his life story." January 2, 2024. https://

www.youtube.com/watch?v=K4dbHY8qoHs&t=1s; accessed April 10, 2024.

79 **Wayne's delinquent stepson:** When Wayne's stepson was 15, he was removed from the home after accusing his stepfather of sexual abuse. The allegations were unproven, and Wayne was never charged.

79 **organic coconut creamer:** Wayne was OK with the creamer.

Chapter 8: The Delgado Protocol

82 **"the stamina of a young stallion":** See "Stellar Life" podcast, March 26, 2019. https://podcasts.apple.com/no/podcast/161-anti-aging-longevity-and-performance-with-dr/id1091011049?i=1000433458407; accessed September 8, 2024

83 **Mark was pale and flabby:** Might the Delgado Protocol have helped him beef up?

83 **"it's more of a tax write-off":** The "Mastering Love, Sex & Intimacy" aspect of The Delgardo Protocol is outlined at the Delgado Protocol website: https://delgadoprotocol.com/\mastering-love-sex-intimacy/?srsltid=AfmBOoqMUAaI7jdHvC8cgR5fBkENBSxKidkrJPPVQn03X1xCtsKQQQn9; accessed 9/8/24.

83 **"the best correlation to longevity":** OC Wellness Blog, https://www.ocwellness.com/blog/lasting-love-sex-and-intimacy-special-guest-dr-nick-delgado/, July 10, 2023, accessed 9/8/24.

84 **"let that stuff go":** Ibid.

92 **"tripped her mid-stride":** Lisa, p112.

Chapter 9: Best Man

97 **sentenced to death:** Johnson was executed in August 2023. Angie was present at the execution. A documentary about the case, *The Worst Crime*, directed by Ben Scholle—in which Angie declined to appear—was released in 2019.

98 **the best man:** Officially, there were two Best Men—Mark and another friend, Tommy Martin.

PART TWO

Chapter 10: "Something's Not Right"

105 **"He left his phone at home":** Rose Gruner interview. Regarding Wayne's phone: apparently, he had more than one phone, although he did forget them all. Mark texted a friend on 4/2/14: "can you send me Angie's phone number or send her a message let her know that wayne left his phone behind at the office and doesn't have it right now."

110 **"noise flash diversion device":** See GLOBAL INVESTIGATIONS AND ENFORCEMENT | MAY 2022, "HOW TO PREPARE FOR AND DEAL WITH A DAWN RAID OR SEARCH," Holman Fenwick Willan LLP, https://www.hfw.com/downloads/004001-HFW-How-to-prepare-for-and-deal-with-a-Dawn-Raid-or-Search.pdf. Accessed January 5, 2024.

Chapter 12: Accessory Before the Fact

132 **"They refused to answer any of our questions":** Neighbors desperate for answers in doctor's murder, WINK News, published June 30 2015, accessed April 3 2024.https://winknews.com/2015/06/30/neighbors-desperate-for-answers-in-doctors-murder/

135 **"You could even face the death penalty":** This is Taylor's testimony of the conversation. In court, Michael Downs said that he didn't recall suggesting she might be part of a murder conspiracy, and that if he did, "I don't see that as being a threat. It's more of a broad statement." See State of Florida v. Jimmy Ray Rodgers, Case No. 15-CF-000673 A, October 11, 2019, p2579.

137 **"grateful for every donation":** Information in this chapter drawn from: crime scene report; sworn statements and police video interviews with Angela Marie Wright, July 12, 2015; Edward Moran 7/12/15; Kathy Moran, 7/12/15; 7/14/15; Robert Wideman, 7/15/15; Taylor Shomaker 7/16/2015; Detective Nick Schuenemann #310 CFI #10-064, CCSA #CA10788 Criminal Identification Division Jefferson County Sheriff's Office, 08/25/2015 Seized Evidence List, 10154 Westbriar Drive, Cadet, Missouri 63630.

Chapter 13: "Love Is Patient, Love Is Kind"

142 **"Don't overthink it":** Lisa, p131.

142 **"a gurney with a black body bag":** Ibid., p125.

143 **over 450 people in attendance:** See Homily for the Celebration of the Life of Dr. Teresa Ann Grace Sievers—July 6, 2015, Rev. Dr. Judy Lee, accessed October 7, 2024, https://judyabl.blog/2015/07/06/homily-for-the-celebration-of-the-life-of-dr-teresa-ann-grace-sievers-july-6-2015-rev-dr-judy-lee/.

144 **"Thank you for being there for Mark and the kids":** Ibid., p12.

144 **Crime scene personnel had remained:** Trial transcript, State of Florida v. Mark Sievers, Case no. 15-CF-000673-B. November 20, 2019. p2377.

145 **"vigorously—that's an understatement":** "New details in Sievers murder investigation," WINK News, https://winknews.com/2015/07/16/sheriff-scott-calls-sievers-murder-fascinating-says-hes-getting-case-updates/; accessed February 21, 2024.

PART THREE

Chapter 14: The Reid Technique

149 **"blunt force trauma utilizing a hammer":** See arrest affidavit, p14.

150 **"natural hostility between hunter and hunted":** David Simon, *Homicide—A Year on the Killing Streets*, Picador 2006, p206. Note 39.

150 **adequate Miranda warnings:** See Richard A. Leo, "Inside the Interrogation Room," 86 *Journal of Criminal Law and Criminology* 260, 280 (1996).

152 **"sympathetic monologue":** James Orlando, Connecticut General Assembly Office of Legislative Research Report Interrogation Techniques, https://www.cga.ct.gov/2014/rpt/2014-R-0071.htm; accessed January 8, 2023.

153 **Apparently, it was impressive:** In an intercepted undated prison letter to an unknown correspondent, Jimmy writes, "Hook me up and tell all your friends about me and my big cock. I'm sure they're going to want to see it and I'm not shy . . . I'm not joking when I say it does not fit in both my hands."

Chapter 15: Hindsight Bias

157 **What if they weren't the person I thought they were:** "Hindsight Bias: A By-Product of Knowledge Updating?" Ulrich Hoffrage, PhD, Ralph Hertwig, PhD, and Gerd Gigerenzer, PhD, Max Planck Institute for Human Development; *Journal of Experimental Psychology: Learning, Memory and Cognition*, Vol. 26, No. 3.

158 **better predictions in the future:** Ibid.

158 **Carrie Kain was an ex-girlfriend of Wayne's:** Mark's texts taken from Florida v. Sievers, case #15-268513, State's exhibit #96B, p2589-2621. Texts used in this chapter: 33092 (4/28/2014).

158 **called the Crimestoppers hotline:** The police later concluded that Carrie's tips had "no evidentiary value."

158 **"long walk" on the beach:** This was Teresa's closest friend in Bonita Springs, Michele Petrites.

159 **A friend of Annie's named Rebecca:** Lisa, p132.

159 **he apparently spied on her:** Ibid., p115.

159 **"just standing in one place staring at his house":** Fox 4, WFTX Digital Team, "Neighborhood was on edge in eight months before arrest of Mark Sievers," posted 9:29 A.M., October 1, 2019: https://www.fox4now.com/news/local-news/neighborhood-was-on-edge-in-eight-months-before-arrest-of-mark-sievers; accessed January 12, 2024.

160 **"on our porch out of nowhere":** Ben Brasch, Melissa Montoya, Michael Braun, Frank Bumb, and Cody Dulaney, 10 Tampa Bay, "Mark Sievers Arrested for Wife's Murder in Lee County," https://www.wtsp.com/article/news/mark-sievers-arrested-for-wifes-murder-

in-lee-county/67-61620511 February 27, 2016; accessed January 12, 2024.

160 **"he could have shot me!":** "Neighborhood was on edge," op cit.

160 **"funny, funny feeling":** Ibid.

161 **"half-baked people":** Bryan Anderson, NBC2 News, https://www.facebook.com/BryanAndersonNBC2/videos/973003639389645/; accessed January 10, 2024.

163 **"TS does not seem to be the type":** Comment about swinging by "1&2&3," Websleuths, December 30, 2015, comment #199. https://www.websleuths.com/forums/threads/2015-12-29-breaking-news-new-discovery-docs-now-released.297486/page-10#post-12264025; accessed September 2, 2024.

163 **"I believe none of the comments made by Mark":** Comment about Mark's comments by "Swflorida" ("verified patient of Dr. Sievers"), Websleuths, December 1, 2015. https://www.websleuths.com/forums/threads/2015-12-01-sievers-husband-hired-killers-investigation-shows.295797/page-9#post-12219214, comment #168. Accessed September 2, 2024; https://www.websleuths.com/forums/threads/2016-05-17-batch-6-discovery-docs-graphic-content.308281/page-29; accessed September 2, 2024.

163 **"spoof Teresa's phone":** "spoofed" comment by "FelicityLemon," June 27, 2016, Websleuths Sievers Sidebar #4, comment # 400. https://www.websleuths.com/forums/threads/sievers-sidebar-4.309312/page-20#post-12661860; accessed September 2, 2024.

163 **"longstanding, deep emotional needs":** "emotional needs" comment by "AlwaysShocked," June 2, 2016, post #556.

https://www.websleuths.com/forums/threads/2016-05-17-batch-6-discovery-docs-graphic-content.308281/page-28#post-12604406; accessed September 2, 2024.

163 **"NBC is doing a live update":** "looking for Mark," comment by "mckazpm," Websleuths, comment #165, https://www.websleuths.com/forums/threads/2015-12-01-sievers-husband-hired-killers-investigation-shows.295797/page-9#post-12219214; accessed September 2, 2024.

163 **"in the window of suspicion":** "window of suspicion," comments by "RiversintheDesert," Websleuths, comment #186, https://www.websleuths.com/forums/threads/2015-12-01-sievers-husband-hired-killers-investigation-shows.295797/page-10; accessed September 2, 2024.

163 **set off a bunch of fireworks:** Mark seemed to have something of an obsession with fireworks. He'd often annoyed people in the past by setting them off from the roof of his house, on one occasion almost getting into an altercation with an angry neighbor.

164 **three chess pieces:** Information in this chapter drawn from: Affidavit (proffer), State of Florida v. Curtis Wayne Wright, Jr., Lee County Sheriff's Office, case #15-26851327, August 27, 2015.

Chapter 16: State's Evidence

165 **"betrayal oozes out of him":** Freud, S. (1977). *Introductory Lectures on Psychoanalysis.* W. W. Norton & Company. xii. Page 15. I. Part I. The Parapraxes (1916).

166 **inmates playing spades:** The prison system's most popular card game.

169 **such crimes are surprisingly common:** See, for example, *In the Name of Love: Romantic Ideology and Its Victims* (Oxford, 2008), Aaron Ben-Ze'ev and Ruhama Goussinsky.

170 **when, where, and how the murder was planned:** Other information in this chapter drawn from: Deposition of Mark D. Petrites, MD, November 7, 2019, p6-7. Letter from Michele Petrites, in Sievers, Mitigation. Transcript and police video of interviews with Mark Sievers, 7/1/15; Annie Lisa, 7/1/15; Bonnie Sievers, 7/1/15; Mary Ann Groves, 7/2/15; Lenka Spiska, 7/2/15, Lee County Sheriff's Office, case #15-268513. All texts taken from Florida v. Sievers, case #15-268513, State's exhibit #96B, p2589-2621. Delta passenger history, CSR #5270. Texts: 44072 (2/3/2015); 44111 (2/4/2015); 44231 (2/6/2015); 44245 (2/7/2015); 44326 (2/9/2015); 44616 (2/16/2015); 44662 (2/17/2015); 44810 (2/20/2015); 44847 (2/21/2015); 44887 (2/22/2015); 45201 (3/3/2015); 45697 (3/16/2015); 45667 (3/15/2015); 45717 (3/16/2015); 45734 (3/17/2015); 45802 (3/18/2015); 45876 (3/20/2015); 45913 (3/22/2015); 45915 (3/22/2015); 46141 (3/27/2015); 46648 (4/10/2015); 46669 (4/11/2015); 46922 (4/16/2015); 47095 (4/22/2015); 47248 (4/27/2015); 47209 (4/28/2015); 47354-47359 (4/29/2015); 47746 (5/4/2015).

170 **four years' shuffle room:** In Florida, an inmate must serve, at minimum, eighty-five percent of their sentence.

170 **specter of forthcoming retribution:** See "Literary Justice vs. Justice in Literature," Ira Nadel, *Interdisciplinary Literary Studies*, Vol. 20, No. 1 (2018), p40.

171 **outweigh even scientific evidence:** See Brandon L. Garrett, "Contaminated Confessions Revisited," *Virginia Law Review,* Vol. 101, Issue 2, 395, 396 (2015) (stating

that many recent cases of DNA-based exonerations have been "dominated by false confessions").

171 **"shapely confessions":** Anne M. Coughlin, "Interrogation Stories," *Virginia Law Review,* Vol. 95, Issue 7, September 4, 2013. https://virginialawreview.org/articles/interrogation-stories/; accessed December 15, 2024.

Chapter 17: Double-Cross

177 **transference of guilt:** The theme recurs in Highsmith's work, as it does in the movies of Alfred Hitchcock, which may have been what drew him to make his incomparable 1951 adaptation of the novel.

178 **"A pure murder":** Patricia Highsmith, *Strangers on a Train,* Norton, 2001, p26.

179 **On their "real" phones:** Information about Jimmy's childhood from interviews with Jimmy Ray Rodgers, 12/01/2023, 1/09/2024; Taylor Shomaker, 11/30/2023; Jackie Rodgers, impact statement, December 12, 2019. Other information in this chapter from David Lebid interview and photographs, State of Florida v. Jimmy Ray Rodgers, August 27, 2015; Affidavit, State of Florida v. Curtis Wayne Wright, Jr., Lee County Sheriff's Office, case #15-26851327, 27 August 2015; Facebook page, State of Florida v. Jimmy Ray Rodgers, August 27, 2015; Jimmy's prison emails 04/19/2016; 04/02/2016.

180 **graduated from law school:** In fact, Jackie Rodgers, Jr. graduated with a J.D. from Pepperdine in 2017.

Chapter 18: The Hit

184 **telling people they were going to Florida:** In his police interview on February 19, 2016, Wayne told the

investigators that, in the summer of 2015, a major mandatory upgrade needed to happen on the office servers, involving all the medical procedure codes for insurance and hospitals, and Wayne needed to be at the office in person to do it. It also needed to happen on a weekend when the office was closed. Wayne said he'd planned to make the trip to Florida to do the upgrade the weekend Mark and Teresa were out of town, which is why he'd discussed his trip openly with people. At the time, according to Wayne, he didn't anticipate that Mark would later decide this should be the weekend of the murder.

184 **hit the beach:** Account of the crime comes from Affidavit, State of Florida v. Curtis Wayne Wright, Jr., Lee County Sheriff's Office, case #15-26851327, 27 August 2015.

186 **"keeping u safe!":** Mark's texts taken from Florida v. Sievers, case #15-268513, State's exhibit #96B, p2589-2621. Texts used in this chapter: 7377 (11/7/2011); 28041 (1/14/2014); 47305 (4/28/2015); 47701 (5/4/2015).

188 **tree-lined ditch:** Unbeknownst to the oblivious hit men, this retention ditch is a protective site for the gopher tortoise, one of a number of local areas "intended to help prevent intentional and unintentional harm to gopher tortoises and their burrows." See https://myfwc.com/education/wildlife/gopher-tortoise/signage/.

192 **there wasn't blood on the ceiling:** Trial transcript, State of Florida v. Jimmy Ray Rodgers, Case no. 15-CF-000673 A. October 11, 2019, p2448.

194 **"lay the ground for an insanity defense":** Telephone interview with Jeff Giordano, 4/3/24.

194 **"People were cheering":** Fox 4, WFTX Digital Team, "Neighborhood was on edge in eight months before arrest of Mark Sievers," posted 9:29 A.M., October 1, 2019: https://www.fox4now.com/news/local-news/neighborhood-was-on-edge-in-eight-months-before-arrest-of-mark-sievers; accessed January 12, 2024.

194 **"He did the unthinkable":** Morgan Rynor and Jack Lowenstein, "Former Lee County Sheriff remembers Mark Sievers arrest for wife's murder," Published: December 5, 2019. Updated: December 5, 2019. https://winknews.com/2019/12/05/former-lee-county-sheriff-remembers-mark-sievers-arrest-for-wifes-murder/; accessed December 5, 2024.

195 **vice versa:** An image of Wayne identified as Mark appears in the Fort Myers *News-Press*. "Mark Sievers, on Florida's death row for wife's murder-for-hire, seeks files 'destroyed' by Ian." Tuesday, July 5, 2023. https://deal.town/the-news-press/news-alert-mark-sievers-bonita-springs-man-on-death-row-for-wifes-murder-for-hire-seeks-files-destroyed-by-ian-P3YBGPRJD9; accessed January 10, 2024. Ironically, in an Australian article, Wayne is identified as Jimmy. See "11/15/2019—U.S. Expert Witness News: FBI Expert Witnesses Testify in Jimmy Rodgers Trial." https://witnessdirectory.com/newsdetails.php?id=114; accessed December 15, 2024.

PART FOUR

Chapter 19: Murder-for-Hire

202 **"killing you or me or our kids":** Jimmy's emails taken from Collier County, Florida Jail, inmate email records 12/04/2015-05/08/2018. Emails used in this chapter: 3/10/2016; 3/13/2016; 03/23/2016; 04/01/2016;

04/02/2016; 04/09/2016; 06/01/2016; 06/02/2016; 06/25/2016; 06/26/2016; 07/02/2016; 08/27/2016; 05/21/2016; 04/02/2016; 04/01/2016; 04/09/2016; 03/11/2016; 03/24/2016; 08/27/2016; 03/27/2017; 04/04/2017; 4/24/2017; 4/17/2017.

204 **"Lake Boyz":** The judge in the "Lake Boyz" trials, Bruce Kyle, was also the judge in the Rodgers and Sievers trials.

204 **murdered in Cape Coral:** The murders were later attributed to Wade Wilson, who was convicted and received two death sentences on September 4, 2024.

206 **filmed by a documentary production team:** A docuseries on the Sievers case, "Brother from Another," directed by Lysa Heslov with George Clooney as executive producer, was reportedly in development at the time of the trial.

206 **Law and Crime Network:** Both trials are available to view in their entirety from the Law and Crime Network on YouTube. See https://www.youtube.com/watch?v=Dm99EZVXP3Q&list=PLoW1SIeAWaWYEyMIbIp6PsKNJoV8m2zrB. Accessed February 15, 2024.

207 **"most high-profile case of my career":** Personal communication by email, April 21, 2024.

207 **child werewolf Eddie Munster:** Incidentally, Butch Patrick, the actor who played Eddie Munster, was accused in 2013 of murdering pharmacist and racetrack owner Ken Schulz-Juedes in Wisconsin. He was eventually eliminated as a suspect. Schulz-Juedes's wife Cindy was found guilty of the crime.

208 **"quite a bizarre relationship":** Trial transcript, State of Florida v. Jimmy Ray Rodgers, Case no. 15-CF-000673 A. October 10, 2019. p2257.

208 **"the perfect alibi, and the perfect murder":** Ibid., p2212.

208 **"very sad, very tragic":** Ibid., p2449.

208 **"another man's madness":** Ibid., October 21, 2019. p3867.

210 **"to save his own worthless skin":** "The Plot to Kill Dr. Sievers," CBS *48 Hours* https://www.youtube.com/watch?v=5tk4LwJXXT0 35.21. Accessed February 15, 2024.

212 **George Clooney:** Trial transcript, State of Florida v. Jimmy Ray Rodgers, Case no. 15-CF-000673 A. October 18, 2019. p3856.

212 **"She's a grifter":** Ibid., p3850.

212 **"I accept and respect it":** Personal communication by email, April 21, 2024.

Chapter 20: Capital Crime

214 **"I'd visit him in jail":** Interview with Jeffrey Giordano, 4/3/24.

215 **retired white women:** Those over the age of seventy are excused from jury duty in Florida, so these may have been younger retirees, or people over seventy who still wanted to perform their civic duty.

215 **older jurors are more certain:** Rothman, Max B.; Dunlop, Burton D.; and Hirt, Gretchen M. (2000) "Jury Selection in Aging America: The New Discrimination?" *Marquette Elder's Advisor,* Vol. 2, Issue 2, Article 10. Available at: http://scholarship.law.marquette.edu/elders/vol2/iss2/10. Accessed December 15, 2024. 20204. See also PL, Heath WP, Grannemann BD. "How type of excuse defense, mock juror age, and defendant age affect mock jurors' decisions." *Journal of Social Psychology* August 2007; 147(4): 371-92. doi: 10.3200/SOCP.147.4.371-392. PMID: 17955749. Accessed December 15, 2024.

215 **fact-oriented arguments of fellow jurors:** Douglas O. Linder, "Juror Empathy and Race," *Tennessee Law Review*, Vol. 63, 887 (1996). Available at: https://irlaw.umkc.edu/faculty_works/411. Accessed December 15, 2024.

216 **stylish glasses:** Controversies related to glasses-wearing defendants are analyzed at length in Sarah Merry, "'Eye See You': How Criminal Defendants Have Utilized the Nerd Defense to Influence Jurors' Perceptions," *Journal of Law and Policy* 21 (2013). Available at: https://brooklynworks.brooklaw.edu/jlp/vol21/iss2/17. Accessed December 15, 2024.

216 **notes on a legal pad:** Mark's stepmother, Jennie Weckelman, attributes this partly to Mark's bad memory (he is careful to document everything as much as possible). She also pointed out that "His much-criticized, intense notetaking during trial was partly a way for him to keep distracted and maintain the blank countenance insisted upon by his lawyer."

218 **"Mike was sincere and optimistic":** Email communication, 3/27/25.

218 **"'cue ball' look":** "Doppelgänger," @FrancescaLD; "cue ball look" @Raccoon_Mama. "mini-me" @kurtrichards6899, See comments: https://www.youtube.com/watch? v=CYQWrH WKI1s&list=PLoW1SIeAWaWZ9fQCpZstYW_l5Y9Jdmx8s&index=3; accessed August 9, 2024. Incidentally, the attorney at Mark's evidentiary hearing in October 2025, John LoBianco, was also completely bald.

218 **his first name, Curtis:** An interesting note: at both trials, everyone referred to Wayne as "Curtis"—even those, like Taylor Shomaker, who knew him well. Were they

simply following the lead of the prosecutors, or might they have been trying to distance themselves from him, perhaps unconsciously?

219 **if any members of the jury were homophobic:** Mummert mentioned this at Mark's evidentiary hearing on October 13, 2025.

219 **vomit loudly into a nearby trash can:** "Mark Sievers gets sick in court," FOX 4 Now, https://www.youtube.com/watch?v=qNEru3kMFYM. Accessed December 15, 2024.

220 **teach her to shoot:** Mark's texts taken from Florida v. Sievers, case #15-268513, State's exhibit #96B, p2589-2621.Texts used in this chapter: 5600 (8/27/2011); 7990 (12/18/2011); 8305 (12/25/2011); 1770 (9/29/2010); 11171 (6/18/2021); 11265 (6/24/2012); 11719 (7/22/2102); 12898 (10/10/2012); 8444 (1/19/2012); 34736 (5/28/2014); 45756 (3/17/2015); 45776 (3/18/2015).

221 **"kind of a perv":** During his testimony at Mark's evidentiary hearing on October 14, 2025, Jimmy testified that he did recall meeting Mark at Wayne's wedding, and didn't like him. "He was the kind of guy who had to one-up you all the time," he said.

221 **"Jimmy Rodgers was C":** Trial transcript, State of Florida v. Jimmy Ray Rodgers, Case no. 15-CF-000673 A. October 10, 2019. p2237.

221 **"the will of his double":** Patricia Highsmith, *Strangers on a Train*, Norton, 2001, p143.

222 **Mark's one-time doppelgänger:** "LCSO deputy arrested during standoff at Buckingham home," WINK News, February 19, 2016; accessed April 10, 2024. https://

winknews.com/2016/02/19/lcso-deputy-arrested-following-standoff-at-buckingham-home/.

222 **glistening domes:** According to Mark's stepmother, Jennie Weckelman, "Mark's behavior, dress, and clean bald head were mandated by his lawyer. While in jail awaiting trial, he had let his fringe of curly hair grow."

223 **Jimmy's involvement, and the burner phones:** There was some discussion beore trial about whether it would be appropriate to refer to the prepaid phones as "burner phones" because, as Kathleen Fitzgeorge pointed out, "*Burner phone* sort of implies you're up to no good. You're doing something. You have this because they're not traceable." Trial transcript, State of Florida v. Jimmy Ray Rodgers, Case no. 15-CF-000673 A. October 10, 2019. p2251.

223 **his jealousy of Nick Delgado:** Nick Delgado was, in fact, in the witness list for Mark's trial, but was never called.

223 **"An unconscionable act":** State of Florida v. Mark D. Sievers, in the Circuit Court of the Twentieth Judicial Circuit, in and for Lee County, Florida, Case no. 15-CF-000673-B, Transcript of Jury Trial Proceedings, December 4, p4091.\

224 **"five-time, bipolar convicted felon":** More than once, Wayne's diagnosis of bipolar disorder was used against him in court. This seems inappropriate. When people diagnosed with mental illness are involved in acts of violence, most are the victim, rather than the perpetrator.

224 **"sit where Mark sits now":** Ibid., p4184.

225 **According to Florida statute:** This was the case until April 2023, when Governor Ron DeSantis signed the bill, following the House's approval, that it's only

necessary to have eight jurors agreeing to the verdict. Florida is currently the state with the nation's lowest threshold for juries to recommend death sentences (Alabama requires ten).

225 **two motherless children:** After a short battle with Bonnie Sievers, Mary Ann had been granted custody of Emma and Olivia in 2016—but the girls wanted to stay in Florida, continuing their schooling, violin and karate lessons, and friendships. This meant that, although she had full custody, Mary Ann had to move to Florida for two years, renting a condo, until the girls could finally be persuaded to move to Connecticut with their grandmother (the difficulties of the situation caused enormous stress to the family). The girls were subsequently raised by Mary Ann, Annie, and other family members.

225 **could have been a celebrity:** Clips from *Pathways 2 Healing* and Teresa's other television appearances can be seen on YouTube: https://www.youtube.com/@teresasieversmdmsmsfaarfma5197; accessed February 9, 2024.

226 **talking on the phone whenever possible:** In between the verdict and the sentencing phase, defense attorneys had come across a five-page letter written by Michele Petrites contradicting Mark Petrites's testimony that, prior to Teresa's murder, his only connection with Mark Sievers was through Teresa. Michele's emotional letter, written before she left for law school, expressed how fortunate she was to have the Sievers family in her life and thanking the family for their friendship over the years. Of Mark, she wrote, "I am so grateful to be included under your umbrella of protection. I do not know of

anyone who is so willing to safeguard his wife's friends in such a sacrificial way as you do." But the letter was disallowed as part of Mark's mitigation process.

227 **death penalty to be imposed:** Mark Sievers, Appeal from the Circuit Court in and for Lee County, State of Florida, Initial Brief of Appellant, 3.22.21., p13.

227 **"retribution for what was taken":** Personal communication, April 28, 2025.

228 **"wrongful conviction":** Information in this chapter drawn from Sievers, Mitigation; personal interviews with Jimmy Ray Rodgers, 12/01/2023, 1/09/2024; Taylor Shomaker, 11/30/2023; in the Circuit Court in the Twentieth Judicial Circuit in and for Lee County, Florida. Case #15-CF-673 B, State of Florida v. Mark Sievers, Jury Trial Transcript.

Chapter 21: Death Row

229 **1,800 other inmates:** Union Bay Correctional Institution is situated about thirty miles north of Gainesville, Florida. It currently holds 1,950 inmates at different security levels, including death row prisoners.

230 **twenty-three years:** See https://deathpenaltyinfo.org/facts-and-research/dpic-reports/dpic-year-end-reports/the-death-penalty-in-2023-year-end-report; accessed February 15, 2024. Unfortunately, there are also instances where inmates are executed while their appeal is still in progress. This happened to Anthony Wainwright, convicted of rape and murder in 1994, who was executed on June 10, 2025, despite never having his constitutional claims reviewed by a federal court due to his attorneys missing a filing deadline, among other errors.

230 **"a measure of true life":** paraphrased in Elizabeth Hardwick, "The Life and Death of Caryl Chessman," *Partisan Review*, 1960.

231 **alone in their cells:** Death Penalty Information Center, https://deathpenaltyinfo.org/death-row/death-row-time-on-death-row; accessed May 23, 2025.

231 **"extreme, debilitating, and inhumane":** https://deathpenaltyinfo.org/news/florida-becomes-latest-state-to-end-permanent-death-row-solitary-confinement-after-settlement-of-conditions-lawsuit ; accessed February 15, 2024.

231 **socialize, play cards, and watch television:** Info from the Florida Department of Corrections (DOC) Annual Report 2021-22; accessed February 15, 2024.

231 **"killed within the first ten years":** Interview with Jeff Giordano, April 3, 2023.

231 **"services of a state-appointed attorney":** Personal communication, July 12, 2025.

232 **"Your son Mark Sievers":** Twentieth Judicial Circuit in and for Lee County, Florida, State of Florida v. Mark Sievers, Case # 15-CF-673B, Motion for New Trial based on Newly Discovered Evidence of Actual Innocence, Filing # 140867610 E-Filed 12/22/2021 05:03:17 P.M. Appendix, p11.

233 **"murder-for-hire yarn":** Twentieth Judicial Circuit in and for Lee County, Florida, State of Florida v. Mark Sievers, Case # 15-CF-673B, Motion for New Trial based on Newly Discovered Evidence of Actual Innocence, Filing # 140867610 E-Filed 12/22/2021 05:03:17 P.M. p6.

233 **"the facts in his letter":** Ibid.

233 **death row appeal denied:** Mark Sievers, convicted in 2015 murder-for-hire of wife Teresa, denied death row appeal. Fort Myers *News-Press,* Retrieved December 29, 2022.

238 **death row at UCI:** On the subject of doubles, there is, bizarrely, another inmate in the Florida Department of Corrections named Curtis Wayne Wright, Jr., who also goes by Wayne. His date of birth is 10/04/1971, making him just three years younger than the "real" Wayne Wright. The "wrong" Wright is serving a life sentence at the Walton Correctional Institution in Defuniak Springs, Florida.

238 **no execution date:** Given his claims of innocence, Mark has said he would, by far, prefer execution than life in prison without the possibility of parole.

DISCUSSION QUESTIONS

(1) When a woman with no obvious enemies is killed in mysterious circumstances, the police generally turn to the husband as the first suspect. Do you think this is always appropriate? Could it lead to unfair bias against suspects?

(2) This case got a great deal of media attention, with emphasis on how beautiful Teresa was, and her fondness for high heels. Would you agree this seems demeaning, or could it be seen as a flattering tribute to her sexy, sparkly personality? Can you imagine a more appropriate way for her to be portrayed in the media?

(3) Do you think the texts about "swinging" and sex partners should have been introduced into evidence in court? Might they have implied that Wayne was sexually obsessed with Mark and jealous of Teresa, so much so that he might even kill to be with his "brother"?

(4) How would you explain the strange secret bond between Mark and Wayne? Do you believe they might have been lovers?

(5) Everyone agrees that Mark was a good father and loyal to his family. In your opinion, does this make the murder more horrifying, or does it make Mark seem less monstrous and more sympathetic?

(6) Have you ever known someone like Mark—an apparently good person who does something that seems shockingly out of character? If so, did you go back and reconsider that person's past behavior?

(7) Jimmy was a convicted felon but also young, naïve, and admiring of Wayne. Do you think this in any way mitigates his involvement in the murder?

(8) How do you feel about Taylor's and Angie's roles in this case? Do you think they were innocent victims, or complicit in the crime? What makes women stand by untrustworthy men, especially those who have committed terrible crimes?

(9) How do you feel about the death penalty in general? Mark Sievers was shown to have organized the conspiracy to kill Teresa, but he had nothing to do with the actual crime. Do you think the death penalty was justified in his case?

(10) Mark continues to insist he had nothing to do with the murder, and that Wayne acted alone. Do you think there is any possibility that this could be true, however slight? If so, what possible motive would Wayne have?